T0285156

# HOUSEWIFE

# HOUSEWIFE

## WHY WOMEN STILL DO IT ALL AND WHAT TO DO INSTEAD

## LISA SELIN DAVIS

LEGACY
LIT

NEW YORK   BOSTON

Copyright © 2024 by Lisa Selin Davis

Jacket design by Shreya Gupta. Jacket images: woman in kitchen by Picture Kitchen/Alamy Stock Photo; © Getty Images; © Shutterstock.com. Jacket copyright © 2024 by Hachette Book Group, Inc.

Legacy Lit
Hachette Book Group
1290 Avenue of the Americas
New York, NY 10104
LegacyLitBooks.com
Twitter.com/LegacyLitBooks
Instagram.com/LegacyLitBooks

First Edition: March 2024

Legacy Lit is an imprint of Grand Central Publishing. The Legacy Lit name and logo are trademarks of Hachette Book Group, Inc.

The publisher is not responsible for websites (or their content) that are not owned by the publisher.

The Hachette Speakers Bureau provides a wide range of authors for speaking events. To find out more, go to www.hachettespeakersbureau.com or email HachetteSpeakers@hbgusa.com.

Legacy Lit books may be purchased in bulk for business, educational, or promotional use. For information, please contact your local bookseller or the Hachette Book Group Special Markets Department at special.markets@hbgusa.com.

Print book interior design by Taylor Navis.

Library of Congress Cataloging-in-Publication Data

Names: Davis, Lisa, 1972- author.
Title: Housewife : why women still do it all and what to do instead / Lisa Selin Davis.
Description: First edition. | New York : Legacy Lit, 2024.
Identifiers: LCCN 2023020942 | ISBN 9781538722886 (hardcover) |
    ISBN 9781538722909 (ebook)
Subjects: LCSH: Women--Employment--History. | Housewives. | Women--Social conditions.
Classification: LCC HD6053 .D38 2023 | DDC 331.4--dc23/eng/20230719
LC record available at https://lccn.loc.gov/2023020942

ISBNs: 9781538722886 (hardcover), 9781538722909 (ebook)

Printed in the United States of America

LSC-C

Printing 1, 2023

*To my mother-in-law, Susan Sherwin, who managed to have a wonderful career and raise wonderful children*

# CONTENTS

# INTRODUCTION

# Happy Wife, Happy Life

*Because for so many years people thought that I did nothing while raising my kids I had to learn how to do everything.*

—Alana Joblin Ain, "Poet's Guide to Home Repairs"[1]

*Other countries have social safety nets. The U.S. has women.*

—Jessica Calarco[2]

I learned about how to be a modern woman when I was seven years old, from a TV commercial for Enjoli perfume. *I can bring home the bacon, fry it up in the pan, and never let you forget you're a man,* crooned a blond woman in a peach bathrobe, then a powder-blue suit, then a lavender evening gown. Enjoli was "the eight-hour perfume for the twenty-four-hour woman."[3]

The late-1970s jingle was a rehash of Peggy Lee's 1963 "I'm a Woman," fashioned for the dawn of the eighties. It was also a prescription. Women not only could but *should* achieve each of these archetypes: career woman, perfect mother, and sexpot. No image of the woman eight hours *after* the sweet perfume faded, harried and exhausted, passed out under a pile of unfolded laundry on the couch.

Women bought the product—and the message attached to it—in droves. One ad exec called it "the most successful introduction in fragrance history."[4]

The Enjoli vision of womanhood became, to some extent, my own. By the dawn of the new millennium, I expected that I'd have four children, starting at age twenty-eight. I loved to craft and cook, and I pictured a life of domestic bliss, but of course I would still be a writer. Those things didn't seem incompatible, because I had no sense of what it took to be either writer or mother, financially or emotionally. I'd been raised mostly by a single mom in a feminist household, and she did *everything,* from painting our rooms to knitting our sweaters. I assumed I'd be similarly capable.

None of it happened as I'd envisioned.

I moved to New York City from western Massachusetts after graduating from college in 1993, staying on my brother's futon couch in his honest-to-goodness tenement apartment in the pre–Rudolph Giuliani East Village in Manhattan (when it was more drugs and crime than wealth and upscale restaurants). He told me about a Brooklyn neighborhood where other fresh-from-college types, educated but low-earning, were shacking up—relatively safe and really cheap.

I had assumed that I'd find someone to procreate with by the end of that decade, but I didn't. I only started writing in my thirties, which is when I met my now husband. In all that time, the neighborhood transformed from a place to which both working-class and impecunious-but-educated people would flock, to a place where wealthy people from Manhattan would relocate instantly upon receiving a positive pregnancy test. Often, I sat typing in cafés literally penned in by strollers during family sing-along, steeping in a kind of marbleized resentment and jealousy swirl. How I both disdained and envied them, those moms with expensive pants and thin thighs and a purpose in life beyond their own careers.

At the same time, it also just seemed so embarrassing, women with PhDs dropping five dollars in a jar as an ambitious but desperate young musician alternately crooned "Wheels on the Bus" and "I Wanna Be Sedated." I didn't realize then that the mothers weren't offering cash tips because they'd liked the song as younger women, but because they felt bored or fried or confused or anxious and craved Xanax. They, too, wondered what the PhD had been for and if this was what they ought to be doing—for their children, themselves, our country, humankind.

But I didn't understand any of that until, at the ripe old age of thirty-seven, I finally became a mom. From the department of TMI: my older daughter was conceived on the night of Barack Obama's first election (how's that for liberal bona fides?). Two weeks after she was born, my husband's work schedule intensified at his corporate creative job, which provided the health insurance and paid the bulk of our rent. So I spent my days tending to our child and our apartment: cooking, cleaning, knitting hats, and meeting up with my local moms' group—the first group of any kind I'd ever joined.

On some small level, I had the life I'd wanted, even if I was a decade older than I'd hoped to be when it began, and I wasn't living in a Craftsman bungalow in a college town but in my same duct-taped-together fourth-floor walk-up. My compulsion to write vanished, replaced by this shimmery thing I vaguely recognized as happiness. My daughter had cured something in me: my ambition. Temporarily, anyway.

In the moms' group, we forged common bonds in the odd set of circumstances in which most of us found ourselves: career women whose trajectories had come to an abrupt halt, or at least an indefinite pause, when our children arrived, smack-dab in the middle of the Great Recession. We were living through an economic crisis in a country with no universal day care or mandated paid parental leave. Almost nobody in the group had grown up in Brooklyn or had extended family nearby to help. To those of us without enough income to justify a full-time nanny, how we would resume our pre-kid working lives remained a mystery.

As the months went by, and some mothers returned to work, the dynamics of our makeshift community changed. From the women who'd nannied up and slipped back into their suits, there wafted a slight smugness, albeit often followed by guilt. From those a year in and still breastfeeding and co-sleeping and attachment parenting escaped a slight sense of superiority, often accompanied by a hint of inadequacy and insecurity. Regardless of the choices we made, even for those of us lucky enough to be able to make choices, we felt bad.

Meanwhile, those of us married to men started noticing that the emotional and domestic labor divide felt very 1950s, despite the fact that 72 percent of mothers work.[5] Working mothers spend more time on household labor and childcare than fathers but are less likely to have paid family and medical leave, paid sick days, flexible work conditions, and affordable childcare.[6] These statistics manifested in my life as utter confusion. At the time, I worked five hours a week, writing for a real estate blog. I typed during my daughter's nap and occasionally hired a babysitter, but it confused me. Yes, research claims that when mothers work outside the home, it benefits children and parents alike.[7] But if I paid someone else, how would I turn a reasonable profit? I had absolutely no idea how the seemingly opposing trajectories and desires for both a career and motherhood could peacefully coexist.

Then I had another child, a delicious, sweet baby who seemed to be asking with every blink of her chocolatey eyes how she could make our lives better. Yet my domestic bliss pixelated into panic. As we accumulated more and more cheap stuff from Amazon, and our clutter clogged the railroad apartment's long hallway, I found myself regularly overwhelmed with a visceral rage—at the state of our place; at myself for not training my children to tidy; at their dad for the Pigpen-like genes he must have bestowed upon them, the tendency to leave a trail of mess behind them as they walked. Rage at both of us for not having thought to create more financial security for our nuclear unit, and at myself for not achieving a single Instagram Momfluencer moment.

How did the women around me have clean houses and styled hair while holding jobs, cooking healthy meals, and raising nice children? My kids didn't know how to make scrambled eggs or sew a button. They couldn't get themselves out of bed in the morning or ready themselves for school. And the expense of two children meant my minuscule income would no longer suffice. In our achievement-focused neighborhood, I so often felt like a failure. Our mess—both physical and emotional—morphed into an indication of my dereliction as a woman and mother. The euphoria I felt from having children was now accompanied by a dull heartbeat of defeat. As President Trump nominated Amy Coney Barrett, mom to seven, for the Supreme Court, I began to fantasize about a reality show called *Childcare Arrangements of the Rich and Famous*. What was the secret? There seemed to be no map for the road I was traversing.

Still, the joy, the joy: my babies.

In the moments without rage or child-centered euphoria, fatigue invaded my bones, my brain. No energy for the sewing projects and homemade snickerdoodles I'd envisioned as integral facets of motherhood. How had my single mother, who at times worked multiple jobs to provide for me and my older brother, also made us beautiful meals and sewed our clothes? Maybe it was just because she had her first kid at twenty-two instead of thirty-seven, I reasoned. Maybe she was just more *awake*.

One woman in our moms' group was a little different. I didn't know this woman at all. I'm not sure how she came to be living in the epicenter of hipster parenting, where most of the moms had assumed not just a job but a career before procreating. But she once wrote on our listserv, "I was a housewife before I was a mother so I had something lots of others didn't have... TIME!"

Having never heard a woman of my generation refer to herself as a housewife, I was fascinated. My childhood had been filled with hippie women's libbers, women with hairy armpits, wearing Birkenstocks and fighting for abortion rights and the ERA. Most of my friends' parents were divorced, and the mothers *had* to work. I hardly even knew anyone with a stay-at-home mom and when, as a kid, I met one, she seemed like a mythical creature, somehow extracted from the fictional world of 1950s TV. When I was little, my grandmother was one of the only women I knew without a job, but even she had worked as a law office secretary until she married my grandfather. Her own single mom raised five kids in the Jewish ghetto on Manhattan's Lower East Side and then Williamsburg, Brooklyn. Working motherhood threaded through our familial legacy.

As this mom proclaimed herself a housewife, it conjured for me such a specific image: the kitten heels and hourglass dress, the ranch house, the white, middle-class woman who watched soap operas and presented her husband with a martini upon his return from the office. Here in the land where stay-at-home moms wore expensive athleisure wear and took homemade baby food–making classes, did anyone live like that? Who gets married and just... stops working? Or never had a job in the first place?

My wondering included a tinge of disdain, an assumption that there was something lesser about this version of womanhood or family life, perhaps because it had never occurred to me not to pursue a career. Then again, such a choice was never possible. No one asked child me, "Who do you want to marry when you grow up?" The question was, "What do you want to *be*?" To be a housewife required a husband or a spouse willing to support a wife. I'd never been presented with that option.

But, upon reflection, I might have liked to hitch my wagon to someone, confident that he or she loved me enough that I could be comfortable in a state of financial dependency. Of course, my fantasies of wealth always involved marrying into it; I had perhaps never believed in myself enough to fantasize about becoming wealthy on my own, maybe because I'd been financially disadvantaged enough in my early childhood to qualify for free lunch.

Along with delivering my beautiful children, though, I had been delivered a set of peers and a purpose, so I hadn't really considered that I was now in a state of financial dependency myself. As a freelancer, I had no paid parental leave. My husband and I didn't discuss the fact that he was the main breadwinner, though when I brought up from time to time that maybe I was happier *not* working, his face twisted into some combination of surprise and panic. He had married a feminist, a working writer, and neither expected nor wanted to be fully financially responsible for our family.

By the time I attempted to resurrect my full-time writing career, the publishing industry had changed. Magazines were often paying *10 percent* of what they had before I'd given birth. Over and over again, I asked myself if it made sense to keep working. Was anything I had to write about worth the time away from my kids? Weren't they better off *with* me?

Yes, I thought.

But also: No?

How does one do the calculus, add apples and oranges, wage work and housework, to arrive at modern motherhood, at equality, at good parenting, at a functional family? I thought back to that Enjoli commercial, which directed me in how to live: Keep a perfect house, earn money, make food, look sexy, rear children. Where did that woman's kids go all day, how much did it cost to send them there, and when did she sleep?

I had gotten so much of what I wanted: to have family and to be a writer. (Admittedly I was missing a couple of things I also really wanted, like an IRA and a home I owned.) How could I be living better than 80 percent of the world and still feel so aggrieved, exhausted, and discombobulated? Some of that is my lack of gratitude and disagreeable personality, but I found that even more naturally optimistic women than I felt trapped in some weird iterative cycle, that some version of Betty Friedan's "problem that has no name" was rinsing and repeating generationally.[8]

Then I wondered: Was that self-proclaimed housewife in the moms' group, who'd long ago disappeared into the suburban wilds...*happier*? If I finally gave up my ambition for a career and instead nurtured ambition to be a great mom and homemaker, would *I* be happier?

The question of the housewife burned on a low blue flame in the back of my mind. All the time. That's how life was until 2020.

And then: pandemic.

IT WAS ONE of the weirdest moments of the relentlessly weird Trump reelection campaign. Standing at a rally in Michigan in October 2020, staring out at a crowd of thousands, President Trump made a promise to the women in attendance: "We're getting your husbands back to work."[9]

*How strange*, I thought, as I desperately tried to hold on to my freelance work while being forced to homeschool my kids, after the pandemic shut down their school. In the wake of Trump's election, more women had been elected to Congress than at any time previously. More women voted than ever before. But the pandemic took a disproportionate toll on women, especially working mothers. Those with education and resources were pressed to choose between their careers and their kids' education. Those without resources were pressed to choose between paying rent and their kids' education.

The pandemic exposed the American "mother-as-social-safety-net" problem—why spring for universal childcare when mothers do it all for free?—and our lack of family-supportive policies. For the first time, many major news outlets reported on the mom crisis; it seemed like, for once, the nation cared.

Women held 54 percent of the jobs lost, and these were not side jobs to make a little extra cash or keep a woman busy while her husband worked. Sixty-four percent of working women are their families' co- or primary breadwinners; for Black women that's 84.3 percent.[10] In September 2020 alone—just in time for school to start, or not start, as the case was for most—865,000 women dropped out or were forced out of the workforce, four times the number of men.[11] Though three-quarters of women with children under eighteen work,[12] and as 2.2 million women were purged from the workforce, Trump prioritized men, yammering on about "suburban housewives."

"The suburban housewife loves trump [*sic*]," he tweeted.[13]

And: "The 'suburban housewife' will be voting for me."[14]

And: "The Suburban Housewives of America must read this article. Biden will destroy your neighborhood and your American Dream."[15]

Strangest about Trump's use of the term was how much of a unicorn this kind of woman was. The white, middle- or upper-class married woman in a homogenous, affluent suburb, safe from urban ills, perfectly coiffed and padding about the ranch house—she hardly existed anymore. According to the Pew Research Center, as suburbs have grown poorer and more diverse, these days the woman most likely to be an American housewife is a poor, non-white immigrant, who can't work legally, or can't earn more than the cost of childcare, or comes from a culture that disapproves of working mothers—or, perhaps, that embraces the option of housewifery. The largest groups of stay-at-home moms are Hispanic (38 percent in 2012) and Asian (36 percent). Some 26 percent of white mothers and 27 percent of Black mothers stay at home. As Pew noted, "Stay-at-home mothers are younger, poorer and less educated than their working counterparts."[16] Some 34 percent of stay-at-home moms are poor, they noted; 12 percent of working mothers are poor. (What might not be measured in these statistics is how many of these women toil in shadow economies, cleaning homes or watching children off the books.) As of 2016, only one in five American families had a "stay-at-home" parent.[17] Still, the number of stay-at-home moms has risen steadily since the turn of this century, after steeply dropping in the 1980s and '90s.

As I would learn when I researched the history of the American housewife, that June Cleaver type Trump was evoking? She was mostly an illusion, and many of the women who did live the real-life version of her fictive presence became utterly miserable. Yet the housewife is such a powerful and persistent myth and archetype that 74 million people cast their ballot for it—an idea of a certain kind of family, and a woman's place within it, retains that much power. The word was out of favor, yet its mystical influence remained.

This book is about the history of that archetype—where it came from, how it has changed, why we cling to it even as we devalue it, and how it manifests, both in our public policy and our private lives.

The shape of this book is like a tree. Part I is the trunk: the history of the idea and ideal of the housewife from the Paleolithic Era (really) to the pandemic. Part II branches out from there to talk about how our attachment to this ideal has left women financially vulnerable, egalitarian marriage rare, and public policy family-unfriendly—and what we can do to make things better.

The book will focus mostly, though not entirely, on lower-middle- and middle-class women, and some upper-middle-class women, because women living in poverty have so much stress beyond figuring out modern motherhood. But the policies I explore, the cultural changes I suggest, benefit all women. In fact, they would benefit all families, and society at large.

As I researched, I found that the meaning of the word *housewife*, and the kind of woman it evoked, shape-shifted over generations and eras and depends on class and race. I found that the hunter/gatherer binary, which we often think of as a corollary to breadwinner/homemaker, was far more complex, and that our ideas of women's work are as much about ecology as biology. I found housewife political movements. I found housewife sexual fetishes. I found that the most visible woman in all the land, the First Lady, is the housewife of the nation—and thus doesn't get paid for a more than full-time job. I found increasingly difficult expectations of women from one generation to the next, with less support for them in each iteration, upping the ante and setting up women and families for defeat. And I kept wondering: Who *gets* to be a housewife, and who's forced to be one?

Mostly what I found is that, because the ghostly shadow of the housewife, its unsustainable ideal, hovered over them, women felt that whatever they were doing wasn't right, wasn't good, wasn't enough. There's a pervasive and poisonous capitalistic American notion that women's work and their unpaid labor is un-valuable, that somehow selling dental equipment or delivering packages is more important than changing diapers and breastfeeding. But in fact, the unpaid labor of women is *in*valuable. Paid labor cannot be accomplished without it.

The pandemic and the accompanying crises presented a very rare opportunity to reevaluate and reinvent women's work and worlds, to call for a new women's labor movement. The best thing not just for women but also for men, children, families, society, and the economy is to explode the paralyzing myth that housewives and the nuclear family are the only normal, natural, and right way to live, and explore the map of the democratic family in a fairer, more supportive society. There is no one way to be a wife, mother, worker, or woman, and no one right way to organize a family.

Housewife is an archetype, an insult, a dirty word, but most of all it is an enduring idea of what women should do and be. Until we understand how it has shaped policy and perceptions across decades and centuries, we will not be able to move forward.

# PART I

# CHAPTER 1

# The History of "Housewife"

Martine never imagined that she, a Black woman of working-class roots, would end up a housewife, a word that conjured images of white, middle-class, suburban ladies. She was teaching English in Vietnam, where she met a white American soldier and eventually moved with him to Oklahoma City, then Sweden. It made sense to get married. The military pays married men more. Only spouses can shop alone at the commissary, not girlfriends or domestic partners, who must be accompanied by their active-duty partners to get on base and make purchases at the commissary or PX. And she needed health insurance.

Martine's mother had gotten pregnant with her at nineteen, when Martine's dad was twenty, and her parents had managed to stay together and get by financially. But it wasn't easy, and they wanted more for her: more security, more education, better decision-making. To not get knocked up too early or out of wedlock. There was still the expectation in the ether that a woman of a certain age—she was twenty-eight—needed to be married.

But the transient military life meant Martine couldn't settle long enough anywhere to establish a career. While her husband was at the base all day, she did some part-time work and, later, taught online. But mostly Martine dedicated herself to keeping the house clean, cooking meals, paying bills, earning her keep.

She liked building a nest, but without money of her own, and not feeling close enough to her husband to want to have kids, Martine felt destabilized: dependent, but somehow distant. It was the strangest place to find herself, in her twenties, educated, married, only marginally employed. And to her surprise and sometimes dismay, she was a housewife—a word hardly used anymore, and which she never in a million years thought would apply to her.

## REAL AND FAKE HOUSEWIVES

EARLY IN MY research, I created a Google alert for the word "housewife." Almost every reference that graced my inbox detailed the antics of those in the *Real Housewives* franchise—a phenomenon I had managed to avoid my entire life, but also a media brand whose staying power was undeniable. America loved to watch rich, idle women behaving badly.

Of course, few of these women actually fit the bill of "housewife" in the traditional sense: a woman who manages the household and doesn't work outside it. Some presided over empires or earned money as influencers, not to mention millions per episode. A few remained unwed. None tended full-time to domestic duties or their children. The franchise's creator, Scott Dunlop, was riffing off the popular show *Desperate Housewives* when he aimed to expose the lives of entitled people for voyeuristic pleasure in 2006. The producers who bought his idea said to focus on the women, and to call them "housewives" because the desperate ones were in such demand. That word created a strange sparkle amid the public, an allure.[1] It touched the nerve of a cultural mythology.

But it also became an identity. Cast members are Housewives, capital H, not in any kind of literal sense, but to distinguish them as members of a very particular tribe who wear bejeweled frocks and whose every outing, every interaction, is partially choreographed not just for the camera but to include the other women with whom they are embedded, entangled, and, at times, pitted against. Maybe the fictional Desperate Housewives were narratively desperate, but the fact that the Real Housewives are not real housewives seems to bother no one, perhaps because the Millennials who came of age with them use the word *literally* to mean *figuratively*, and know how to interpret irony in some kind of sincere way that this Gen-Xer can't. That is, they embrace that reality TV has little to do with reality.

I do understand this much: The word "housewife" situated these women not in a role with specific responsibilities, but in a social and cultural class. It's a class of McMansions and real mansions, of gold-digging, of money—and bridges—to burn and time to waste. In some ways, it's the steroidal version and vision of the idealized 1950s housewife detailed in chapter 5, who had access to new technologies like the washing machine, and with them an unprecedented luxury called leisure time. The 1950s housewife might not possess obscene wealth, there in her tidy Cape Cod in brand-new Levittown, but she might own a magnificent thing called a dishwasher, which would free her up for soap operas and canasta.

On the one hand, Real Housewives expressed a bastardized version of that 1950s ideal. On the other, they *were* indeed real. They were human—angry, conniving, gritty, glamorous, competitive, backstabbing, emotionally messy—in a way that those polished and coiffed mid-century housewives weren't. As one writer pointed out, "The 'fake' housewife is the one we carry as an imagined, beatific maternal housekeeper in our collective unconscious. The fake housewife is Donna Reed."[2] The nurturing, domesticated mother once confined and defined by the word "housewife" is now a free-spending party animal who catfights with others of her ilk. By the twenty-first century, the word "housewife," in American popular culture, seemed to retain almost none of its original meaning at all.

Still, the vision "housewife" conjures, of tract houses and sodded lawns and stay-at-home moms, is imprinted on the nation's soul. Or at least, it's the surreal fantasy that the Marvel superhero Wanda spun as a psychiatric response to losing the love of her life in the TV show *WandaVision*; she reinvents Vision, her deceased partner, as a 1950s suburban dad and herself as housewife. That is, when someone with supernatural powers wields them to create utopia, it looks like Levittown. But Levittown, as we shall later see, spun discontents of its own.

Outside of Wanda and the not-real Real Housewives, there were mentions in the odd obituary,[3] or occasional cheeky uses of the word in American media. A regular local TV news installment called "The Harried Housewife®" (yes, it's registered) offered recipes and home-making tips.[4] But since the Harried Housewife herself, a cookbook author and media personality named Cynthia O'Connor O'Hara, was paid for her work, it's unclear if she's actually a housewife. If she just has a part-time job, and it's centered around domestic duties, perhaps she can still claim the term?

We've seen a few twenty-first-century TV series portraying vintage or historical housewives, like Jessica Biel in *Candy*, about a sweet little 1980s housewife who ends up killing her friend.[5] Or Elizabeth Olsen in *Love & Death*, about a sweet little 1980s housewife who, er, ends up killing her friend. Or Renée Zellweger in *The Thing About Pam*, about a sweet little 1980s housewife who, um, ends up getting killed by her friend.

To find headlines *not* referring to Real Housewives or murdering housewives or dead housewives required a bit of Boolean finesse, asking Google to edge out any reference to "real." Then I accessed a strange new crop of entries. Most non-*RH* franchise mentions in my inbox referenced women across Asia and Africa who'd been murdered or otherwise in trouble with the law. The word "housewife" implied that the crimes were sensational because of the women's status as upstanding citizens: married and not working outside the home. As members of a storied class, we expected them to remain above reproach, fulfilling their womanly duties.

"Gunmen Abduct Housewife, Children in Delta Community," according to an article about a woman named Faith who had disappeared from a Nigerian town.[6] Another Nigerian headline: "How Bandits Who Plotted to Rape Housewife Were Nabbed in Kaduna Forest."[7] "Housewife stabbed dead," reported the United News of Bangladesh.[8] "One arrested over rape of housewife in Pirojpur," reported another Bangladeshi news source.[9] What made these stories newsworthy was that the housewives featured in them should not have been newsworthy.

These days, "housewife" is also the translated name of a Croatian cookie, Domacica, manufactured in a Zagreb factory since 1957.[10] In 2022, the company designed a campaign to add other professions to the labels—housewife and artist, housewife and lawyer—to "remember that women, in addition to their work, are those who most often take care of the household on a daily basis as well," per the company's press release.

You'd think this would be a win, acknowledging the uneven distribution of labor, and that working women in heterosexual marriages still do the bulk of domestic duties and childcare. But the campaign apparently didn't go over well with Croatian feminists. They interpreted it as saying a housewife—even as a shortbread cookie dipped in chocolate—was not, on its own, enough, that women only retained worth if they contributed financially and vocationally outside the home.

For an almost completely outdated word, people still have a lot of opinions about it. Much as was the case with the word "tomboy," the subject of my last book, long after the word had gone out of favor in the United States, it endured and caused trouble in other parts of the world, conjuring a vision we'd moved past here—or, at least, a vision we *thought* we'd moved past.

## BEHIND THE WORD

THE WORD "HOUSEWIFE" emerged in the thirteenth century, a combination, obviously, of "house" and "wife."[11] *Hus* is Old English for dwelling. In Middle English, *wif* or *wyf* referred to woman or female, but not a woman married to a man. It was also related to a verb that meant "to neuter," though as far as I can tell, no one has officially discerned a connection between becoming a wife and metaphorically or physically castrating a husband.

At some point, the word *wifman* appeared, the eventual source of "woman."[12] Some believe it's related to the word "weave." Apparently nobody knows how "bride" and "woman" became conflated.[13] Eventually, "housewife" came to mean, as the Oxford English Dictionary describes it, "A (typically married) woman whose main occupation is managing the general running of a household, such as caring for her family, performing domestic tasks, etc."

The word "hussy" also meant "female head of household" or thrifty woman, because the *house* in "housewife" was sometimes pronounced "huss."[14] By the middle of the sixteenth century, "housewife" also meant a "frivolous, impertinent, or disreputable" woman or girl. In the nineteenth century, the meanings split. "Housewife" came to contain the neutral or positive embodiment of a woman running the home, and "hussy" the negative: a woman gone astray.

In the 1900s, "housewife" was also the name of a sewing kit—a woman's tools in a box. No one seems to have figured out just why this is.

Though it conjures whiteness today, "housewife" wasn't always limited to white women. A late-nineteenth-century magazine called *The Housewife*[15] advertised in both white and Black newspapers.[16] Ads in African American newspapers for household products used the word, often for salves like Mexican Mustang Liniment, which housewives could leverage for "general household use" while the "Lumberman needs it in case of accident."[17] Articles about cooking and cleaning, referencing the "American housewife," included Black women.[18]

In 1911, one Mrs. Julian Heath, née Jennie Dewey, founded the National Housewives' League, of which she remained president until 1932. Heath had worked with Jacob Riis, the photographer and activist dedicated to drawing attention to and improving the lives of the poor, but later she turned her attention to home economics, growing her membership to as many as 800,000 women.[19] She founded *National Housewives* magazine and permitted food manufacturers to advertise in it or pay to display their goods within the league's headquarters. In 1924, Heath began to appear on WJZ radio, eventually taking to the air five days a week to talk to women about the ways they could and should be handling home affairs. In other words, Heath became a shrewd businesswoman, marketing herself and her media to housewives, while not technically being one—an early version of the kind of housewife influencer that would shake up social media in the twenty-first century (see chapter 12).

Not all housewives were associated with purity; some banded together to demand change (more on that in chapter 4.) A 1914 article on the Housewives' League of the United States—a different organization than Heath's—noted that, together, housewives could wield real power in protecting families against predatory merchants, who would put lead weights in turkeys before selling them to housewives by the pound or artificially raise the price of milk.[20] In the 1930s, working-class housewives, who understood the strength of unions, organized strikes and pickets to bring down food prices and lower rents.

An open letter in the 1941 *Afro-American Courier* urged women to join the National Housewives' League—a third such organization, this one founded by a Black woman—"since women spend or control the spending of 85 percent of all the money passing through the marts of trade."[21]

In the 1970s, conservative activist and author Phyllis Schlafly would organize tens of thousands of housewives to successfully campaign against the Equal Rights Amendment.

In other words, housewives have been, at many times, a political class.

## HOUSEWIFE, OUTDATED AND TIMELESS

IN A 1976 edition of *Good Housekeeping*, First Lady Betty Ford took issue with the common phrase "just a housewife"—a phrase women uttered apologetically when asked what they did for a living.[22] "We have to take the 'just' out of 'just a housewife' and show our pride in having made the home and family our life's work," she opined, noting that women satisfied as homemakers were just as liberated as the mythical bra burners, and just as important. She was one such satisfied person, she said. (Though, as shown in chapter 10, First Lady is more than a full-time job.)

Ford suggested replacing "housewife" with "homemaker." That one magazine article may not have single-handedly eradicated the use of the word "housewife," but she was on to something. "Homemaker" was perhaps more palatable to a changing America, less passive wife and more active caregiver. By the 1970s, "homemaker" had outshined "housewife."[23]

Then came the '80s, and, as we'll see in chapter 13, even "homemaker" quickly became antiquated. By the '90s, stay-at-home mom became the corollary to career woman and working mother—which had also become the name of a magazine in 1979.[24] (No magazine titled *Working Father* followed.) The singular archetype now fractured into what looked like multiple paths. (Stay-at-home, meanwhile, was actually a vintage term, a name for people who didn't travel. When "mom" was first tacked on, the term was written in quotes.[25])

Throughout the latter decades of the twentieth century, the percentage of mothers who worked kept veering upward, and the moms who didn't—whatever we should call them—hit a record low in 1999: 23 percent. Then it climbed again. Pundits interpreted this shift as mothers with degrees "opting out" of the workforce to pursue full-time parenting. But, according to historian Stephanie Coontz, those moms likely stayed home because of the recession; they couldn't find work.[26] To be a housewife wasn't always a choice; sometimes it was a last resort.

It's still hard to figure out how to divide mothers into categories according to employment, and what to call them. If "full-time mom" is what some women prefer, those to whom the moniker doesn't apply might take offense. Am I only a mother part of the time? Surely the fact that, regardless of my activity, my children occupy 99 percent of my brain space makes me a full-time mom, too? "Working mother" is problematic because, well, motherhood is work no matter what. (LinkedIn recently added "stay-at-home mom" as an official job title, to smooth the way for women to return to work after taking time off, or being forced to take time off, and prevent those glaring resume gaps.)[27] We could say "remunerated mothers," but it sounds like they're being remunerated for motherhood—an idea some politicians are currently considering—plus, that's a hard word to spell. Mothers who work outside the home? Mothers with jobs? Mothers without paid work? Should we go back to homemaker? Is that going forward?

Some now consider housewife an insult. Conservative commentator S. E. Cupp offered a small but potent example. A political campaigner came to her door to canvas and asked if her husband was home. "When you go door to door, campaigning for local office, don't say to the woman who answers (me), 'Hello! Wow. You look so put together...for a housewife,'" she complained on Twitter. It was straight out of the 1950s. "When a woman answers the door, she's your voter. Talk to HER. And just because she's home doesn't make her a housewife. It might make her the ruler of her domain. Stop looking past us. We are running it all," she wrote.[28] Inherent in this feminist rant was the assumption that a housewife didn't rule the domain.

Today, stay-at-home mothers tend to be married not to wealthy breadwinners but those in the lower echelons of wage-earning. These women can't find work that pays more than the staggering cost of childcare. Educated, wealthier women are those less likely to stay at home.[29] Among the extant traditional 1950s-style white middle-class families with a homemaker mom, few seem comfortable talking about their lives openly. However, sometimes they take to Reddit. There, husbands joke about their wives being "subs"—meaning submissives, not sandwiches—but say their wives wanted it this way, and the whole family is happy. She makes him a PB&J sandwich every day and puts a love note in his lunchbox.

A woman going by LittlePikaDuck asked if 1950s housewife kink was a thing. (It very much is, if you look on the sexual fetish website FetLife.)[30] She fantasized about being a '50s housewife, she said, and supported by a husband, and wanted to know: Is that bad? She'd been told off by feminists for her desires, and though she considers herself independent, well, she wants to be looked after, too.

One person responded that it's a relatable desire, but "I've found that the men who want to treat you like a 50s housewife are typically BAD. NEWS." Most of those dudes, she said, believe a woman needs taking care of, and treating women like housewives goes to their heads. Sometimes "cis men take it too far," she said, and you can tell that it's not just a kink for them.

Other than a group of women who romanticize 1950s housewives and claim the term as a badge of honor (chapter 12), random Redditors, a trans woman who embraces the term "housewife," and a woman in a submissive/dominant sexual relationship using "housewife" as a way to express the balance of power, I found few people associating themselves with it.[31] "Housewife" was a mostly dormant term to many of us, until President Trump awoke it during his 2020 campaign.

## THE HOUSEWIFE TRAP

FOR MARTINE, BEING a housewife manifested as a trap. "Nothing I ever did was enough," she said. "I was doing so much work: all the grocery shopping and all the cooking and all the cleaning." Her husband resented any life she forged outside their shared domestic space, the working life she held on to. She didn't fit his idea of how a woman should be, but had wrangled herself into a state of dependency. After they moved to Sweden, she decided that the marriage wasn't going to last.

But four years later, when I spoke with her, they were still married, because of the recession and the gig economy and the late start she got—she still needed the low-cost health insurance, and neither of them had expressed any desire to marry again. It wasn't until she took a full-time job that she finally decided to file for divorce, though he hasn't yet been particularly cooperative.

Martine sees nothing wrong with people choosing to be homemakers. But she resents how women in homemaking roles have so little economic and social independence, and how hard it is for them to find work when they're ready to surrender the homemaking role.

"Housewife," whether a popular term or not, has stayed with us, burdened and besieged us for centuries, deep into the past, its tendrils still reaching into our future. It undergirds our private families and our public policies. The path to freedom—to choice—is to reimagine what constitutes women's work.

# CHAPTER 2

# The Neolithic Housewife

*The Greek word oikos, meaning house, is the root of the word ecologist, which could be defined as, among other things, housewife.*

—Rebecca Solnit[1]

During the five weeks they'd been digging at Wilamaya Patjxa, a site of barren grasslands high in the Andes where the sun was bright and the air cold and thin, the archaeologists and their local Aymara collaborators had already excavated dozens of 9,000- to 11,000-year-old projectile points and five skeletons. But this skeleton, WMP6, was different.

As archaeological assistants Mateo Incacoña Huaraya and Nestor Condori Flores carefully dusted off the emerging bones, they found the skeleton crouched on its left side, surrounded by a "big game hunting kit": projectile points for dispatching vicuña and deer alongside cutting and scraping tools for processing animal hides.

"He must have been a great chief, a great warrior," one of the excavators said. Lead archaeologist Randy Haas, assistant professor of anthropology at the University of California, Davis, thought: *That's possible.*

After carefully documenting the findings, the team gently placed the bones in tissue paper, set them in a box, and carted them back to their lab in the nearby town of Puno, on the shores of Lake Titicaca. There, a few weeks later, anthropologist Jim Watson of University of Arizona began an analysis of the 9,000-year-old skeleton. The bones belonged to a seventeen- to nineteen-year-old, but he found that the long bones, like the femur, tibia, and fibula, were lighter and thinner than he'd expect for a male.

Forensic scientists Glendon Parker and Tammy Buonasera had invented a way to test the sex of an ancient skeleton through analyzing proteins in tooth enamel, so Haas had them test WMP6. "That was the moment of, 'My gosh, our hunter was a huntress,'" Haas said.

Haas didn't approach archaeology from a feminist perspective. He hadn't set out to prove a hypothesis about division of labor among the sexes in the early Americas. "I didn't come into it thinking about the gendered aspects of human economies," he told me. His interest is in inferring human behavior from material remains that people leave behind. Haas wants to know what people were doing.

And yet, his discovery presented a challenge to the oft-told tale, the archetype of man-the-hunter and woman-the-gatherer. Historically, many believed those archetypes translated to man-the-breadwinner and woman-the-housewife. If once woman roamed the plains in search of berries, nuts, and seeds, later she roamed the aisles of the supermarket—or, these days, the pages of Instacart—in search of provisions to feed her hungry young. But people often assumed it was the meat, or, later, the money to buy it—men's work—that *really* mattered.

Haas might have assumed something similar had he not stumbled upon what he called this "serendipitous" discovery. He then compiled data from published archaeological investigations of 429 burials, from between 8,000 and 14,000 years ago, finding twenty-seven with determinable sex who'd been buried with hunting instruments. Of those, sixteen were male. Eleven were female. His meta-analysis, "Female Hunters of the Early Americas," was published in *Science-Advances* in 2020. He concluded: "Early females in the Americas were big-game hunters."[2]

"I think what these data are telling us are that sexual division of labor that we understand in Western society is not a given; there's nothing intrinsic about it," Haas told me. "There is much more fluidity in probably the first ninety percent of our species' existence, over which most of our cultures and biology evolved."

That is, the sexual division of labor might have been fundamentally different in the past, and the man-hunter/woman-gatherer trope may be more myth, and misunderstanding, than settled history.

## RETHINKING THE WAY-BACK

FOR YEARS, ARCHAEOLOGISTS and anthropologists didn't ask the sex of someone who'd been buried and unearthed with hunting materials, because they assumed such a skeleton belonged to a man. Sex was determined not by science but by gender bias. Take the case of Bj 581, a 1,000-year-old Viking skeleton discovered in 1878 by Swedish archaeologist Hjalmar Stolpe. Bj 581 had been buried with "a sword, an axe, a spear, armour-piercing arrows, a battle knife, two shields, and two horses, one mare and one stallion; thus, the complete equipment of a professional warrior," per a study by Charlotte Hedenstierna-Jonson and others in the *American Journal of Biological Anthropology*.[3]

In 1975, the Swedish History Museum inventoried the remains of Stolpe's digs. When an osteo-archaeologist named Berit Vilkans logged Bj 581's bones, she found the thin, slender bones of the forearm and what was left of the pelvic bone resembled a woman's more than a man's, and suggested perhaps the master hunter was female. Her fellow scientists were unconvinced.[4]

In 2016, Anna Kjellström, an osteo-archaeologist from Stockholm University, looked anew at Vilkans's report and came to the same conclusion, but she encountered resistance, too. Then, in 2017, scientists tested the DNA. A genome-wide sequence data confirmed the absence of a Y chromosome: Bj 581 was female.

Some scientists remained skeptical, suggesting that the weapons had been used as scrapers or knives, not to kill animals: women's tools. Maybe she'd been buried with her hunter husband, but his skeleton had decomposed. Maybe the graves had been mixed up.

But other scientists and historians realized that they had to rethink their assumptions and generalizations about the gendered organization and social orders of ancient cultures.

After all, some past societies, including Vikings, had complex gender roles. Vikings were indeed patriarchal, but women might have had more freedom than they did in later Christian Europe. They fished and could travel and divorce their husbands. Maybe that had been lost on the men dusting off bones in the nineteenth century. Even back in the Middle Ages, stories of fierce female Viking warriors abounded, but those stories had been downgraded to myths by later Europeans.

Since the 2000s, archaeologists have been studying a 2,500-year-old tomb[5] in southern Russia.[6] It contained the remains of four female warriors, from ages twelve to fifty or so, buried with iron arrowheads and knives, animal bones and jewelry, among other items. These women were likely part of a nomadic tribe called the Scythians, thought to be the inspiration for the mythical Amazons. Archaeologists also found another eleven burials of women with weapons. Female hunters were certainly not limited to the Americas.

When WMP6 proved to be female, Haas found himself rethinking the generalizations that had permeated his own education and research. Paleolithic societies especially seemed to have quite different gender roles than modern, or even Neolithic, societies. Haas believes that communal hunting, rather than a strict, gendered division of labor, has "deep evolutionary roots."

## THE PALEOLITHIC HUNTRESS, THE NEOLITHIC HOUSEWIFE

ANATOMICALLY MODERN HUMANS—THAT is, people like us—likely evolved around 250,000 to 300,000 years ago. But up until about 12,000 years ago, during the Paleolithic Era, or the Old Stone Age, humans lived what Haas calls a "residentially mobile lifestyle." As nomads, they roamed the land in search of food for which they could hunt or forage, with the rudimentary tools they'd figured out how to engineer.

At the end of the last Ice Age, sometime between 14,000 and 20,000 years ago, humans likely crossed a land bridge from Siberia across the Bering Strait and made it to what we now call Alaska. If this is true, these would have been the first Americans, our indigenous people; archaeologists call them Paleoindians.[7]

This, said Haas, might have been the best time and place to be human, and to be a woman. In nomadic tribes, women didn't have to leave children behind to secure food. That painful choice between tending to children and providing for them hadn't yet evolved. Let's assume that living in a small clan, a communal society, was the equivalent of accessing paid family leave and universal childcare. Reproduction rates were high, and so were the number of resources. Enough people existed for a supportive community but not so many to invoke massive competition for the Americas' abundant game: woolly mammoths and giant sloths, massive camels and enormous bison.

When the main source of food was live game—very, very large live game—that's where the community would have focused its resources. "[Big game] is what gives you the most bang for your buck," Haas said, so it made sense from an economic perspective that everybody invested efforts and resources pursuing big game together.

Haas believes that somewhere between 30 and 50 percent of females participated in hunting. As an early gender-neutral activity, it may have been our first co-ed sport.[8] Some of that has to do with the hunting technology, because even then men on average had evolved to be bigger and stronger than women. Pre-pubertal females might have been the right age to master the atlatl, or spear-thrower, but later, heavier bow-and-arrow technology might have been easier for males.[9]

Of course, women wouldn't be chasing massive bison while breastfeeding or caring for toddlers too young to hunt, but since their home bases were temporary, females had no separate domestic sphere to inhabit.

Then ecological conditions changed. Haas believes that because humans were a novelty for much of the big game in the Americas, the naïve animals weren't particularly rattled by them. "Flight-initiation distance"—the distance at which one can approach an animal without it running away—might have been pretty small in the Paleolithic Era, rendering big game easier to catch and thus easier to overhunt. Some of those mammoths and giant camels might have gone extinct in part because humans were populating the landscape at a higher rate than the animals; lots of demand, and a supply that finally dried up.

Thus, people started eating lower-ranked resources like plants and smaller game like vicuña and alpaca. When their "diet breadth" expanded, their mobility patterns and how they organized their use of the landscape shifted. Rather than fully nomadic tribes in frequent motion, moving home base to be near big game and moving again when the resource was depleted, humans began to slow down some. They placed a home base in a location central to resources, called "central place foraging": setting up camp according to migration patterns or which plants are in season. "You go out, you harvest those resources, and you bring them back to your house," said Haas.

Now that there was a thing called home, somebody had to stay behind and tend to it. It no longer made sense for everyone to participate in hunting. It was time to divide the labor, raising the question: If some people have to stick near home, and others have to roam farther and stay away longer in search of calories, and then head back—well, who's going to do what?

Traveling with infants is a challenge, especially when humans had to voyage farther to hunt. So is keeping them quiet when the game grew scarce and the flight-initiation distance increased. A division of labor by sex probably started to seem logical. "All of these things contribute to a family unit saying, 'Look, it's probably going to make more sense now if we let males take care of the hunting side of the economy and females take care of the gathering side,'" Haas said. "And this is something that I think probably would only have happened in the last ten thousand years." (Not all anthropologists agree with Haas, of course.)

The man-the-hunter, woman-the-gatherer model that many of us think of as the natural order of things has only been our way of life for a tiny fraction of our existence, and this happened less due to biological destiny than as a result of shifting ecological conditions; the landscape shaped our division of labor.

The introduction of agriculture reinforced and further constrained gender roles. Hunter-gatherer women were likely pregnant or breastfeeding for most of their adult lives, which causes "physiologically induced amenorrhea"—a woman can't get pregnant if she's constantly breastfeeding. Thus, the birth rate was relatively low.

But once we stopped hunting and foraging, humans lived more sedentary lives and stored food to feed children, which led to an increase in the birth rate. And that's what tied women to the domestic sphere. Once we solidified the notion of home, we also set a woman's place within it: the idea of housewife. But that took thousands of years.[10]

## THE MAKING OF MAN-THE-HUNTER MYTHS

So why the pervasive narrative of man-the-hunter and woman-the-gatherer, confirmed by plenty of research? Anthropologists compiling ethnographies in nineteenth- and twentieth-century North and South America "seemed to show a fairly strong sexual division of labor pattern," Haas said. "In many indigenous societies, men tend to do the hunting, and women tend to do either processing of some of those hunted goods or foraging of plants and small game and fishing and things like this."

Yet when ethno-ecologist Jeanine M. Pfeiffer combed through 220 ethnographic studies to create a meta-analysis, she discovered that the hunter/gatherer narrative wasn't cleanly supported by the research that promoted it. Rather, women in both ancient and recent societies hunted wild pig, monkeys, kangaroos, python, mongoose, and caribou, across multiple continents. They participated in game hunting—big and small alike—and dived for wild seafood.[11]

Women might use different technology or techniques than men. Bun women in Papua New Guinea and Baka women in southwest Cameroon use nets or make dams to fish, but men use botanical toxins. In other cultures, women and men fish for different species, leading to "gender-based knowledge systems."¹² Even if they didn't hunt themselves, women sometimes contributed knowledge of tracking patterns. "Women's insider knowledge," says Pfeiffer, "enables households, whether they're female-headed or not, to survive and thrive in a way that they never would if they were solely male-headed."

In almost every culture, the gendered division of labor starts early, but it isn't always divided the same way. Chipewyan women were likely to hunt if they didn't have children, while in other agrarian societies, younger men steered clear of tending to plants, but doing so was a respectable activity for older men.¹³ In some cultures, weaving, preparation of skins, or gathering fuel is women's work. In other cultures, it's men's. Gender roles in these cultures aren't always static, or unaffected by age, ability, or environment—or always similar to Western roles. It made sense to divide labor by sex, but there's still no overarching human agreement about which sex should do what.

Meanwhile, many of us thought that hunting mattered more than gathering, or that male caloric contributions exceeded female contributions. But some studies have shown that women provided the majority of household calories in certain communities, and that gathered foods have, for thousands of years, made up a much larger percentage of diets than hunted foods.

"Throughout history, including all the way up to the present, women are far more engaged as primary breadwinners than we have ever been given credit for," Pfeiffer told me. By primary breadwinners, she means women as gatherers and hunters and fishers, providing up to 80 percent of the sustenance of a household, plus "all the uncompensated labor that women do."

One thing that does seem common across cultures: Women tend to carry what Pfeiffer calls a "triple load": agricultural tasks and/or gathering of natural resources outside the home, childcare, and household maintenance—like most modern Western working mothers. Time-budget surveys around the world show that generally women do the literal and figurative heavy lifting or work longer hours at menial tasks.

The division of labor by sex thus is not necessarily about which sex is superior, or about what women and men should do respectively. It's really just about efficiency.

## THE MISSION CHANGES

So HOW DID we continue to get the story so wrong, so narrow, when the reality is so broad? As Pfeiffer put it: "Cultural naïveté among Western academicians studying other societies can lead to narrow assumptions about men's or women's roles in those societies."[14] Some of these cultural blind spots developed because men ventured into indigenous communities and spoke only with other men; they didn't always see with their own eyes what women did. What you come away with depends on whom you talk to.

One oft-made assumption was that a society's elders are the most knowledgeable, and since men tend to have more status in indigenous societies, ethnographers would end up interviewing older men. In some of these societies, men's and women's lives and roles were quite different, so any information about women was filtered through men's perspectives. Sometimes men and women spoke different dialects, but often translators were male; they might not even have been able to communicate with women, excluding entire subcultures of them. These write-ups really were *his*tory, not *her*story. (Though the field of archaeology remains predominantly male, women have made steady gains and may overtake men in the future—contributing to different data sets.)[15]

Some archaeologists and anthropologists struggled to comprehend shifting modern and ancient gender roles because they assumed that modern hunter-gatherer societies retained much in common with ancient ones. But modern hunter-gatherer societies lived differently than they might have thousands of years earlier. They might not have been watching TikTok or perusing the Walmart's pink and sparkly girls' clothes section, but they'd been reached by missionaries and anthropologists with Western gender views. These indigenous communities, even if remote, weren't untouched by the modern world.

"The foragers that live today or lived recently are embedded in world economies," Haas said. "They're influenced by missionization. They're influenced by agriculturists. They're part of those economies." So we can't rely on them to tell us about gender roles of bygone eras.

"The ethnography we're looking at is only [from] the last hundred years. A hundred years out of two hundred thousand years is just a drop in the bucket," Haas said. "Why should we expect the environment that recent hunter-gatherers inhabit today was anything like what it was ten thousand years ago, twenty thousand years ago, thirty thousand years ago?"

## HUNTER-GATHERER HIERARCHY?

EVEN ONCE SUCH a thing as "women's work" existed, long past the Neolithic Era, people didn't automatically devalue the work associated with women. Several studies have shown that, Haas wrote, "both women and men in ethnographic hunter-gatherer societies govern residence decisions."[16]

In 1896, archaeologists began to excavate a 650-room building called Pueblo Bonito in New Mexico's Chaco Canyon.[17] Chaco society lasted from roughly AD 850 through 1250, with Pueblo Bonito as the largest building in this particular settlement.[18] There, archaeologists found a burial crypt containing the remains of fourteen people.

When they recently analyzed those remains' nuclear genome data and mitochondrial DNA, they determined "the persistence of an elite matriline in Chaco for 330 years": a female-led dynasty.[19]

Also consider the Tibetan Khasi, both matriarchal and matrilineal: Women inherit the property, and upon marriage the man relocates to the woman's house.[20] Historically in this culture, women assumed the breadwinner role, but more recently both sexes work. And while we're at it, consider that the female hunter who's so unfathomable to modern humans is a staple of ancient polytheistic religions. The ancient Mesopotamian goddess Inanna has been called "a raging destroyer feared by deities and humans alike," and Athena was born with shield and helmet, ready to fight.[21]

Gender roles evolved over time and culture and landscapes and conditions, largely due to external circumstances—not because men were better than women, or more deserving of leadership positions, but because ecological considerations led to the most logical division of labor. Think of it as early egalitarianism, of cooperation. Ecology, not just biology, adumbrated the boundaries of women's work.

Contrary to the pervasive myth that men have always been hunters and women gatherers, the lesson these complex histories teach us is this: Working mothers have been the norm from the beginning of human history.

# CHAPTER 3

# Interdependent Housewives

Meera grew up in a close-knit Indian immigrant community in Japan, where none of the mothers worked. "They were housewives in the truest sense of the word," she said. Her grandparents lived a fifteen-minute walk from her house, and she regularly spent afternoons there, or stayed overnight.

Despite the wonderful aspects of her childhood, the insularity of the community felt stifling. These families had arrived from India mid-century, bringing with them the traditional values of their homeland. They didn't really assimilate, because doing so would mean loosening the grip on their identities and their history, and they maintained their own community institutions, protected from the larger world.

Early on, Meera developed a love of reading and writing and dreamed of a career crafting words, but there were so few professional opportunities for women in Japan. One of the driving forces behind her coming to the United States to attend college was that she felt strongly that she wanted to live a life outside the home, and America presented that possibility. "I was going to do something different from the women I grew up around," she said.

The people she met once she arrived confirmed her beliefs. The parents of her college friends really did seem to live in egalitarian households, with chores divided fairly. Moms worked outside the home; dads did childcare. "It just felt much more in line with the common values I was looking for," she said.

After school, Meera moved to New York City and took a job at a magazine. She was living the dream. She met her husband, then an architect who later went into real estate management. But as she thought about having kids, Meera saw how hard being a working mom was. The female editors with kids were stretched so thin. "That was my first sign that the career path I was going down wasn't going to be a really good fit for being the sort of mother I wanted to be," she said. Meera left the magazine to freelance, spending five years carving out a different track before giving birth to her son.

She wondered, though: Was she tempering her ambitions, lowering her expectations of herself, or was she being realistic about what was possible? Six months after giving birth to her son, Meera hired a part-time nanny and returned to work. In theory, she had it all. She could still do what she loved without the relentless, enervating juggle or without staying home full-time. Having the privilege of choice, Meera chose the middle path between her mother's world and the world she'd seen modeled at the magazine.

So why wasn't she…happier?

Some of it was the feeling that her work mattered less than her husband's, which led her to question the validity, the importance of the career she'd so carefully nurtured. He was clearly the breadwinner, and once her son got older and started school, that left Meera as the parent perpetually on call. With at least one three-day weekend a month and parent-teacher meetings always scheduled in the middle of the day, the school calendar depended so much on one parent staying home. It just didn't allow for the kind of egalitarianism she'd admired when she first arrived in this country. If Meera ever had to ask a "favor" of her husband, to pick up or drop off their son at school, it wasn't an easy conversation. He didn't have the kind of workplace culture that made it seamless for men to prioritize family. Maybe America didn't, either, Meera was learning.

She balked at a culture where paternity leave seemed so optional, so exceptional. Men could take it or leave it, but women were expected to take time off, even without pay. There were so few community and governmental supports.

She was so . . . alone.

During the pandemic, Meera stopped working completely, helping her four-year-old with online school. She loved spending time with him, but the decision inspired a new round of angst, an identity crisis. Who was she now?

And then she began to miss something else: the family, the world, she'd grown up with, the institutional support generated within. As limited and limiting as that community was, it offered her that cross-generational connection with her grandparents and the institutions that they inhabited. "Now I look back on the fact that it was this consistent, reliable form of childcare, away from my parents, that they had for years and years and years," she said.

For a long time, Meera thought she found working motherhood hard because she'd seen no role models of it growing up. But then she realized her challenges stemmed from a fundamental problem with America and its attitude toward the family, the pressure it puts on mothers, each nuclear family fending for itself.

But it wasn't always this way.

## NECESSARY NEEDINESS

INDEPENDENCE. THE OFFSPRING of manifest destiny, it's held up as the American ideal. God may have deemed the United States fated to spread democracy and capitalism, but stoic American families made it happen. Independence is so woven into our political system that each family is expected to bootstrap up the ladder of the American meritocracy on its own.

The earliest American families didn't have it easy, by any means. The average American housewife in the 1700s and early 1800s reared six children in multi-generational households, usually without running water or electricity.[1] Men chopped firewood; women stoked the fires. Men harvested the produce; women canned it. Housewives, especially in rural areas, performed plenty of physical labor outdoors, from milking cows to milling flour. These were not days of brandishing a feather duster while shuffling about the carpeted apartment in heels.

Today, homemade goods are the province of the privileged Etsy set, while the cheapest and quickest food is the most processed and unhealthy, and the cheapest clothes are those of fast fashion, made possible by exploitive labor. But back then, almost everything was crafted at home: soap, clothes, bread. Women called their domestic acts "my Narrow sphere" or "my humble duties."[2] Cooking wasn't an art form, leading to Instagram-ready glittering dinner pics. Done over an open hearth with a spare assortment of utensils, meals were unfussy and made of whatever could be locally sourced. Rather than an expression of femininity to perfect, chores were simply something to get done.[3]

A housewife possessed both the skills to manufacture those goods and, if she was lucky enough to afford it, some support staff; she might manage others who manufactured goods for her and her family. Or, if possible, she'd take on a "hired girl" as needed. Housewives made sure everything on the home front ran smoothly, allowing their husbands to concentrate on providing for the family economically. His work simply could not be done without her free labor.[4] Perhaps it was better to be a housewife, because you got to have a house and be a wife, as opposed to the various single women serving the housewife. Black women, almost all enslaved at the time, rarely even had the privilege of being shunted into the housewife role.

While she may have been the boss in the kitchen, and of the others who worked in it, a housewife's boss was always her husband, "a moral arbiter as well as the ultimate decision-maker in the marriage," Glenna Matthews writes in *Just a Housewife*.[5] Father knew best. Experts warned mothers not to be too doting or affectionate, lest it make their kids soft. Somehow these housewives should manage a staff while promoting their own submissiveness.

Yet colonial families, albeit with an icy mom and stern dad, weren't entirely on their own. They took support from civic, political, community, and government institutions and groups. Families relied on "neighbors, church institutions, courts, government officials, and legislative bodies for their sustenance," historian Stephanie Coontz wrote in *The Way We Never Were*.[6] Community parades and festivals took prominence over, say, gathering the family for Thanksgiving or Christmas.[7]

The history of the American family, from the beginning of this nation, is one of *inter*dependence. Without government and community help, no early American settlers would have thrived. Americans "have been dependent on collective institutions beyond the family, including government, since the very beginning," wrote Coontz.[8]

Families were seen as vehicles for the colony, for the economy, and for supporting institutional functions. The poor, the elderly, the ill— they were taken care of within families; if not their own, then within other families paid by the government to attend to them. Little of this neediness, reliance on others, was looked down upon in the colonial era, no matter one's class. Owing money to the government, or to your local grocer, and gift-giving, charity, favors, dependency—these were signs of connectedness, of trust, of a colonial code of familial and community conduct.[9] These days, of course, they're signs of personal failure.

Lest we romanticize this time as one of utopian interdependence, remember one practical reason for spreading the eggs to so many baskets: The average marriage lasted only for a little over a decade—not due to divorce, but because of the death rate.[10] To emotionally invest only in his or her partner wouldn't be in a spouse's self-interest. Meanwhile, Americans couldn't have built the new world without killing off the native people who already inhabited the land. But they couldn't have built this new world without helping one another prosper on the land they stole.

And housewives? They may have been working very, very hard without being paid for it, but rarely did they toil all alone.

## REPUBLICAN MOTHERHOOD

DURING THE REVOLUTIONARY War, women assumed "male" responsibilities in their husbands' absences: raising money, farming, taking care of finances. But once the fighting stopped, the revolution no longer extended to women. What to do with the now-uppity ladies who'd tasted more agency and power but whom men needed to return to hearth and home after the war? (This will be a recurring theme.) Convince them that their patriotic duty was located in the home.

This was the dawn of "Republican Motherhood," in which mothers' and housewives' premier task was raising children to become proper American citizens; women stayed home to rear and educate the kids (especially sons) so they could venture out into the world. The family served the Republic.[11]

The idea may have been inspired by philosopher John Locke, who in his *Treatises of Government* portrayed women's job of raising future patriots to be of equal value to men's jobs, because there'd be no one to fight for the sanctity of the nation without moms. This rendered women's domestic roles important, yet somehow maintained women's powerlessness.

Before the American Revolution, boys received much more education than girls; Mount Holyoke, the first women's college to rival the curriculum at a men's school, didn't open until 1837. So perhaps Republican Motherhood's most curious facet was that it required that women be educated, that they in turn could properly teach their children. Eighteenth-century writer and women's rights advocate Mary Wollstonecraft wrote that "if children are to be educated to understand the true principle of patriotism, their mother must be a patriot... but the education and situation of a woman at present shuts her out."[12]

Benjamin Rush, former treasurer of the United States Mint, penned a 1791 treatise, "Thoughts upon Female Education" (not to be confused with Wollstonecraft's 1787 *Thoughts on the Education of Daughters*), in which he offered opinions "contrary to general prejudice and fashion" such as: "female education should be accommodated to the state of society, manners, and government of the country in which it is conducted." He suggested that the advancement of men, and the achievement of American prosperity, "cannot be done without the assistance of the female members of the community."[13]

Though Rush founded the Young Ladies' Academy of Philadelphia, where women learned math and science, the entire nation didn't rush to embrace girls' education. Many feared education would create audacious women who would demand their rights. Eventually, of course, the Suffragists would prove their fears founded.

## O PIONEERS!

IF NORTHEASTERN MIDDLE- and upper-class families focused on rearing good citizens, nineteenth-century families out west set up shop under a different reigning ideal. Girls of my generation devoured *Little House on the Prairie* books by Laura Ingalls Wilder. In real life, Wilder's mom, Mrs. Ingalls, was tough, pistol-wielding, and pregnant with her third child when her husband moved the family from Wisconsin to Kansas to start anew amid the Civil War, western expansion, and, though not represented as such in the television adaptation, an ongoing genocide of native peoples.[14] They represented a typical independent frontier family.

Or so we were told.

In reality, families who moved west in the nineteenth century weren't particularly self-reliant. Frontier families were, in fact, "the most heavily subsidized in American history," per Coontz.[15]

Railroad companies paid immigrants—the Swedes to Kansas, the Poles to Nebraska and North Dakota—to relocate to lands that had become settleable thanks to government military operations and state-sponsored genocide.[16] Federal land grants and state investments literally and figuratively paved the way for new Americans to inhabit these territories.

The feds gave squatters on government land the option to buy it for less than market value. Single men over twenty-one or widows were eligible to make those purchases under the Preemption Act of 1841. The Donation Land Claim Act of 1850 brought thousands to Oregon. The Homestead Act of 1862 granted 160 acres for a $10 filing fee to those willing to inhabit and improve the land over five years.

It turns out these "rugged, individualistic" settlers were actually the beneficiaries of the kinds of government handouts often met with scorn by those who embrace what's thought of as a typical American western mentality. At the least, the stoic, rugged, self-contained pioneer family is an embellishment. At the most, it's a lie. No western family would've accessed water, land, transportation, or economic development without government assistance.[17]

Community-created institutions performed functions we'd think of as familial today: lodges opened by immigrant groups to assist financially and socially; funeral aid societies and sick or death benefit associations assumed by laborers; unions and religious institutions, taking as their mission helping members and parishioners in monetary or emotional need. The Catholics had godparenting. Some Native Americans had "blood brothers." Black communities had "going for sisters."[18]

Many families couldn't have survived otherwise. Three-fifths of families retained no savings. Even middle-class families depended on government subsidies and community assistance—and this didn't provoke shame. It was expected. Blood "was not always thicker than neighborhood, class, ethnicity, or religion," Coontz wrote.[19] Self-sufficiency was actually a community experience; the community helped families take care of themselves, and that wasn't seen as an oxymoron.

## THE FAMILY TURNS INWARD

BACK ALONG THE eastern seaboard, new ideas about what constituted women's work sprung up, some created by women themselves. Perhaps the most famous purveyors of housewifely dogma in their era, Catherine Beecher and her younger sister, Harriet Beecher Stowe, together wrote the 1869 classic *The American Woman's Home*. They developed a vision of home as haven, a safe place that shielded housewives from the evils of industrial capitalism.[20] (It's almost the opposite in the mid-twentieth century, when the home became a pipeline to industrial capitalism, as noted in chapter 5.) The Beechers included floor plans, laying out where the running water and windows should be to maximize efficiency and safety, and suggested open shelves with boxes to hold napkins and utensils. The more efficiently designed the home, the better it would run, resulting in more time and energy for a housewife to concentrate on her husband and children, rather than sullying herself by competing with men in paid work.

The Beechers preached a particular kind of life for those able to attain it, but considering their literary output, they likely weren't quite following their own advice. They were among the many women who would, over the years, earn a living instructing other women how to perform housewifery properly and not make a living themselves. Both *Good Housekeeping*, whose mission was "to produce and perpetuate perfection as may be obtained in the household," and *Ladies' Home Journal* debuted in the late 1880s. Cyrus H. K. Curtis founded the latter and installed his wife, Louisa Knapp, as editor (she didn't use her legal name, Louisa Knapp Curtis, as a byline); she wasn't crocheting and polishing silver while he went off to work, but commissioned plenty of ads and articles about how to succeed at doing so.

Working women of Knapp's status remained rare then. At the turn of the twentieth century, most women who worked outside the home were young and single. The U.S. Census categorized just 20 percent of women as "gainful workers," only 5 percent of them married.

African American women were far more likely to work outside the home than white women (and still are). In 1880, 35.4 percent of married Black women and 73.3 percent of single Black women participated in the labor force, compared with only 7.3 percent of married white women and 23.8 percent of single white women. Black women who entered the workforce while single tended to remain in it after marrying, while white women often dropped out after getting hitched.[21]

But let's not assume that marrying and leaving the paid workforce equaled some kind of prize, especially in a world without running water, central heat, or electricity, when only well-off housewives could afford a full support staff. In *Divided Lives*, author Rosalind Rosenberg wrote that "economically speaking, wives might be viewed as the last large class of indentured servants in America. Under the terms of the marriage contract, a husband promised to support his wife in return for her promise to serve and obey him."[22]

And with good reason, according to an evolving ideology known as the "Cult of Domesticity" or "Cult of True Womanhood," in which women must maintain piety, purity, submissiveness, and domesticity.[23]

As the Industrial Revolution precluded the need for much hard labor from women and wives, they and men alike began to hold romantic views of love and nurturing as female qualities that could temper men's participation in their capitalistic pursuits. In turn, men began to hold romantic views about women as relentlessly generous and self-sacrificing—and came to expect them to be that way. As physician Charles Meigs wrote in 1847, "A woman has a head almost too small for intellect but just big enough for love."[24] Women must remain in the domestic sphere, keeping all that is good and true away from the land of men, work, and money. Thus, the cementing of the breadwinner/ homemaker divide.

A credo of romanticized male individualism developed alongside this romanticized vision of female domesticity, with liberty, equality, and fraternity adding up to the image of the self-made man.[25] Alas, such a man's independence was, you guessed it, really a product of *inter*dependence—behind every great man a woman toiled silently in the background to render his life outside the home possible. Men could embrace self-reliance because women embraced (or were forced to accept) dependence.

Meanwhile, middle-class women could retreat to this rarefied yet restrictive place only because technological advances and the exploitation of lower classes allowed them to. Poorer women worked in textile mills, preparing cloth wealthier women used; the raw materials in those mills had been harvested by enslaved people.[26] Thus, despite the ethos of self-reliance, an entire economy ran beneath it, allowing a select group to claim this fallacious identity. The notion of altruistic families, and in particular altruistic mothers, grew alongside the free market and a new middle class, giving birth to the enduring American ethic of individuality—one few Americans could have actually lived up to.[27]

As the ethos spread, community and civic institutions decentralized, putting more pressure on families, and specifically women, to fill the gaps. Rather than something necessary to succeed, interdependence slowly shape-shifted into something shameful. Though normalized in most cultures, interdependence became anathema to American ideals.[28]

Most of us look back now at the Cult of True Womanhood and see it as benefiting men. After all, they continued to lead public lives while women retreated into domesticity. The truth, of course, is more complicated. Some women formed romantic bonds in their separate spheres or started businesses. Sarah Josepha Buell Hale, mother of four—five, until one of her children died—authored *Mary Had a Little Lamb* and later edited the magazine *Godey's Lady's Book*, directed at women. She, too, earned a living selling ideas of domesticity.

And just because men were thrust solely and squarely into the breadwinner role outside the home doesn't mean that it ultimately benefited them. In the twenty-first century, books about confidence crises among girls and women ceded to those about crises among boys and men, falling behind academically, emotionally, and financially. After decades of concerted efforts to raise the profiles of women since the 1970s, today we worry that boys are suffering, less able to articulate their emotions and ask for help, still stifled by the expectation of self-sufficiency.

It's easy to romanticize the past, and I don't suggest that the hard physical labor, the demands, the lack of power weren't enormous stressors before the Cult of Domesticity, during the more interdependent era. But because there was once an expectation of interdependence, I do propose that housewives at least had some support for their difficult lives, as families weren't expected to figure out how to feed, clothe, educate—morally and academically—their children all alone. And I suggest that we need to take the stigma out of American interdependence today.

So many of us still feel the pressure to make our nuclear families successful without assistance. We shudder in shame at not being able to afford day care. When we fail to live up to the Enjoli perfume commercial image of womanhood, we experience it as personal failure, rather than cultural and political failure. We may no longer beat our laundry on a stone, or hide in the home surrounded by needlepoint projects, but we've still been tasked with a difficult load, lest we've been lucky enough to draw on endless wells of cash and create a capitalistic version of interdependence, by way of hiring nannies, housekeepers, and cooks.

As our society and economy evolved, the expectation of self-reliance would become increasingly cemented not just in our ideology but in our policies and laws. We shifted from interdependence to independence, from a housewife whose work is valued as part of a patriotic project to one whose work is cordoned off away from the world and devalued, from family buoyed by government, civic, and community assistance to family expected to fend for itself. For decades to come, these tensions would surface, over and over again, in the lives of American housewives.

# CHAPTER 4

# Militant Housewives

I t was all about business. After hearing a lecture by Alben L. Hol-sey of the National Negro Business League about the importance of investing in Black-owned businesses, the Reverend William H. Peck organized the Booker T. Washington Trade Association in April 1930—an early version of For Us, By Us.

The Reverend's wife, Fannie Peck, had also attended the lecture, and she understood housewives' essential role in supporting Black-owned businesses, too. Housewives controlled household budgets, even if they didn't contribute to them monetarily; women managed about 80 percent of family income at the time.[1] So on June 10, 1930, amid the Great Depression, she formed an association of her own: the Housewives' League of Detroit.[2]

She began with fifty members, all tasked with spending their household budgets within their own community, or at businesses that hired and supported African Americans. Their motto: "Don't buy where you can't work." This not only helped fortify Black-owned business but also helped more Black Americans find employment. Peck preached self-reliance, common sense, and pride to housewives.

With so many housewives successfully exerting common power,

Peck helped other Housewives' Leagues form: in the Ohio cities of Cleveland, Cincinnati, and Toledo, in Pittsburgh, Indianapolis, Jacksonville, and Kansas City, Missouri.

Holsey himself got word of Fannie's prowess, and in 1932, he encouraged her and some fellow League members to create a national committee. Thus began the National Housewives' League of America, Inc. Their first president: Fannie Peck. By the next year, they were meeting in Durham, along with the National Negro Business League.

Peck's organization was among several housewife groups in the '30s and '40s, women who banded together to agitate for change using their collective power. These weren't always demure women, hemming their husband's garments at home, or proper ladies like Peck. Some of the women took to the streets and raised hell.

I found much of this out through the work of Dartmouth historian Annelise Orleck, author of the article "We Are That Mythical Thing Called the Public: Militant Housewives in the Great Depression," and the book *Common Sense and a Little Fire: Women and Working Class Politics in the United States*. She chronicled unruly housewives from lower economic echelons, largely absent from history and from the cultural memory of housewifery. From the late 1920s through the 1940s, she wrote, there was "a remarkable surge of activism by working class American housewives."[3]

## WOMEN HAVE A BIG PART TO PLAY

IN 1933, ELEANOR Roosevelt authored a book called *It's Up to the Women*. A call to action for women and housewives in response to the Great Depression's economic and psychological destruction, the book also commented on a sad and little acknowledged truth. While men comprised the bulk of the nearly 13 million unemployed, women dealt with the aftermath of dwindling or dried-up familial funds. Practically every woman, Roosevelt noted, was living on a reduced income, whether they earned it themselves or not.

Roosevelt's husband, Franklin Delano Roosevelt, had been elected to get America out of the economic morass, but his wife took it upon herself to give the ladies their own notes. "We are going through a great crisis in this country," she wrote, and "women have a big part to play if we are coming through it successfully."[4] Almost a quarter of the country's workers were unemployed. For those still working, wages descended more than 42 percent.[5] Factories and farms shuttered.

The way to surmount the national problem was not just through her husband's New Deal social programs but through personal and familial sacrifice. Women had been doing as much since the *Mayflower* landed, Roosevelt noted, and without them, we'd never have won the Revolution. They had carried on at home while their husbands toiled in battle, keeping home fires burning, meals cooked, injured bodies cared for. Now women must "look at ourselves critically" and give up "pleasant things," realizing it had always been a luxury to have them.

I see this as a recurring trope, calling on women to personally, individually solve problems that should rightly be addressed societally, structurally: the personal as substitute for the political (think of recycling your #2 plastic versus large corporations embracing green policies). And of course Roosevelt was nodding here to women who actually had pleasant things to give up—or whose ancestors hailed from the "right" European countries and came over on the *Mayflower*.

But Roosevelt really was interested in making life better for all women. One idea was for older women to help younger women tend to children, a kind of grandmother doula program, we might call it now.

(When I told friends about this, some said it was already common in their ethnic Hispanic cultures. Others practically drooled at the idea of Borrow-a-Gramma.) Having a middle-aged woman "who has been through many of the difficulties she is now facing, come in to help her" would make life easier, "but as a rule the expense entailed in this country makes it impossible," Roosevelt wrote.

The Depression had a destabilizing effect on the family. The marriage rate fell to what was then an all-time low[6] (it hit another major dip in 2018[7]). Some men eschewed marriage if they couldn't achieve breadwinning status. The government even floated the idea of subsidizing young couples delaying marriage because of money. Roosevelt herself cautioned women not to be disappointed in men or their husbands for their reduced income—don't emasculate fellas because they couldn't get paid.

Even if women earned less than half of what men did, and women of color earned less than half of what white women did, those marriage delays allowed some women to become more independent, financially and emotionally.[8] More than 6 million such women contributed to their families' financial health during the era.[9] As a result, some could envision emancipating themselves from housewifery.

These economic dire straits increased what historian Elaine Tyler May called "shared breadwinning"—a model closer to earlier, agrarian families, in which both parents tended the land.[10] Now, amid crisis, both parents needed to work in some families, or if a husband lost his job, a wife might help make ends meet through taking on women's work—"pink collar" jobs such as nursing, doctor's aides, dental assistants, teaching—that wouldn't take men's work like factory jobs, which might threaten men's sense of masculinity.

Through the economic and emotional cloudiness, silver linings burst: There were more chances to embrace interdependence. Many people lived with extended families again—while not by choice, of course, they were nonetheless reestablishing kinship networks beyond the nuclear family. As one newspaper put it, "Many a family has lost its car but found its soul."[11]

The Depression *could* have been the first step toward a future of more equitable marriages, a reinvention of gender roles and the financial expectations attached to them. But of course, that's not what happened. Many of FDR's policies designed to get men back to work made it harder for women to do so, or even to stay employed. Section 213 of the Economy Act of 1932 dictated that if two spouses were employed federally and there were layoffs, the wives went first; some 1,600 women were dismissed from federal employment.[12]

The government proscribed women's work in so many ways. Some 75 percent of cities excluded married women from teaching. Eight state laws prohibited women from working for the state.[13] The government might offer financial relief to an unemployed breadwinner, but wouldn't provide assistance for women's employment needs, like subsidizing day cares.

What the government and culture really pushed women to do, after the roaring, independent, and feminist 1920s, was go home. One Works Progress Administration official opined, "The best service a mother can do is to rear her children in the home."[14]

## HOUSEWIFE SELF-HELP, FOR OTHERS

YET MANY WOMEN didn't stay home. Instead, they took a stand.

With children growing hungry, women had to figure out how to make food stretch, to reduce, reuse, and recycle as never before. Some housewives began to form self-help groups and bartering clubs, swapping labor for fish, fruit, grains, and vegetables. People pitched in to gather and distribute food and goods,[15] or sew clothing, to harness the power of community when the government fell short.[16]

As prices for basics like milk and meat crested sharply, these progressive-minded women grouped into neighborhood councils to demand improvements in living conditions, especially in ethnic slums. There were housewives' councils and women's auxiliary clubs like the Chicago Committee Against the High Cost of Living, the Mother and Child Unit of Communist Organizers, and the United Council of Working Class Women.

In New York City, many were spurred on by Ukrainian Jewish immigrant and organizer Clara Lemlich Shavelson, who as a young girl had worked in Lower East Side sweatshops under abominable conditions. Shavelson later formed the International Ladies Garment Workers Union (ILGWU), but after birthing three children, she concentrated on rallying wives and mothers, believing that they could not only improve their own lots but also those of larger swaths of society.[17] After helping arrange kosher meat boycotts in 1917 and rent strikes in 1919, Shavelson, along with other communist women, formed the United Council of Working-Class Housewives in 1926. They helped fight evictions, organize sit-ins and marches, and made the case that housewives, in charge of consumption, were inextricably linked with production.

When meat prices rose during the Depression, working-class housewives took action. On May 27, 1935, a coalition of New York City housewives picketed butcher shops, demanding an end to what was for some a 62 percent increase in meat prices. Convinced shops were artificially limiting supply, they insisted on a 10 percent price decrease.[18] Though meat wasn't the only unaffordable product, it retained symbolic value as a central and highly caloric provision, the "big game" of the times.

Black and Jewish housewives assembled into picket lines to protest meat producers. Black housewives in particular targeted white-owned businesses suspected of price-gouging their most disenfranchised customers.[19] Within the second week of striking, as many as 5,000 butcher shops may have been closed.[20]

Word spread. The Chicago Committee Against the High Cost of Living began organizing meetings in the streets outside meatpacking stockyards, announcing their discontent.[21] Housewives testified before the Detroit City Council: "What we can afford to buy isn't fit for a human to eat."[22]

A 1935 issue of the Communist Party's publication *The Working Woman* included a two-page spread with a cartoon lambasting rich factory owners—"haves"—and encouraging have-nots to strike on June 8. "Buy No Meat," it read. "Tell Your Friends Not to Buy. Prepare to Picket Large Packers."

Housewives by the thousands answered the call. Coalitions of Polish, Irish, Italian, Black, and Jewish housewives launched consumer protests. Some 10,000 housewives in Los Angeles picketed. Housewives in Boston, St. Louis, and Kansas City started their own. Protests later sprung up in Indianapolis, Miami, and Denver. None would buy meat, they said, until prices came down.

After the June 8 strike, a caucus of housewives marched on Washington, then demanded to meet with Secretary of Agriculture Henry Wallace. Some politicians were suspicious of the protestors. Their high heels, their pearls and purses, their fancy hairdos led U.S. Representative Clarence Cannon of Missouri to assume the women wanted attention more than justice.[23] To discredit them, Cannon accused the housewives of being middle class, more interested in feeding their egos than their families. He couldn't conceive of the fact that immigrant housewives had organized such an effective campaign. He even wondered if perhaps the meatpackers themselves had orchestrated a "fake food strike."

On July 27 that year, somewhere between 200 and 500 housewives marched through the streets of Hamtramck, Michigan, a Polish enclave outside of Detroit, demanding that butcher shops reduce prices.[24] They carried signs that read: "Strike Against High Meat Prices. Don't Buy."[25] To many, the strike seemed shockingly effective, considering that the strikers were "just housewives." Some store owners insisted there must be a powerful Communist Party influence behind their organizing and actions. A cigar factory worker named Joseph P. Schultz claimed the strike was his idea, only to complain later that "[t]hese women became too hot to handle."

In fact, the leader of the Hamtramck strike was a petite, thirty-two-year-old, 100-pound Polish American housewife named Mary Zuk. Wife of an unemployed autoworker and daughter of a mining union activist, Zuk headed the Detroit Committee for Action Against the High Cost of Living. She organized the strike, she told the local newspaper, when she "began to notice how deeply meat bills cut into the food bills of her family." Zuk became known as "generalissimo of the campaign" and "the mother of the meat strike."[26] The post office received letters from housewives in other cities and states, addressed to "Mrs. Zuk—Detroit."

The strikes weren't all peaceful. Picketing women beat a man in front of a sausage store when he refused to give up the meat he'd bought. Several men crossed the picket lines only to find the housewives weren't sweet little ladies gently requesting a reduction in cost, but fierce and furious women literally fighting for their children's lives. Some women slapped the men, pulled their hair, and wrested away their packages. The *New York Times* reported the men were "scratched and bruised," and the women "kept police scout cars dashing from one picketed butcher shop to another."[27]

But they were triumphant—at least at disrupting business. "Housewives in Meat Strikes Close Hamtramck Stores," the *Detroit Times* reported.[28] Butchers claimed they'd lost $65,000 worth of business. By the beginning of the second week, butchers put signs in their windows that prices had dropped by 20 percent.

The butchers were forced to admit, wrote Annelise Orleck, that the boycott was "95 percent successful."

In August 1935, Zuk and five others finally stormed into Secretary Wallace's office and made demands: Cut prices by 20 percent; sever the meat processing tax; prosecute price-gouging meatpackers. Wallace's first move was to try to kick out the press; he perhaps didn't want to be seen refusing the housewives, whose main aim was to feed their kids. The press didn't leave, but eventually Wallace did, and the next day, the *Chicago Daily Tribune* headline read: "Secretary Wallace Beats Retreat from Five Housewives."[29]

Rather than take their concerns seriously, other newspapers made fun of the rebelling women. Yet they were serious, and not just about meat prices. Jewish housewives in New York barricaded themselves in tenements to prevent evictions. In Cleveland, Black mothers draped damp laundry over utility lines until the power company turned the lights back on for families unable to pay their bills. A woman named Myrtle Hoaglund declared she was founding a statewide Michigan housewives' organization because "We feel that we should have united action."[30] She shared with her city council a sack full of letters from housewives across the nation who wanted to learn to organize boycotts in their own cities and towns.

The news coverage added fuel to the housewives' fire, and for some housewives, that fire was literal. They burned meat warehouses in the Midwest and mid-Atlantic. Polish housewives in Chicago burned meat at Armour and Company's warehouse.

As strikes continued, and militant housewives gained more press and at least the appearance of power, many began to face a conundrum: Straddling organizing and home life, they found a balance difficult. Some newspapers warned that women's straying so far from demureness and the domicile would result in the family's demise. As is so often the case, the presence of women outside the home—organizing, fighting for rights, pushing for equality—caused a panic that children would be harmed.

Some struggled to maintain the domestic front while protesting, and some union husbands demanded that their wives abandon political work. *The Working Woman* magazine offered a hamper full of canned goods to women who could come up with the best retort for such an imposition. The winner: a Bronx housewife who advocated for shared childcare. A Pennsylvania housewife wrote in to say "There can't be a revolution without women."[31]

## INWARD, OUTWARD

PERHAPS THESE REVOLUTIONARY actions weren't such a stretch for working-class women. This wasn't the romantic mid-twentieth-century white suburban housewife, pure and unsullied in the domestic sphere, but the poor, ethnic version that preceded it. The term "housewife" "did not mean that they weren't then or had not previously done wage labor outside of the home," Orleck explained to me. Many had held jobs, some of them within unions, before becoming mothers. Others had witnessed or been involved in boycotts and rent strikes in the 1900s and 1910s. A 1930s training film for British housewives showed them scrubbing the floor with a wire brush and washing dishes in cold tubs—housewives, in some cases, were hardly more than unpaid maids.[32]

These working-class women embraced the term "housewife" because it bestowed on them a certain amount of political capital. They reclaimed a mildly derogatory designation, pinned on them by politicians and policymakers and corporate leaders. "They owned it. They politicized it. And they made use of the image of the housewife as the consumer," Orleck said. They essentially used "implements of their trade, to get across their desires for fair treatment." Writer Rebecca Solnit called this "the secret of the housewife theory of history: These women take the qualities that are supposed to render them irrelevant and use them defiantly as well as strategically."[33]

Reared in the land of union organizers and socialist groups, not genteel, single-family houses, these working-class housewives may have seen their homes—often tenements and apartments—as connected to fields and factories: What happened out there industrially affected them and their families domestically. In their tight-knit, densely populated communities, it was easy to rally large groups in the name of civic improvement, to face outward and collectivize for better conditions. They applied the tactics and language of union organizing to the domestic front.

Orleck notes that militant housewives likely wouldn't have considered themselves feminists, though this was happening just about fifteen years after women won the vote. (Two years after that, in 1921, a coalition of Black women requested the National Women's Party's help in securing voting rights for Black women; the NWP rejected them.) Their activism, Orleck told me, "is not done in the name of being a housewife, but of being a mother"—for families, not for women. As their concern was for children's education, a safe food supply, and affordable prices, the women were still selfless on some level. Even when slapping a man carrying his sausage (not a euphemism), they performed the role of protector, in service of their kids.

Eleanor Roosevelt was late to the word "feminism" herself. While never publicly supporting the suffragists, she'd long been sympathetic to the plights of immigrant and working women and became more politically active once she learned of her husband's affair with her own social secretary, Lucy Mercer.[34] Women could fight relentlessly to improve the quality of life for other women without becoming attached to the adjacent phenomenon called feminism.

Nor were these working-class housewives assimilated into what we think of as whiteness now. They were still defined by their ethnicities, separate from those *Mayflower* descendants: Irish, Italian, Jewish among them.

But some of those poor and ethnic white women took advantage of just how much worse things were in the Depression for women of color. Some hired Black migrants from the South to work inside their homes under appalling conditions that NAACP investigator Ella Baker and journalist Marvel Cooke exposed. They called it the "Bronx Slave Market" in which "human labor [is] bartered and sold for slave wage."[35] Black women would wait "expectantly for Bronx housewives to buy their strength and energy for an hour, two hours, or even for a day at the munificent rate of fifteen, twenty, twenty-five, or if luck be with them, thirty cents an hour." Some of those women, Baker and Cooke reported, worked in grand homes before the Depression rendered them desperate enough to seek employment with a "lower middle-class housewife, who, having dreamed of the luxury of a maid, found opportunity staring her in the face in the form of Negro women pressed to the wall by poverty, starvation and discrimination."[36]

Some housewives banded together. Others used the era's desperation to exploit Black women.

This isn't to stay that there weren't middle- and upper-middle-class housewives then. Wealthier women, the mistresses of their own domain, faced inward in the solitude of single-family homes. In a 1934 short film called *What a Housewife Must Know*, a white woman darns, her husband and children nearby, as a narrator explains that "[h]ousekeeping still remains the most important business of the world." He continues:

It engages the hearts and minds of more people and calls for higher qualities than any other occupation. Each woman faces it single-handedly. She must know how to cook, know food. She must know how to set her table attractively. She must know how to make her home comfortable and inviting. She must know the worth of labor-saving devices, and how best to conserve her time and energy. She must know clothes—how to buy and how to make them. She must face death to bring children into the world. She must raise them, care for them, and pilot them safely to the threshold of manhood and womanhood. To her husband, she must be a companion, a sweetheart, a wife, and a mother. She must stir ambition, pull him through fears, and keep success from hurting him. She must make social contacts. She must widen her own horizons and find time for culture.[37]

Such expectations must have been particularly difficult to meet when it was hard to buy food and clothes, when men's self-esteem was in the toilet.

## HOUSEWIFE POTENTIAL

MILITANT HOUSEWIVES MADE headlines, they made heads turn, and they called attention to the power of housewives when they rallied.

In Hamtramck, the price of meat had fallen some. But late in August, a Michigan circuit judge approved the plea of meat market owners Julius Friedman and David Rosenberg to bar the women, claiming their business had been cut by half because of the housewives' pickets. The women had been so effective that they had to be stopped by a court of law—and they were. The government largely dismissed or ignored the housewives' demands, though the U.S. Supreme Court declared a meat processing tax unconstitutional in 1936. Housewives stopped the strikes. They had moved the needle, but it was hard to tell exactly how far it had budged.

Organizing housewives did result in some longer-term effects— that is, some of the men's fears came true: Women were no longer content to return to the kitchen to cook the meat they'd fought so hard to afford. Their penchant for politics spread beyond the butcher shop. Several developed a taste for affairs of state and picked up a range of important skills along the way: learning to speak and write effectively, to lobby, to hold powerful men accountable, and even to address uneven distribution of power at home. They "shattered the notion that because housewives consume rather than produce, they are inherently more passive than their wage-earning husbands," Orleck wrote.[38]

Organizing revealed to them their own potential within the home and beyond it. Some former militant housewives ran for office in Washington State and Michigan, elected in 1934 and 1936 by calling on the government to regulate utilities and food prices. Zuk herself ran for Hamtramck City Council and became the first woman to ever win a seat there, largely because of the support of fellow housewives and on the promise to fight for affordable food, housing, and utilities. Upon winning, Zuk announced, "A mother can organize and still take care of her family."[39] On Mothers' Day, 1936, 700 of Zuk's supporters took to City Hall to demand childcare centers, a health care clinic, better playgrounds, and community spaces. These things were "owed to mothers," they said.

As for Fannie Peck, her organization continued until 1996, and she was beloved for her contributions. The annual Fannie B. Peck Day began in 1946, to celebrate Fannie and all she'd done not just for Black housewives, but for the communities in which they lived. The city of Detroit honored her in 1950. Noted the *Michigan Chronicle*, "A whole generation of youngsters in Detroit owe their improved position economically and their presence in a constantly improving community in part, if not entirely, to the efforts of Mrs. Peck."[40]

But the notion of the housewife had changed by that time. In the '40s and '50s, the working-class, striking housewife would be supplanted by the middle-class, suburban housewife, holing up at home.

# CHAPTER 5

# The Making of the American Housewife

The amazing thing about *The Donna Reed Show* was…it was called *The Donna Reed Show*. It was all about *her*. She was the star. Carl Betz played her husband, Alex, but how many people remember *his* name?

If *I Love Lucy* featured one of the most powerful women in TV playing a housewife—in fact, playing someone often failing at house-wifery to big laughs—*The Donna Reed Show* showcased the also pow-erful Reed, navigating the mild foibles of a classic 1950s housewife, one Mrs. Donna Stone.

Season 2, Episode 19, 1960: "Just a Housewife."[1] A radio announcer broadcasts "The Housewives' Corner" from McClure's grocery store, where Donna and a myriad of nearly identical perfectly done-up white housewives peruse the well-stocked aisles. He asks his first inter-viewee what she does. "Oh, I'm just a housewife," she answers. (Who else is grocery shopping in the middle of the day, in pearls and heels?)

This rankles Donna. "Have you ever noticed how women seem to apologize when they say that?" she asks her friend. After the announcer makes his way to her, he notes: "Housewives mold public opinion and are instrumental in shaping public policy," only to ask her about upside-down cakes. Donna fumes. The disrespect!

"Men don't say, 'I'm just a salesman' or 'I'm just a scientist,'" she complains to her husband later. "You don't say, 'I'm just a doctor.'"

"'Housewife' is a word like 'mother' or 'moon' or 'antidisestablishmentarianism,'" he tells her. That is: She's imposing too much meaning on a simple descriptor. After all, Alex says, you *are* a housewife.

"Not the way he used it," Donna says. He "makes it sound like a faceless glob." The problem isn't housework, she's sure to point out. The problem is the assumption that she's lesser than because of her lack of paid work outside the home. The problem is that "housewife" translates to: *You're of inferior intelligence and retain no power.*

Her husband agrees to call her "Maharani of the mop." Then he asks, "Don't you think it's about time to start dinner?" Their son enters, asking them to fill out a school form. *Father: pediatrician*, he writes. And of Donna, he asks, "Mother, are you anything, or just a housewife?"

Their daughter says, "Housewife is such a blah word," and announces that within ten years a woman will be president. "The modern woman will no longer be chained to the stove," she declares, and Donna and she condemn the boys to do the dishes—for one night only.

"I know you're sensitive about the word, but how else do I describe a woman who stays home, runs a house, cooks, cleans, looks after the kids?" Alex asks.

"How about 'mule'?" Donna responds.

Back at the grocery store, another woman explains that she started out to be an anthropologist, but, "You know how it is. You often get married and have children."

"Oh, so you're stuck," the announcer says.

"Well, I wouldn't say that…"

Donna schools him. "Every woman you call 'just a housewife' is a nurse, a psychologist, a diplomat, and a philosopher," she opines. "Every housewife has a personality. We're not part of a herd. We're not 'just housewives.'" The speech turns Donna into a town celebrity, invited to speak at women's clubs and to a reporter from the local paper. Her children find new respect for her.

One friend announces her husband is taking her out to dinner for the first time in a year. "You've liberated us," another friend says. "We have the men worried."

In fact, the men of the town interpret Donna's remarks as meaning "Every housewife must leave home, husband, and children." They tell her husband, Alex, that he can't handle his wife.

But he can. Instead of praising her, Alex asks her to retrieve him a fresh set of pajamas from the dresser he stands three feet from. "Nothing has changed. You haven't accomplished a thing," he tells her.

By the end of the episode, the name of the radio show is changed to "Shopper's Corner," but the women interviewed still identify themselves as "just a housewife." The change is symbolic, but not structural. Her husband is right. The family laughs. Order is restored.

The irony about Donna Reed is that, in order to portray a classic housewife on TV, she herself worked full-time. But another funny thing about this "classic housewife": There was nothing classic about Donna Stone at all.

From our twenty-first-century perch, it's easy to look back at the mid-century era and perceive it as the rightful reset in postwar America, a return to tradition, creating newfound safety and prosperity. The roles of breadwinner and housewife were embraced anew. That's what Trump harked back to in his 2020 speeches, the nostalgia he tugged on to secure votes, which got me curious about housewife history.

So I was surprised to discover that in reality, this cultural shift was a return to a normalcy that had never really been the norm—a way to live nostalgically in the present as if it were a rosy recapitulation of the past. The real-life version of Donna Reed, the 1950s housewife, was simultaneously an ideal and an everyday occurrence and a modern myth. She was an anomaly, an aberration, constructed and crafted by multiple economic, political, ideological, and infrastructural forces: appliance manufacturers, mortgage subsidies, governmental agencies, and housing developers among them.

The baby boom, and the mothers staying home to care for those babies, didn't just *happen*; it was sold and bought, promoted, supported, embraced by Hollywood and the publishing industry, by individuals and corporations, fueled by a powerful ideology of domestic containment that responded not just to a postwar economic boom but a terrifying Cold War. Good lord, I realized after all this research: The "traditional" 1950s housewife was a *product*. An unprecedented demographic shift, accompanied by a complete rejiggering of how Americans lived, was packaged as the way it always was and should be.

Historian Stephanie Coontz called the 1950s nuclear family "the most atypical family system in American history."[2]

## THE WAY IT COULD HAVE BEEN

IMAGINE A WORKING mother's utopia: a federally funded town, surrounded by industry, where their deepest needs and concerns are met. At the center sit three childcare centers, large-windowed facilities where thousands of children of mothers working in nearby factories are looked after, fed, and educated for mere dollars.[3] Racially and economically integrated, it's staffed with a crew of maintenance workers to tend to minor repairs on the modest homes. Nearby health centers quickly and efficiently treat kids or parents who take sick. Public buses run from housing to childcare centers and on to job sites. Mothers can purchase inexpensive, precooked meals to feed their children when they pick them up at the end of the day, to maximize family time.[4]

It sounds like socialist Shangri-la (which I know for my Libertarian and conservative friends is an oxymoron), something America could only dream of. And yet Vanport City, Oregon, was very much a reality. Developed in 1943 courtesy of "father of shipbuilding" Henry J. Kaiser, and nicknamed Kaiserville, this newly manufactured town surrounding Kaiser's shipyards blossomed from the federal government's $26 million investment. The centerpieces were indeed three Kaiser Child Service Centers,[5] costing $250,000 each, where some 7,000 children were cared for.

But let's be honest about how this happened: Kaiserville was erected not out of concern for mothers and children but out of political will, as a way to support the war effort. Congress passed the Lanham Act in 1940, which secured public funds for childcare—but only for communities with war-related industries.[6] Lanham funded more than 3,000 childcare centers, allowing mothers to earn money and contribute to the patriotic project of doing "men's work," while their husbands fought in World War II.[7] Because it was in service of manufacturing guns and ships, the public funding of childcare didn't read as socialist; it read as American as apple pie.

Kaiser himself made very little profit on the housing, which was bare bones and lacked curb appeal. His profit came from what his workers made, from the Rosies riveting on the ships sent off to war. Just a few years before, middle-class women were told that by nature of their sex, they were incapable of this kind of physical labor, but now their "delicate hands" made them a natural fit for "precision work." After being urged to stay out of the way of men's work in the '30s, now "Women *must* keep 'em rolling," as a pamphlet from the early '40s implored, showing images of [white] women young and old in the "male job" of factory work.[8] Their femininity now ren-

dered women suitable for once exclusively masculine gigs—as long as the purpose was to support male soldiers.

Even so, they were warned not to change personalities or to get too uppity. One wartime pamphlet cautioned that "women avoid arrogance and retain their femininity in the face of their own new status…In her new independence she must not lose her humanness as a woman."[9]

The government urged housewives to participate in the national project by scrimping and saving—not just money but cooking fat to tote to the butcher, so it could be used in explosives. Bacon fat as bombs equaled housewife patriotism.[10]

**Housewives!**
**SAVE**
**WASTE**
**FATS**
**FOR**
**EXPLOSIVES!**

*Take them to your*
*meat dealer*

But just because the government marketed these new visions of womanhood didn't mean all men were on board. To the 1943 Gallup poll question "Would you be willing for your wife to take a full-time job running a machine in a war plant?" only 30 percent of men answered yes.[11] Twenty percent of housewives working in plants did so despite their husband's lack of support.

Government and industry encouraged the shift because it was always supposed to be a temporary, negative side effect of war. When the war ended on May 8, 1945, the Lanham Act terminated, and with it the experiment of supporting working moms—and possibly a sane and equitable future for women and families, even though few of us knew this working-mother-supportive blip of history existed. Rosie the Riveter was a powerful but fleeting phenomenon, with an abrupt demise.

Vanport City was dismantled, the day cares shuttered once soldiers made their way home. After the war, Kaiser himself smartly shifted to single-family home development and made a bundle.

Though some studies indicated improved long-term outcomes for kids served by Kaiserville and other day cares, no such programs replaced them.[12] The government created no policies to assist women who'd gone to work and were now cut loose, even though the majority of them didn't want to cede their newfound independence, identities, and jobs.[13] After women proved they were capable of so much more than domesticity, what could have come out of the war was a model of egalitarianism—with both parents working and sharing financial and emotional burdens, and childcare seen as everyone's work.

Instead, after expending a lot of energy convincing women to go to work, now the government and the media had to convince women to go back, and stay, home.

## PATRIOTIC PROCREATION

MANY OF US think of the mid-twentieth century as the era of peace and prosperity, but this next iteration of America unfolded as the Soviet Union conducted its first successful weapons test on August 29, 1949. Anxiety threaded through the abundance. The salve: procreation.

And procreate we did! Americans married younger and more often—some 14 million girls got engaged by age seventeen, and by the end of the 1950s, the average age at marriage was twenty. The divorce rate decreased, the birthrate increased, and voilà: baby boom.[14] Between 1947 and 1961, the number of American families grew by 28 percent.[15] A sign of optimism, prosperity, choice (with birth control), and free will, a larger family projected man as successful provider and woman as successful housewife.[16] Children became the center of the family, giving meaning to a mother's newly re-contained life.

Women's magazines sold motherhood and housewifery as duty, destiny, and delight to this burgeoning demographic, beseeching women to be "feminine, wistful and gay" and hone their "romantic look" to land a man. *Ladies' Home Journal* encouraged women to be both alluring and standoffish, paying careful heed to their grooming but withholding attention and physical affection to keep him wanting more and more—until he produced a proposal and a ring.[17]

Television programs like *The Adventures of Ozzie and Harriet* and *The Donna Reed Show* pitched picture-perfect, white suburban nuclear families, with only the smallest and most solvable of problems. These shows were essentially advertisements for how the family could and should transform, even though they only represented a small segment of American society. Some 25 percent of all American families were poor; 50 percent of two-parent Black families were poor. Coontz called such programs the "media's denial of diversity."[18]

Despite options for women's higher education actually increasing during this postwar era, women endured pressure not to leverage that education into a career. Why pursue a degree in math when you can get a "Mrs." degree—marry, and raise well-educated, proper children, as in the era of Republican Motherhood?

In 1957, *Ladies' Home Journal* asked, "Is College Education Wasted on Women?"[19] They predicted that "increasing numbers of women, disillusioned with their present roles or with what the workaday world can offer, will turn toward motherhood as the happiest road to fulfillment."[20]

Some publications went further. *Life* called women's employment "a disease."[21] The celebrated 1946 book *Modern Woman: The Lost Sex* said that "independent woman" was a contradiction in terms and called feminism "at its core, a deep illness."[22] *Esquire* called working women "a menace."

The biggest fear was that women's liberation would cause the collapse of the family, that educated career women would lead to a decline in procreation among white people, inciting "the old eugenic cry of 'race suicide,'" according to historian Elaine Tyler May's book on mid-century families *Homeward Bound* (from which I am cribbing liberally).[23] A *Newsweek* article opined that it was "the higher educated wife, rather than the husband, who brings down the birth rate."[24] Or as *Ladies' Home Journal* put it, "Women who lead very active lives, under conditions of nervous stress and strain, often do not conceive, and when they do, they miscarry."[25] One doctor argued that miscarriage was caused by "an unconscious rejection on the mother's part of repeated pregnancies and of motherhood."[26] He suggested therapy rather than physical examination—ironic considering how doctors would go on to medicate the heck out of women's unhappiness in the Mothers' Little Helper decade after (see chapter 6).

A new breed of popular and persuasive parenting experts and psychologists cautioned that working women, divorce, and bad mothering would lead children to delinquency, communism, or even—gasp—homosexuality.[27] In an era of norm-busting beatniks, an underground gay rights movement pressing against an overt anti-gay ideological fervor, and wrong-thinkers with Communist Party memberships, procreation now became women's most patriotic offering—as opposed to manufacturing widgets a few years earlier. Good mothering would prevent wayward children and create the next generation of leaders, warriors, and peacemakers—scientists who'd build better mousetraps and fight the Commies.[28] FBI director J. Edgar Hoover implored "homemakers and mothers" to fight the evils of crime and communism by rearing proper kids.[29] "I feel there are no careers so important as those of homemaker and mother," he said in 1956.[30] (Of course, the guy never married, or, it seems, even had a romantic partner.)[31]

But even that wasn't enough! These housewives also had to sexually satisfy their husbands lest they stray—either to communism or homosexuality. Men must be fulfilled in the bedroom so they could perform properly outside it, and submissive housewives—sexpots behind the bedroom doors—were the antidote.

Coontz wrote that "the federal government made a concerted effort to establish one particular family form as the norm: a nuclear family headed by a man whose wife was legally and economically dependent on him."[32]

## THE BAD-ENOUGH MOTHER

LEST WE SURMISE that mid-century society extolled motherhood as a panacea for cultural ills and deviations, note the increasingly popular pastime of critiquing moms. Author Philip Wylie's 1943 smash hit *Generation of Vipers* introduced Americans to the concept of "momism," a pernicious kind of overly intensive mothering that, rather than preventing a son from becoming a sissy, could turn him into one.

Of course, the opposite was a problem, too. In other narratives, mothers who were too elusive, cold, or neglectful caused some sons to turn to crime. The important thing, as women's magazines reminded their readers, was to never put the children before the husband. But don't smother the kids, either.

To the problem of the imperfect mother, a solution emerged: the unimpeachable father. Television began to feature family dramas like *Father Knows Best* and *My Three Sons*, with fathers as central figures, much as in early America. If overbearing mothers caused neuroses, stern fathers provided the cure. Some magazines advised that fathers start participating in childcare during their child's infancy, to keep children, especially sons, from being "dominated by women."[33]

## LEAVING FOR LEVITT

THIS NEW GLOWING era of the modern housewife couldn't have happened without a shiny new model of the American hometown in which to achieve domestic perfection: suburbia. With the massive uptick in returning soldiers, their newly returned-to-the-kitchen wives, and the boom of babies came a need for new homes—and thus a housing shortage.

A crisis for some presented an opportunity for others. The Federal Housing Authority created low-cost mortgages, and private investors infused their cash into the housing market. Financed mostly by the government, the 1956 Interstate Highway Act drew 41,000 miles of national highways across the landscape. Funds siphoned from public transit that served dense cities were funneled into roads that supported private transit in less densely inhabited, less urban new frontiers.

Mid-century suburbia thus bloomed—not as a natural cultural swing but rather the product of a collision of supply and demand, forged by policy and financial investment. Nearly half of suburban homes were financed by the government. Well, what do you know? It turns out that as a nation we *do* believe in public assistance and welfare—just for certain kinds of citizens and families. Even the technology used to create those homes had been subsidized—the prefab walls, the aluminum drop ceilings, the plywood paneling: all from government-funded research, writes Coontz.[34] Incentivized by discounts and cheap mortgages, families fled cities for these newly crafted suburbs, cementing the breaking of the extended family unit down into its new, smaller version: the nuclear family.

The most iconic suburb: Levittown, New York, the creation of William J. Levitt, who erected hundreds of nearly identical modest two-bedroom Cape Cod–style homes thirty miles outside New York City, on the site of an old potato farm. So much private and governmental support existed for single-family home ownership, it was generally less expensive to buy a home there than to rent an apartment in the city.[35]

Demand was already high before supply arrived. Three and a half hours after sales began in March 1949, Levitt had sold $11 million worth of homes. Levittown became so popular among budding families, it became known as "fertility valley" and "the rabbit hutch."[36]

Levittown was Kaiserville's opposite. Everything was designed for domestic containment, separating the home and industrial spheres. A residential oasis with little commerce and few communal spaces, each house took up only 15 percent of the lot or less, creating a private park for each family. Forget public transportation; each house hosted its own private driveway. Windows overlooked the lawns so mothers could watch their own kids while scrubbing dishes. Homes came with built-in TVs and Bendix washing machines tucked into an alcove; no need to leave the house for laundry or entertainment.

Suburbia thus created "an architecture of gender," literally building in the homemaker/breadwinner divide.[37] As Dolores Hayden wrote in *Redesigning the American Dream*, "These houses encode Victorian stereotypes about 'a woman's place.'" Developers, governments, media—they marketed this vision of the future to a generation dedicated to breaking from the past. Social regression presented as modernity sold, beautifully.

But it sold to a select market. Though Levitt said, "As a Jew, I have no room in my mind or heart for racial prejudice," Levittown was for whites only because, "if we sell one house to a Negro family, then 90 to 95 percent of our white customers will not buy into the community."[38] Though today suburbs are among the most racially diverse towns in America, they were crafted as white enclaves, creating a generation of white homeowners and leaving inner cities to people of color in the era of "white flight."[39] Many suburbs engaged in redlining, deliberate exclusion of non-white families by restricting who could get mortgages, where. Banks refused mortgages for most integrated communities and female-headed households, so the racial and gender segregation of Levittown—white dads worked, white moms stayed home—was built into both the town's design and financing. All of this contributed to the archetype of the white suburban housewife.

But she might not have been considered white before she'd moved. Suburbs were also home to ethnic whites from segregated, urban neighborhoods—Jews, Italians, Eastern Europeans who had been "othered" by dominant and WASPier white society—now melted into a kind of homogeneous whiteness in suburbia. Social psychologist William White called suburbs "the second great melting pot," where ethnic whites shed some of their differing identities and histories and became simply American.[40]

The most American thing about these suburbs, however, was their relationship to consumerism. As early hotel technology was miniaturized, and industrial products like vacuums shrunk to fit the single-family home, manufacturers needed a market; that's where the housewife came in.[41] Between 1947 and 1961, national income increased 60 percent, growing the number of families with discretionary spending; the amount of spending on home goods rose by 240 percent.

Sure, they didn't work outside the home, bringing in wages or paying taxes, but housewives contributed enormously to the GDP. Their spendings on drapes and playpens and lawn furniture kept the economy rolling: washing machines, irons, fridges, ovens, toasters, oh my! Much as Amazon sold books to gather information about purchasers to eventually sell them *everything*, appliance manufacturers targeted the home for a new kind of consumerism, marketed as patriotism: Americans bought it, literally and figuratively.[42] By the end of the 1940s, Americans had purchased, according to May, "21.4 million cars, 20 million refrigerators, 5.5 million stoves, and 11.6 million televisions." Each year, they relocated to more than 1 million new units of housing.

Breadwinner plus homemaker plus single-family home became the dominant American aspiration and the ultimate sign of status. The image of the happy and contained suburban housewife adorned countless magazines and TV shows.

Yet in reality, suburbia, like Cold War motherhood itself, was anchored in fear.

## HOME AS BOMB SHELTER, BOMB SHELTER AS HOME

THE POSTWAR ERA was an unfriendly peace—a cold war, after all—tinged with suspicion and fear, duck-and-cover, the possibility of total annihilation a mere button-push away. Beneath the cheerful hum of 1950s suburban ideals droned a low tone of unease.

The government didn't just subsidize suburbia because it thought it a superior model. Suburbs' decreased density made them safer, especially in the event of a nuclear attack (so they surmised). At the signing of the Highway Act, President Eisenhower extolled how the roads would provide "quick evacuation of target areas."[43] Suburbia thus protected against communist and nuclear threat.

Some suburban homes included bomb shelters, privatizing familial safety in an insecure world, while acting as accoutrements, like a garage or garden shed. Women's magazines advertised them, affixed with signs reading "Home Sweet Home." They ranged from, as May notes, "a $1,350 foxhole shelter" to a "$5,000 deluxe 'suite.'"[44] The latter came with a toilet and a Geiger counter.[45] But should nuclear war never break out, these spaces could serve as playrooms. *Life* magazine even featured a couple who spent their honeymoon in a bomb shelter.

The Federal Civil Defense Administration (FCDA), tasked with creating nuclear evacuation plans, scrapped the large-scale vision and crafted home defense campaigns in which each family could attempt to equip itself to withstand the bomb on its own. The FCDA encouraged women to learn nursing and master "preparedness" for the worst case: personal defense as civil defense. FCDA employee Jean Wood Fuller instructed housewives who couldn't afford full-scale bomb shelters how to create smaller, simpler versions with a board tilted against a wall.[46]

Fuller tapped the National Grocers' Association, American National Dietetic Association, and pharmaceutical companies to help her design guidelines for surviving nuclear war. Their campaign, "Grandma's Pantry," taught women what to store in bomb shelters for three days' worth of survival: canned goods, medical supplies, portable radios.[47] Women should rotate canned goods and change bottled water every three months.

*Mrs. Edmund S. Muskie and daughter, Ellen, put the finishing touches to their Grandma's Pantry, a three-day food and water supply for emergencies, in their shelter area at Blaine House. (National Archives Catalog)*

Even in the event of nuclear disaster, groups like the FCDA insisted, gender roles should remain intact. One civil defense plan from 1950 laid out who should do what: Men would fight fires, rescue people, clean streets, and rebuild. Women would watch children, tend to those in the hospital, do social work, and feed people.[48]

By the end of the baby boom—officially in 1964—a generation of women who once tasted working motherhood had been retrained and constrained in a completely anomalous version of America, which most of us had come to believe was traditional.

## THE NEW NORMAL

MANY AMERICANS ACCEPTED that the 1950s housewife depicted on *The Donna Reed Show* embodied all that America had been and was supposed to be.

Meanwhile, Donna Reed couldn't have been less like the typical 1950s housewife if she tried. Born small-town Iowa farm girl Donna Belle Mullenger and named campus queen of Denison High, she packed her belongings into a jalopy and moved to California after graduating. There she lived with an aunt to study stenography and secretarial skills at Los Angeles City College. She acted in campus plays and was named campus queen yet again in 1940. When the newspaper printed Donna's picture, three movie studios asked her to audition. It was rumored that she delayed her Hollywood debut until she finished her degree.

Eventually, Donna's career began, culminating in her crowning as America's sweetheart by way of *It's a Wonderful Life*. But she didn't have the reputation of a sweetheart on set. After complaining to MGM studio boss Louis B. Mayer, she was loaned to Paramount. Donna described many of the directors she'd worked for as "incompetents" who "hated women, which is why they make their female characters as unpleasant as possible."

Eventually, after making more than forty movies, Donna made her way to TV and her eponymous show.[49] On screen, she was everything a middle-class white woman should be: gentle, modest, practical, subservient, feminine, taking her place behind her hardworking husband.

But by the time her show debuted, Donna Reed had already been divorced. Her second husband, Tony Owen, with whom she had four children, was *The Donna Reed Show*'s producer; she would eventually divorce him, too. She liked what she portrayed, even if she didn't represent it personally. "We have proved on our show that the public really does want to see a healthy woman, not a girl, not a neurotic, not a sexpot," she said in 1964. "I am so fed up with immature 'sex' and stories about kooky, amoral, sick women."[50]

As *The Donna Reed Show* wrapped up in 1966 at Donna's request, a new crop of shows became popular. *I Dream of Jeannie* and *Bewitched*—about a genie and a witch, respectively—both depicted women with limitless powers who chose to limit them to the domestic sphere. Many shows shilled to women the idea of tucking their power away in service of suburban submission and happiness.

But rather than create a generation of happy housewives, this radical shift in expectations in American living would eventually lead to a generation of depressed housewives, who turned to desperate measures to numb their pain.

# CHAPTER 6

# Medicating the Housewife

The patient: sixty-three-year-old housewife Alice Hood Hammatt of Topeka, Kansas. Suffering from "agitated depression" and anxiety, Hammatt had agreed to the operation, hoping it would alleviate her symptoms. But the night before the procedure, she got cold feet. She worried, she said, about them shaving her head.

The doctors: neurologist Walter Jackson Freeman and his partner, neurosurgeon James Watts. Freeman convinced Hammatt to go forward with the operation, assuring her that they needn't remove her hair. But on the morning of the operation, she pushed back while the doctors sedated her, then placed her under general anesthesia.[1] The last things she said before she went under were "Who is that man? What does he want here? What's he going to do to me? Tell him to go away. Oh, I don't want to see him." After that, Hammatt screamed.[2] While she was anesthetized, they shaved her head.

Freeman and Watts then marked six dots on Hammatt's skull with gentian violet, three over each frontal lobe. They drilled tiny holes and inserted an eight-centimeter steel spike with a wooden handle called a leucotome, pressing a plunger that sent a looped wire deeper into the brain. They rotated it, cutting away a cylinder of the white matter between the thalamus and prefrontal cortex.[3] The doctors rinsed the incisions with saline and sewed them up with black silk sutures. The procedure took an hour.

When she awoke from the anesthesia, Hammatt described herself as happy. The shaved head didn't bother her. Freeman pronounced the operation a success.

In some ways it had been. Hammatt had gone from violently thrashing before the operation to passive and pleasant after it. No longer suffering from agitated depression, she didn't have to be institutionalized.

It was 1936, and housewife Alice Hood Hammatt became the first person in America to receive a lobotomy. But in the following week, Hammatt endured complications: Difficulties with language. A convulsion. She at times slipped into agitation or disorientation. She died within five years.

When I started researching this book, I had no intention of writing about lobotomies. I knew vaguely about the "mother's little helper" era—the second part of this chapter—but all I'd recalled about lobotomies was that there was some kind of medical scandal, an operation that turned people into makeshift zombies, which, I believed, legislators had banned many decades ago. But then I discovered that the last person to ever receive a lobotomy was a housewife, too; lobotomies began and ended with housewives in this country.

That fact bore investigating, even if housewives were more common in the middle of the last century than they are today. And indeed, research revealed that thousands of unhappy housewives underwent lobotomies, which only inspired more questions and concern. Why have housewives historically been one of America's most heavily medicated demographics?

One answer: They've been disproportionately led toward operations and pills that would allow them to perform womanhood and mother-hood the way others thought they were supposed to.

## LOSING SPARKLE

BEFORE THE AGE of psychopharmacology, few treatments for the mentally ill existed. During the Depression, the number of mental patients shot up. Overcrowded and understaffed sanitariums teemed with the miserable and insane, who didn't benefit from psychotherapy or behavioral therapy. With no pills to pop to assuage psychological ailments, a psychosurgical cure was potentially miraculous—a welcome alternative to padded cells, straitjackets, a lifetime locked up in an institution.

Portuguese neurologist António Egas Moniz invented the operation in 1935, then called a "leucotomy."[4] The idea was simple: Since the brain caused behavior, if doctors could just get to and tweak the right part of brain, they could stop the unwanted behavior, whether it be psychosis, schizophrenia, depression, or suicidal thoughts. The frontal lobe—really a pair of lobes—controls things like language, memory, and voluntary movement. It helps us organize and plan and make strategic decisions, the building blocks of executive function. For severely mentally ill, despondent, and violent patients, perhaps this was the part of the brain to alter.

Freeman and Watts adapted the operation a year after its invention, performing the first such one in America on Hammatt, the Kansas housewife, at George Washington University; they referred to it as a lobotomy.[5] They published their first data in 1937, case studies of Hammatt and five additional patients whose "insomnia, nervous tension, apprehension and anxiety" improved after intervention. Patients, they said, were more comfortable, more pliant, and more passive. "Every patient loses something by this operation," they admitted. Some had lost "spontaneity," others "sparkle."[6] Out of 200 patients whose cases they later wrote up, 63 percent improved—something people who remember lobotomies only as a medical scandal often forget. What they likely remember is that 23 percent didn't improve, and 14 percent got worse or died.[7]

Those odds don't seem great to me, yet Moniz won the Nobel Prize in 1949 "for the discovery of the therapeutic value of leucotomy in certain psychoses."[8] By 1952, some 50,000 patients had undergone lobotomies in the United States and Canada.[9]

Were this simply yet another story of a miracle cure revealed to be little more than a scam, like the testosterone "rejuvenation treatments" of the 1920s, it would still be shocking.[10] But the gender demographics were so extremely skewed that it adds another layer of scandal.

In the early to mid-twentieth century, the bulk of hospitalized mental patients were men. But by 1942, 75 percent of Freeman and Watts's lobotomy patients were women.[11] A 1951 study of American hospitals found that 60 percent of lobotomies were performed on women. In another study, of Stockton State Hospital's lobotomy program between 1947 and 1954, 245 lobotomies were performed.[12] Despite the fact that there were more male patients in the hospital—many diagnosed with schizophrenia, a common indication for lobotomy at the time—84 percent of the lobotomies were performed on women. Thirteen of the fourteen patients who received multiple lobotomies were female.

Other treatments like electroconvulsive therapy might have been more evenly distributed, though a study on "schizophrenic" women in the 1950s revealed that some were given electric shock to "accept their domestic roles and their husband's dictates."[13] (Were they schizophrenic or just disobedient?) Other medical records hinted that physicians recommended lobotomy for their own benefit as much as their patients'; lobotomies helped "maintain order" in the hospital. These women weren't just defiant or difficult. One patient's "strange behavior" included her mixed feelings about caring for her children, which may have been the then-unknown ailment we now call postpartum depression.[14] In one case, a woman was "fearful of aging" before the surgery, but Freeman pronounced she would "grow old gracefully" after it, and be able to look after her home. If she worried at the erasure of her former sense of spontaneity, her husband was pleased, pronouncing that she was "more normal than she had ever been."[15]

This refusal to embrace performative motherhood, to do housewife right, seemed to help shape physicians' treatment plans—a discomfiting intertwining of psychology, medicine, and gender roles. Think of this phase of American medicine as a preview of *The Stepford Wives*. Unhappy and misbehaving housewives plus hole drilled in the head equals tuna casserole on the table with no complaints. (More recently, in *Don't Worry Darling*—spoiler alert—an emasculated husband anesthetizes his doctor wife, forcing her to live in a VR simulation as a 1950s housewife.)

Doctors also performed the operations on oversexed women, especially those who'd cheated on their husbands. As Jenell Johnson noted in *American Lobotomy*, "After a 'short, painless prefrontal lobotomy,' the woman became a 'happy, respected helpmate for her husband.'"[16] Yet research in Stockton showed that lobotomies actually *increased* sexual desire in some women—and in men, too. In fact, while it didn't stop women from brimming with wanton cravings, it did wonders for frigidity.

Doctors doled out lobotomies in the era of high housewife, when the archetypical woman wasn't roll-up-your-sleeves Rosie the Riveter, but a presumed fount of eternal calm and positivity, vacuuming her way to heaven. When it worked—depending on what your definition of "worked" is—lobotomy diminished a disturbed women's hard edges, but still left her strong enough to keep house.

## HISTORIES OF HYSTERIA

THE LOBOTOMIZING OF the American housewife may seem like a strange medical anomaly, the confluence of technology and the once-in-a-lifetime demographic shift that created the mid-century archetype, and then diagnosed women who didn't achieve it as impaired. But interpreting women's emotions as illness—or at least as problematic—is centuries old.

The word "hysteria" comes from the Greek *hystera*, or uterus; thus the mere state of being female renders a human prone to sickness. Hysteria itself was considered a psychological disorder—"the most commonly diagnosed human ailment in Europe and the United States for two hundred years but is now thought not to exist," according to historian Robert Ostertag.[17] It was written into the American Psychiatric Association's *Diagnostic and Statistical Manual of Mental Disorders* until 1980. But it was always a vaguely defined diagnosis, hedging at a general dissociative state with idiopathic origins.[18] For decades, even centuries, symptoms of hysteria have been absurdly broad and indeterminate: fits and paralysis, trouble swallowing, dizziness, fatigue (describes me, by the way, minus the fits and paralysis).

Sometimes hysteria supposedly stemmed from wild causes like, say, spirit possession, sexual deprivation, or a wandering uterus[19]— an early theory of causation, because physicians thought wombs controlled much about women's health.[20] Fever, irritability, insomnia, anxiety—all linked to the female reproductive system at some point. Thus, physicians trained treatments for these mysterious ailments on women's pelvic area. They told women to have more sex, or masturbate less, or have their clitorises, ovaries, or uteruses surgically ablated.[21] Seventeenth-century French physician Lazare Rivière suggested that should marriage not cure the condition, "'the Genital Parts should be by a cunning Midwife so handled and rubbed, so as to cause an Evacuation of the over-abounding Sperm,'" per Ostertag—and by that Rivière meant "female sperm."[22]

By the nineteenth century, when French neurologist Jean-Martin Charcot slotted hysteria into a Western medical framework, these treatments seemed out of date. Charcot came up with novel approaches like metallotherapy and "moral treatments"—rest, hypnosis, or isolation.[23]

But a cure for unruly women, those performing their gender role wrong, remained elusive. These women were somehow sick—either because they believed themselves to be or because other people considered them so.

By 1870, one American physician determined that three-quarters of medical spending was allocated toward the treatment of hysteria. One who partook of such treatment was Florence Nightingale, mother of the nursing profession, who succumbed to hysteria for the final twenty-three years of her life.[24]

Meanwhile, marketers hawked various housewife-centric ailments and ointments and potions to cure them. An ad in an 1885 edition of the Black newspaper *Huntsville Gazette* read:

> How many women there are working today in various branches of industry—to say nothing of the thousands of patient housewives whose lives are an unceasing round of toil—who are

martyrs to those complaints to which the weaker sex is liable. Their tasks are rendered doubly hard and irks and their lives shortened, yet hard necessity couples them to keep on. To such, Dr. Pierce's "Favorite Prescription" offers a sure means of relief. For all female weaknesses it is a certain cure. All druggists.[25]

That favorite prescription: an herbal mixture of cohosh, barberry, viburnum, valerian, and caulophyllum—a plant used to induce labor. Before surgery, there were potions and snake oils, trying to relieve women of their pain around the unceasing round of toil, and eventually there were surgeries, too.

But rarely did any help alleviate the toil itself.

## ENTER THE ICEPICK

As DEMAND FOR lobotomies increased in mid-century, Freeman pushed for advancement and expansion, searching for an easier and neater way into the brain than drilling holes in the skull—one that wouldn't leave scars. After experimenting on cadavers, he settled on an icepick from the Line Ice Company, taken from his own kitchen. Later he designed his own leucotome, which he carried in a case lined with felt.[26] He called the new operation—an icepick through the eye socket to the brain—a "transorbital lobotomy." It became known, unsurprisingly, as the "icepick lobotomy."

Freeman and Watts performed the first icepick lobotomy on January 17, 1946, in Freeman's D.C. office. The patient: twenty-nine-year-old housewife Sallie Ellen Ionesco, seeking relief from suicidal thoughts and manic depression. Before the operation, her daughter, Angelene Forester, told PBS, "I remember her taking me down [to the basement] and pointing up to the ceiling and saying, 'Do you see those wires? That's what they torture me with.' ...And I remember going to bed at night and she would do things like this—and crying because my mother wasn't like my other girlfriends' mothers." She described her mother as "absolutely violently suicidal" before the lobotomy.[27]

Freeman and Watts knocked Ionesco out with electroshock therapy, then hammered the icepick through the thin bone above her eye, into her brain, wriggling it back and forth to cut off connections to the prefrontal cortex. It took ten minutes. When he was done, Freeman attested that Ionesco woke up without "any anxiety or apprehension." He put her into a taxicab and sent her home.[28]

After the operation, Ionesco could no longer perform some basic functions, and her husband had to do all the cooking. "She resumed not quite as vivacious as she was," her daughter said. "But she came back. She was the person I knew before. And I felt like he had given me a tremendous gift to give my mother back to me. I guess to my father it was not to have to institutionalize her." About Freeman, Forester said, "He did something right."

Freeman wrote editorials and promoted the new procedure in interviews. Sometimes he drove around in a van, the "lobotomobile," and offered lobotomies on the road.[29] He eventually performed transorbital lobotomies on around 2,500 patients across twenty-three states.[30]

After moving to California, he lobotomized Helen Mortensen, who was, of course, a housewife—one of Freeman's very first icepick lobotomy patients in 1946. When her psychiatric symptoms returned, she underwent a second lobotomy in 1956. Eleven years later, she went in for a tune-up: lobotomy number three.[31]

During Mortensen's operation at Herrick Memorial Hospital

in Berkeley, Freeman accidentally cut through a blood vessel in her brain.[32] She died three days later. The hospital revoked Freeman's surgery privileges, and Mortensen the housewife became the last person to ever receive a lobotomy. Freeman himself died five years later. America didn't ban lobotomies. Rather, the medical industry began phasing them out, even before Freeman's last botched operation, because of the rise of a new treatment for psychic disturbances: pharmaceutical drugs.

These, too, would be disproportionately prescribed to housewives.

## BETTER LIVING THROUGH SCIENCE

CHEMIST LEO STERNBACH, who had fled the Nazis for the U.S. in 1941, was working for Hoffmann-La Roche laboratories when he happened upon the first drug in the class that became known as benzodiazepines. These new tranquilizers soothed people without drastically reducing their mental capacity, as opiates or barbiturates had done: calm, but not doped up. The most popular benzodiazepine was an anti-anxiety drug called Miltown, but Sternbach fiddled with the formula, altering the chemical makeup enough to prevent the laboratory from being sued for manufacturing its own version.[33]

What he came up with was Librium, which calmed mice and cats in tests but didn't seem to have any side effects. Hoffmann-La Roche began to market Librium in 1960 with great success, but Sternbach was still noodling with an iteration that could have the same effect with a smaller dose and without the unpleasant aftertaste. Diazepam, known as Valium from the Latin *valere* ("to be healthful"), hit pharmacies in 1963.

Syndromes of the 1960s

## The battered parent syndrome

She's the paradox of our age. Compared to her mother, she has more education, more usable income and more labor-saving devices. Yet she is physically and emotionally overworked, overwrought and—by the time you see her —probably overwhelmed.

What went wrong? Is parenthood something other than the rosy fulfillment pictured by the women's magazines? Is anxiety and tension fast becoming the occupational disease of the homemaker?

Some say it's unrealistic to educate a woman and then expect her to be content with the Cub Scouts as an intellectual outlet.

Or to grant that she is socially, politically and culturally equal, while continuing to demand domestic and biological subservience.

Or to expect her to shoulder the guilt burden of this child-centered age without unraveling around the emotional edges.

Or to compete with her husband's job for his time and involvement.

But whatever the cause, the consequences—anxiety, tension, insomnia, functional disorders—fill waiting rooms.

Sometimes it helps to add 'Miltown' to her treatment—to help her relax both emotional and muscular tension. It's no substitute for a week in Bermuda, or for emotional readjustment. But it will often make the latter easier for her, as well as for the physician.

And 'Miltown' has been doing just that—for a dozen years now—with substantial success.

*Indications:* Effective in relief of anxiety and tension states; adjunctively when anxiety may be a causative or disturbing factor. Fosters normal sleep through anti-anxiety and muscle-relaxant properties.

*Contraindications:* Previous allergic or idiosyncratic reactions to meprobamate. *(Brief summary of prescribing information is continued on next page.)*

Wallace Pharmaceuticals/*Cranbury, N.J.*

when reassurance is not enough **MILTOWN**
(MEPROBAMATE)

Valium didn't slow people's breathing, and thus wasn't a surefire method for suicide. And it was stigma-free, linked with ameliorating the drudgery of everyday life safely, instead of with the indulgences, excesses, and dangers associated with barbiturates, which had killed celebrities such as Marilyn Monroe and Jimi Hendrix.

In her book *The Age of Anxiety: A History of America's Turbulent Affair with Tranquilizers*, Andrea Tone wrote that Valium became "as common as toothbrushes and razors."[34] Inexpensive, fast-acting, and— many thought—harmless, it was "white collar aspirin," "executive Excedrin," or a "peace pill."[35] It became the first $100 million pharma brand. Between 1969 and 1982, it was the country's most prescribed drug; Americans took 2.3 billion pills each year. One paper described the period between 1965 and 1979 as "the benzodiazepine craze."[36]

The majority of those transfixed by this craze were women, who used it in the 1970s twice as often as men. But the overprescribing to women wasn't necessarily seen as a problem. Rather, it was a solution. Valium was "marketed as an antidote for socially dysfunctional women—the excessively ambitious, the visually unkempt, the unmarried and the menopausal misfits," as Tone put it. The pills were also "salves for harried housewives." Women, she wrote, were "popping tranquilizers like cough drops."[37] Downing a Valium at the end of a long, dull day of housewifery became so popular that the Rolling Stones immortalized the practice in the 1966 song "Mother's Little Helper."

Though Valium was also useful for the severely mentally ill, the drug's popularity among the blandly dejected bears mentioning. It came to prominence in conjunction with *The Feminine Mystique*, when the happy housewife of popular culture was crowded out by the trope of the *un*happy housewife, the subject of chapter 7—an undiagnosable problem, a diaphanous sense of discomfort. Though author Betty Friedan named it and offered cures such as hiring help and obtaining meaningful (as in paid, outside the home) work, the pharmaceutical industry offered a chemical intervention. "Better living through chemistry" became the ultimate way to change your mind if you couldn't change your life.

Medical sociologist Ruth Cooperstock surveyed women who took Valium and found that most of their distress "revolved around their traditional roles as wife, mother, houseworker." What ailed them was their role as domesticated women. Author Ali Haggett later noted that "[S]ymptoms of anxiety and depression in women have been directly related to the stresses inherent in domestic work and other disadvantageous aspects of the female role."

This brand of disaffection was not novel. The term "suburban neurosis" was actually coined by a British doctor, Stephen Taylor, in an article in the *Lancet* back in 1938. Granted, England previewed suburbia before the United States, in an urban planning movement called Garden Cities, after the Great War. There Taylor found a rise in women "with anxiety states, the majority of whom present a definite clinical picture with a uniform background." His goal was to show that "environment plays no less a part in the production of what I venture to call 'the suburban neurosis,' than it does in the production of physical disease."[38]

Taylor described mothers in their late twenties who were clean but somehow slovenly. Their list of idiopathic ailments included: "Lump in my throat that goes up and down, or round and round. Trembling all over, and I jump at the slightest noise. Continuous gnawing, nagging headache. Stabbing pains over my heart. Pain in my back which runs up and down. My stomach swells up terribly. Nasty taste in my mouth. So short of breath when I hurry. Terrible buzzing in my ears. I can't sleep at night. I'm getting ever so thin."

He found few physical issues with these women, save for "variable tremor, a definite but variable tachycardia, pendulous flabby breasts, poor abdominal muscles, very brisk reflexes, and nothing else." Such women would be prescribed a random tincture and forgotten, Taylor surmised.

But he detected a commonality in their trajectories. After educating themselves and meeting their husbands, "after two years of saving, and those lovely walks around Box Hill at the week-ends, they took the plunge into a small semi-detached hire-purchase villa on the wonderful new Every suburb estate, adjacent to one of our great by-passes and only twenty minutes from the station." They move. They have children. She grows bored and restless. The symptoms develop. And the legend, or myth, of the Desperate Housewife is born.

The suburban experiment was a completely different way for humans to live, an enormous evolutionary advance rooted in a kind of modernism mixed with consumerism, which may have been short on humanism, community, and extended family. Families were living in the future but had cut themselves off abruptly from the human past.

With their own yards, swing sets, and even bomb shelters, suburban homes became fortresses—bulwarks against war, yes, but also isolation chambers. Television sets replaced the communal movie theater. The washing machine replaced the public laundromat. The swing set replaced the playground. If they allowed more comfort and modern conveniences for the nuclear family, they also "weakened extended-family ties, promoted homogeneity in neighborhoods, intensified racial segregation, encouraged conformity, and fostered a style of life based on traditional gender roles in the home," wrote historian Elaine May.[39]

A 1963 paper called "Housewife's Disease" described a "definite clinical condition which can be looked upon as a psychosomatic syndrome." This was different than the "unceasing round of toil" problem—rather, it was what happened when the toil ceased. The authors described the mysterious ailment's etiology: "After marriage, the hitherto highly developed, mentally and physically active and agile woman of today so often becomes stagnant and isolated—both mentally and physically—from the stimulation of employment and free movement among people." Housewifery, thus, may lead to "a state of acute or chronic dissatisfaction and frustration."[40]

Doctors broke down the stages of the syndrome by age. First, twenty-four- to thirty-year-olds, who became distressed when "the glamour of washing nappies has worn off." Such patients may experience boredom or claustrophobia, libido loss or decreased energy. But it may fade "with the child being big enough to be left in the care of a servant" who "takes over some of the drudgery."

At stage two, now thirty- to thirty-five-year-olds with multiple children, they experience back pain resulting from pregnancies, fatigue, and fear of being impregnated again. Finally, stage three: "forty, fifty, and even fifty-five years." Not only is she undergoing the Change, but, say the doctors, "the family may now have outgrown her." The children are teens. The husband, meanwhile, is likely "at the height of his powers," so the wife must occupy herself with bridge or "a crusading fervor for some particular cause."

Rather than change their role, or this miserable trajectory identified by diagnosing doctors, Valium presented women with the opportunity to accept it. It's the classic American approach to emotions: medicate rather than process, rebranding a normal human experience as a problem solvable by the potent combination of medicine and capitalism.

This phenomenon is sometimes referred to as the "myth of mental illness." According to Tone, pharmaceutical executives worried there wouldn't be enough of a market for run-of-the-mill anxiety drugs because America had become enamored with talk therapy. Thus, they convinced women that their common and reasonable suburban dissatisfaction was a problem eradicable with medical intervention.

This proved terribly effective.

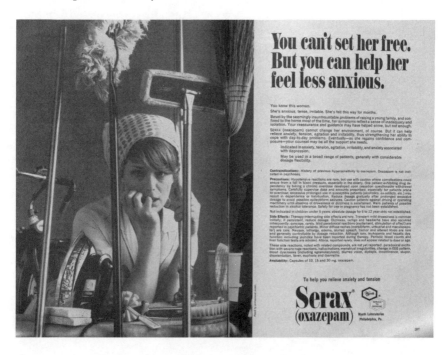

There may be another reason that doctors tended to prescribe tranquilizers for women twice as often as for men,[41] or why today they still prescribe anti-depressants for women at twice the rate they do for men.[42] Women were "more frequently diagnosed with psychoneurosis, anxiety, and other mental instabilities" while benzos were at the height of their popularity, per psychiatrist Jonathan Metzl.[43] Women tend to use psychological and social language to describe their ailments much more than men do, making it easier to see them as having emotional, as opposed to physical, etiologies.[44] Perhaps if men were, on average, more emotionally expressive, the sex ratio of prescriptions would be different, and Valium might have been Father's Little Helper, too.

## ADDICTED HOUSEWIVES

THE VALIUM SOLUTION came with problems of its own. The euphoria wore off, literally and figuratively, when health providers became aware of Valium's addictiveness, and how easy it was to build up a tolerance. By 1967, the FDA had begun to push restrictions on prescriptions, as they'd done for barbiturates and amphetamines, but for many housewives it was too late. They'd become dependent.

Often when an epidemic disproportionately affects middle- and upper-middle-class white people, it garners attention. The housewives' disease made headlines, and by the 1970s, the media often reported on women's drug dependencies. There were articles, books, and even a movie. Congress conducted three investigations into Valium and similar pills.[45]

Dr. Leonard S. Brahen noted in a paper called "Housewife Drug Abuse" that "This abuse extends to the typical middle-class housewife involving legal drugs consciously used for purposes other than pleasure. The problem is that many of these housewives shop from physician to physician to maintain a drug regimen no physician would prescribe."

In 1978, *Ladies' Home Journal* weighed in. "The smartly dressed woman driving a sleek, late model car could be the envy of her neighbors. She has a loving husband, bright children, a beautiful home in the suburbs, and apparently no cares in the world. Except one. This woman is a junkie," they wrote. She's not the "long-haired hippie" junkie, the "culture-culture street people" buying illegal drugs of "pushers." She gets them from her physician.[46] That same year, former First Lady Betty Ford admitted she'd also been sunk by "prescribed addiction." There were "tragic levels of abuse and addiction," wrote Judith Warner in *Time* magazine.[47]

Warner, however, is not convinced that a fake mental illness was invented to justify selling a dangerous drug to overeducated, underproductive women. She suggests that the popular narrative—"the women taking it were essentially perfectly well-functioning mildly neurotic types looking for happiness-enhancing 'brain styling'"—is incomplete. Not quite a lie, but a mere adumbration of the truth. Rather, Warner suggests the bulk of users were extremely distressed and had diagnosable mental illnesses.

"What happens to our long-cherished Mother's Little Helper tale if you replace the notion that women were being singled out and mentally shut down via Valium with the counter notion that those women were in real pain?" Warner asks. The tale would become women with agency seeking support amid a narrow range of options. Better than lobotomy, but still not good.

Some women took these drugs unnecessarily, to make the boring interesting, the intolerable satisfactory. Some became addicted with serious side effects and complications. Some deeply anxious people took them and became more functional. And some unhappy and mentally ill women sought help and got what was marketed and available to them, whether it was the right help or not.

Recalling her mother Sallie Ionesco's lobotomy, Angelene Forester told filmmakers at PBS, "It's a hard decision to make, but inevitably life is just full of decisions like that... For me it was a good thing. I think for Mama it was a good thing. And I think the lobotomy he did on her was a very good thing."[48]

At eighty-eight, Ionesco herself told NPR about Freeman: "He was just a great man. That's all I can say."

# CHAPTER 7

# From Housewife to Women's Libber

She described it as "the problem that has no name." Betty Friedan, née Bettye Naomi Goldstein, Smith College Class of 1942, spent what she called "an unconscionable amount of time" on a questionnaire for her classmates fifteen years after graduation, asking after the state of their lives.[1] She discovered that many of them—educated women turned full-time mothers—endured the same disquieting rumblings she'd been stomaching for years.[2]

"It was a strange stirring, a sense of dissatisfaction, a yearning that women suffered in the middle of the twentieth century in the United States," she wrote in *The Feminine Mystique*, her book inspired by the questionnaire. "Each suburban wife struggled with it alone."[3]

Some housewives felt isolated and overwhelmed, missing using their minds for academic pursuits or employment outside the home, sucked into the "intellectual vacuum" created by the suburban nuclear family.

Friedan, chronicler of the average suburban housewife's discontent and daughter of an unhappy housewife, wasn't such an average suburban housewife herself.[4] There was the matter of her Jewishness, and of her wealth; she was married to an advertising executive and lived in an eleven-room house in a small town north of New York City. Educated at one of the Seven Sisters, without seeking the Mrs. degree, she went on to work for far-left newspapers. While she may have wanted to marry and have kids, she'd never fully untethered herself from career dreams.

Famously, Friedan had been following those dreams in graduate school at Berkeley when her boyfriend complained that he'd never be able to achieve her academic heights, and thus it was pointless for her to keep pursuing her studies and outshine him. Reader, she *married* him, if you can believe it. Sixty years later, it's easy to surmise how the small wound of that moment could end up festering into a cultural complaint that became a best-selling book.

But the book wasn't just about her personal grudge. It was about the limits of the cultural project of the 1950s: to keep certain classes of women, particularly the educated ones, off the corporate ladder so men retained the room to climb it, while also excluding less wealthy classes of women from the luxury of housewifery.

Friedan herself had gotten a degree referred to as the "Ph.T. (Putting Husband Through)." (The University of Florida actually conferred such degrees, awarding wives of students for their "loyal support and unfailing patience.")[5] And she wanted her own turn. So did lots of other women with that degree, it turns out, including writer Judy Blume. "I was pregnant when I graduated and I hung my diploma over the washing machine," she told PBS.[6]

As unluck would have it, that Mrs. degree led to a deeply unfulfilling

*Ph.T. (Putting Husband Through) degrees being awarded at the University of Florida. (Copyright Board of Trustees of the University of Florida)*

life for some, strapping women into multiple hats: "wife, mistress, mother, nurse, consumer, cook, chauffeur," per Friedan.[7] Appliances, marketed as greatly improving women's quality of life, actually led to relentless high-expectation housework. The washing machine, for instance, allowed for less physical labor, but then marketers started selling products to solve problems that hadn't existed, like: to fix a never-before-noticed thing called "ring-around-the-collar." Laundry soap commercials, aired during "soap operas," featured women gently shaming one another because their whites weren't white enough, their colors too dull. An ad for Bold detergent warned women that their laundry "had to be better than clean and white. It had to be clean and white and *bright*."[8]

Better living through science became a contest for who could achieve a "laboratory-clean home." Historian Dolores Hayden argued in her book *Redesigning the American Dream* that "these inventions eroded the autonomy of women at least as much as they contributed to saving women's labor."[9] Oh well!

At least some women had a sense of humor about their predicaments. In 1960, author Peg Bracken penned *The I Hate to Cook Book* and in 1962 its companion, *The I Hate to Housekeep Book*. In the *Atlantic*, writer Caitlin Flanagan chronicles the witty, unhappy housewives of the 1960s; one wrote a chapter called "How to Be Happy When You're Miserable."[10]

Friedan was clear on how the culture—"women's magazines, advertisements, television, movies, novels, columns and books by experts"—had pitched the unattainable housewife ideal to women, then made them beholden to it, shaping hopes, dreams, senses of self, dashed ideals, and disappointments.[11] That's not to say that women's lives in earlier eras, before the suburban explosion, were relentlessly rosy. But perhaps there had been less expectation that life *should* be rosy. The "feminine mystique," Friedan opined, "has succeeded in burying millions of American women alive."[12]

Friedan's critics dismissed her thesis, asserting that it was education that turned a woman from "poetess to shrew." *Newsweek* called their despair "the most recently won of women's rights."[13] But if Friedan sounded hyperbolic to some, the book resonated deeply, if only with the specific class of women in the winter of their suburban discontent, whose existence it chronicled.

*The Feminine Mystique* stayed on the *New York Times* bestseller list for six weeks and sold 1.4 million copies of the first paperback printing.[14] Friedan was keen on the marketing of housewifery as a source of dissatisfaction. Now she marketed the dissatisfaction itself, to great success. Historian Stephanie Coontz noted that "[b]y 1960, almost every major news journal was using the word *trapped* to describe the feelings of the American housewife."[15]

## OUT OF THE KITCHEN, INTO THE OFFICE

THE LIFE OF a housewife, Friedan said, kept women from their "fundamental human drive," which was to realize their full potential.[16] Her solution to the problem that has no name was at once simple and deeply complex: Women must go back to work. Thus, society should create arrangements in which women could use their education without supplanting domestic life—as was the case for men (though, of course, they had wives).

One avenue: national education programs for women, allowing them to continue studying after wifedom and motherhood—still a fantastic policy idea. If they met their human potential, American women would "break out of the housewife trap and truly find fulfillment as wives and mothers," she wrote. To do so, "she must unequivocally say 'no' to the housewife image."[17] Thus: Screw the impossible ideals of domestic perfection, she said. Use instant mashed potatoes and washing machines for what they were intended: to save time. Screw the ringed collars, the dull colors, and the cloudy whites. Then they'd be "once again human beings, not 'just housewives.'"[18]

Ignoring the fact that housewives are human, too, Friedan's vision also failed to recognize that for suburban housewives to achieve such liberation, they must pay others to accomplish the domestic tasks they would abjure. That is, one must contract out, as Friedan herself had three days a week while writing *The Feminine Mystique*, those pesky responsibilities like childcare and housework. For white, middle-class women to be lucky enough to work outside their house, poor women, and women of color, had to work inside it. As Coontz writes, 1950s suburban families (and frontier families before them) "had more of their advantages paid for by minorities and the lower classes" than any others.[19]

Friedan's blind spots became sore spots. She called lesbians "the lavender menace," and almost entirely ignored the needs and realities of Black and working-class women, missing that many women in the 1960s were already desperately trying to balance working and domestic life. Two-thirds of single mothers worked outside the home in the mid-sixties, as did 40 percent of married mothers, the majority women of color.[20] One 1975 article posited a relationship between the husband's job and the wife's unhappiness, noting an "association between manual worker status in the husband and neurosis in the wife."[21] That is, being poorer was harder on a wife's mental health—a well-known fact by now. (The artful name of the article: "Neurotic Wives in a Modern Residential Suburb.")

This narrative—overeducated plus understimulated equals misery—may have masked deep marital dissatisfaction in some cases. Author Ali Haggett suggested that the real sources of anguish for some women were "marital discord" and "traumatic experience during childhood or adolescence."[22] Some pitted onset of symptoms against their husband's infidelity; that is, maybe they fared okay before they got married, or before they became mothers, but it likely wasn't the condition of being a housewife alone that caused their unhappiness. Many had actually enjoyed domestic life, tending to children and home. The reality of their crappy marriages, alas, disrupted the bliss.

To a certain extent, that describes my mom, who met my dad on her first day of college. She was sixteen, an orphan who'd skipped two grades, her education funded through a full scholarship. He was eighteen, gregarious and funny and musical. After college, in the late '60s, and in an attempt to avoid my dad's being drafted to Vietnam, they married, joined the Peace Corps, had my older brother. It was all wonderful. She could afford to hire help in the East African country in which they lived, and their lives were both easy and exciting. They were on an adventure.

Then, three years later, they returned home. He found a teaching job in far upstate New York, and they moved to a slightly bohemian town with a good music scene and remarkably cheap rent. Things were still good. Sort of. She stayed home and did all the cooking and cleaning and sewing and baking and knitting, and he taught English and played music.

While she was pregnant with her second child—that would be me—my dad lost his teaching job. She wasn't working. They had no savings. He began to teach guitar and play in local bands, trying to make ends meet, and at the same time perhaps seeing it as an opportunity to pursue what he'd always wanted to do: be a musician.

My mother had grown up in a poor neighborhood in New York City where most of the women worked. Her own mother, who worked as a bookkeeper and school secretary, had been very ill for much of my mom's life and died many years before I was born, when my mom was still a teenager; her dad had died when she was just a little kid. My mother had, somewhat reasonably, expected that her life would be easier than her parents' lives had been, that her adulthood would be easier than her childhood.

My parents had been living in an apartment, but eventually found a modest house, built in 1871 from some of the leftover materials of the downtown's grand buildings. It cost $13,000; my dad's father lent them $3,000, and they took out a mortgage for the rest. My mom loved the house, and the domestic work she did inside it. But she was also…bored. And weirdly lonely, considering she was married. She wanted to be out in the world a little bit more.

Once I was born, she found being at home kind of stifling, and took a part-time secretarial job at the local college. Now that my father was around more often during the day, she could take classes in library science, one at a time, slowly earning a degree. She might not have realized it at the time, but it was an insurance policy of sorts.

This was the early 1970s, after the problem with no name had been named. The women's movement was in full swing, but my mother saw what it was promoting: working full-time *and* still looking after the kids and house. To her, "liberated women" were working harder than ever before. But there were also more choices. Women were becoming doctors and lawyers. It was a confusing time for my mom, full of both promise and hardship. Culturally, she wasn't chained to the kitchen, but she wasn't quite sure how to free herself from it, either.

It was a confusing time in her marriage, too. My parents had been drifting apart. Once, her brother, my uncle, came to visit. We were out of milk. The next time my mother looked in the fridge, there was fresh milk; my uncle had bought some. *Oh*, she thought. *This is what it feels like to have* help.

Yes, my father watched my older brother and me sometimes when my mother was at work, but he wasn't really there. Eventually, he told her that he didn't want a family—or at least this family, anymore.

When my mother finished her degree, the best job she could find was in Georgia, thousands of miles away. She thought she could provide a good life for my brother and me there. She barely explained to us what was happening. My mom assumed that my father had been so emotionally and physically absent that we wouldn't notice he was gone. (She was wrong, but we eventually got over it. Kind of. Not totally.)

Thinking back on it now, my mother sees how the image of the housewife followed her. When she was very young, in her mother's enclave, people looked down on housewives. Then people put them on a pedestal in the '50s. Then, just when my mother was becoming a housewife, the feminist movement looked down on them again. It was almost impossible to be happy as a housewife in that environment— but her unhappiness really arose because she wasn't properly cared for or loved. In some ways, the unhappy housewife trope is a myth of its own, only applying to a small swath of society, but one that the media was concerned with and catered to.

Which may be why Friedan herself ended up moving beyond it. As the decade went on, Friedan expanded her purview to include more categories of women and condemn sexism in all its forms. She became co-creator and first president of the National Organization for Women—known as "the NAACP for women"—with Pauli Murray, a Black, gender-nonconforming lawyer and activist. Friedan helped found the National Women's Political Caucus with Bella Abzug and Gloria Steinem, among others.

Whatever her faults, the consciousness-raising of Friedan's book helped set the stage for a new dawn of women's activism. She by no means started the second wave feminist movement of the late 1960s and '70s, but she did contribute to the country's loosened attachment to the suburban housewife archetype, allowing for cultural change. Friedan called for a "drastic reshaping of the cultural image of femininity," and in many ways that did happen.[23]

But without enough accompanying structural change—childcare, family leave, fair divorce laws, and the like—women were left in the lurch.

## CONCERNS FOR ALL WOMEN

I ALWAYS TRY to remind young women of these facts when they take women's rights for granted: In the 1960s, most women could not obtain credit cards without a male to cosign their application, and banks could legally refuse to issue a credit card to a single woman;[24] women didn't win that right until the Equal Credit Opportunity Act of 1974.[25] In some states, women couldn't sit on juries, access birth control, or attend some Ivy League schools. Most states still had "head and master" laws, not only bestowing decision-making powers on husbands but legalizing marital rape, which remained legal in all states until Nebraska first made it a crime in 1973.[26] Some help wanted ads were divided into men's and women's jobs.[27] Bored and unhappy at home—that was just the beginning of women's problems.

You'd think, then, that housewives might organize to tackle these laws that cemented their inequality and addressed those problems. But like the militant housewives of the 1930s, many politically active housewives still focused on causes outside of women's rights. Some 50,000 American housewives participated in the November 1, 1961, Women's Strike for Peace to end the arms race. With thinly veiled surprise that such women would have an interest in anything outside the home, *Newsweek* called the strikers "perfectly ordinary looking women," the kind "you would see driving ranch wagons, or shopping at the village market, or attending PTA meetings."[28]

Meanwhile, John F. Kennedy's administration began to consider the plight of women and the government's role in ameliorating it. In 1962, at the behest of Assistant Secretary of Labor for Women's Affairs Esther Peterson, he established the President's Commission on the Status of Women. The chair: Eleanor Roosevelt.

The order's preamble began: "Prejudices and outmoded customs act as barriers to the full realization of women's basic rights." The commission pitched women's equality as an economic issue, key to achieving America's GDP goals, and integral to democracy. Soon every state had its own commission on the status of women.

In 1963, the commission presented to Kennedy *American Women: The Report of the President's Commission on the Status of Women*, "an invitation to action" on behalf of some 96 million American females from "infant to octogenarian, from migrant farm mother to suburban homemaker, from file clerk to research scientist, from Olympic athlete to college president."[29] The report recognized the importance of day care, access to education, and wages—to every woman—and repudiated race-based discrimination as "morally wrong and a source of national weakness," placing "an oppressive dual burden on millions of Negro women." Black women were twice as likely to seek work with young kids at home; most were relegated to low-income service jobs. In too many families of color, the report said, the "lack of opportunity for men as well as women, linked to racial discrimination, has forced the women to assume too large a share of the family responsibility."

The commission aimed to change the material reality of women by changing the social and legal sphere. The Equal Pay Act passed in 1963, and the next year, the Civil Rights Act passed, prohibiting discrimination on the basis of sex.

## CONCERN FOR SOME MEN

BUT WHAT OF the men, especially Black men, whose lack of opportunity the commission had noted? In March 1965, Assistant Secretary of Labor Daniel Patrick Moynihan published a report called *The Negro*

*Family: The Case for National Action*—remembered as the Moynihan Report—explaining why legislation on its own couldn't, and wouldn't, result in racial equality.[30]

Perhaps you're expecting a list of structural reasons for the discrepancy in success between Black Americans and other racial groups, but that's not what Moynihan, a liberal, focused on. Though as many as half of Black families may have been middle class, poor Black families disproportionately suffered high rates of unemployment, out-of-wedlock birth, divorce, addiction, and single motherhood. Despite legal victories like 1954's *Brown v. Board of Education* and the Economic Opportunity Act of 1964, "At the heart of the deterioration of the fabric of Negro society," Moynihan wrote, "is the deterioration of the Negro family."

Moynihan linked broken families to the legacy of barbarous slavery on Black Americans: the psychological and economic manifestation of Black family members auctioned off and separated from kin in early American history, or lynched later on. "The racist virus in the American blood stream still afflicts us," he noted. "Negroes will encounter serious personal prejudice for at least another generation." (Oh, Pat, how naïve you were.) Thus, the best thing for the Black family was to return Black men to their rightful place at its helm, which the slave trade had destroyed.

To Moynihan, Black mothers who'd historically worked and run households, in ways that many middle-class white women wouldn't understand for another decade or so, emasculated Black dads. Dependence on mothers' income "undermines the position of the father," and deprived kids of standard features of "middle-class upbringing." Moynihan was digging into what some researchers call "the myth of the Black matriarchy," that the "domineering Black female" resulted in the "psychological castration of the Black male."[31] "He used this tangle of pathology to describe Black families that are headed by Black

women," Nicole Carr, assistant professor of African American literature at Texas A&M San Antonio, told me.

The fix: Give these families more opportunities to emulate middle-
class white families, relegating Black mothers to the domestic sphere
and allowing Black dads to take over. He told President Lyndon Johnson: "We must not rest until every able-bodied Negro male is working.
Even if we have to displace some females."[32] This despite the fact that
such a model seemed to be making many a white woman miserable.

Though Moynihan understood that to realize this vision, we needed
to pay Black men living wages, enough to support their families, the
report contained no policy suggestions, even if he hoped it would
inspire some. He hinted at the possibility of some kind of universal
basic income, but ultimately Moynihan still saw the nuclear family,
with stern Black fatherhood and demure Black motherhood, as the fix
for what was also a structural and community problem.

His one concrete suggestion: upping the number of Black men in
the military, where they were then underrepresented (the opposite is
now true).[33] These diminished Black men would enter "a world away
from women, a world run by strong men of unquestioned authority."
Weird, because if the solution to diminished Black fatherhood was a
manly Black man at the family center, sending him off to boot camp
wouldn't help Dad be around more.

Moynihan was careful to note that these inequities weren't rooted
in race itself, but in ongoing racism. Still, some left-leaning critics
levied the charge of "blaming the victim," and some conservatives
used the report to assert the innateness of Black struggles. Eventually, liberals abandoned the idea of the broken family as root of
Black inequity; it became the domain of conservative pundits and
some Black centrists today. "We get the 'welfare queen' and we get
this idea that Black communities are impoverished because they're

pathological," Carr said. "Not because the state has stopped giving them services."

## FROM SEXUAL CONTAINMENT TO THE SUMMER OF LOVE

THE CULTURE DID get reshaped, but maybe not the way Moynihan and Friedan had envisioned. Those who grew up in the Depression procreated in the age of middle-class prosperity. Those who grew up in the era of prosperity and uniformity came of age in the '60s, some rejecting from whence they came.

Generational cultural U-turns are normal, but the pressure of conformity had been so forceful in the 1950s that the equal and opposite reaction was a cultural revolution: the upending of gender norms. The cracks in the facade of white middle-class conformity began to show, soon to grow into fissures.

There were Elvis and James Dean, Malcolm X and Martin Luther King, the civil rights movement, the rumblings and rambunctiousness of youth culture. Women's lib drove forward legislation to create equality between the sexes. Oral contraceptives arrived on the market in 1960, conferring on women more sexual freedom than ever before.[34] The number of unmarried couples cohabiting tripled in the 1970s.[35] It increased eightfold for couples under twenty-five with no kids. Eventually, children of the baby boom—an era with the highest birth rate and the lowest divorce rate in history—were responsible for the highest divorce rate and lowest birth rate the country had yet seen.

Americans weren't rejecting marriage per se; they were rejecting marriage to the *wrong person*. No longer sold by the media as a bulwark against all evils, marriage became a relationship one willingly entered into for love, with an increasing expectation of parity.

And if it didn't work out, getting un-married was easier as no-fault divorce became more common. But it still left many women overburdened and financially vulnerable. They usually retained more, or full, custody of their children, so if they needed to work after the new arrangement, there was no government-sponsored childcare to help them, unlike during World War II. Women were treated equally by the law, but that led to inequities.[36] Still, wives' suicide rates dropped by as much as 13 percent after no-fault divorce was adopted, and domestic violence rates within married couples fell 30 percent.[37]

If mothers in the '50s had paid for financial security with dependency, their daughters paid for independence with financial insecurity. But that freedom provided new opportunities. Women now had children later, and fewer of them, allowing them to pursue careers or spend more time working and saving, breadcrumbs along the path toward financial independence. This demographic shift was so explosive that when Ms. magazine launched as a one-off insert in New York magazine in 1971, its 300,000 copies sold out within eight days, garnering 26,000 subscriptions weeks later.[38]

In 1970, a survey of women entering a public university noted that most envisioned their futures as "married career woman with children." In twenty years, the pursuit of a Mrs. degree had morphed into the expectation of a Ms. degree—a bachelor's as a stepping stone to a career. About a quarter of wives from twenty to twenty-four were employed in 1950; by 1980, that number had more than doubled.[39]

More women entered male-dominated professions, like medicine and law, as women pushed open doors that had been stubbornly closed. The image of the domesticated housewife gave way to a new woman; move over, Donna Reed, here comes Mary Tyler Moore. In the '70s and '80s, television programs starring working women and working moms edged out earlier family dramas with women at home. My favorite show when I was little was *One Day at a Time*, about a single working mom and her two daughters, which normalized my life; I wouldn't have been able to relate for a minute to *Leave It to Beaver*. If in 1971 a majority of Americans disagreed with "efforts to strengthen and change women's status in society," by 1975, 63 percent approved.[40]

## WHAT MIGHT HAVE BEEN

WITH SO MANY more women working outside the home, the need for comprehensive childcare became clear, and not just to feminists. In a statement to Congress on February 19, 1969, Republican president Richard M. Nixon announced: "So crucial is the matter of early growth that we must make a national commitment to providing all American children an opportunity for healthful and stimulating development during the first five years of life."[41]

An opportunity presented itself in the form of the Comprehensive Child Development Act of 1971, sponsored by Senator Walter Mondale to create "universally available child development programs" for millions of children.

Building on the Head Start programs of the '60s and emphasizing disadvantaged children and single parents, the bill would establish federally funded, public childcare centers around the country through a "partnership of parents, community, and local government." They would be free for the lowest-income Americans and sliding scale based on income for others.[42] They'd offer services from psychological assistance to nighttime care, ensuring that "no mother may be forced to work in order for children to receive services." Representative Bella Abzug asserted that the CDA was not only a "children's bill" but also "a woman's bill."[43] It passed both the House and the Senate—almost unimaginable in today's politically polarized climate. But President Nixon still had to sign it.

His speechwriter, one Pat Buchanan, urged him not to, as conservative commentator James Kilpatrick asserted that the point of the act was "to Sovietize our youth."[44] It's so easy to scare Americans away from what's best for them with the cry of socialism. (Do you like libraries, schools, and roads? Then you like aspects of socialism.) Though childcare was entirely optional, some parent groups objected to efforts to "federalize America's children," and asked, "Whose children? Yours or the State's?"[45] Support waned among Republicans.

Because of his unpopular planned trip to China in 1972, Nixon felt pressure to disavow anything remotely socialist or communist. A program that interrupted the "traditional" familial approach to child-rearing and replaced it with a state agency, well, that didn't look good to the emerging neoconservative class seeking to gain political power by opposing the counterculture.

On December 9, 1971, Nixon, the guy who two years before had announced his commitment to healthful and stimulating development during the first five years of life, vetoed the bill. He excoriated its "family-weakening implications" and "communal approaches to child rearing over against the family-centered approach."[46] The bill didn't survive the veto.

That was the moment, said Elliot Haspel, author of *Crawling Behind: America's Child Care Crisis and How to Fix It*, "when we lost the plot, because that became the sort of ideology of one political party in this country. The family is one sphere and the public is another sphere and never the twain shall meet." That was the cementing of the "free-market family," when it became transgressive to ask for help so women could work. We briefly had the political will to expose the lie that women could and should do it all alone. But we lost it. Childrearing, from that point on, was commoditized.

## UNDERMINING THE ERA

THAT WASN'T THE era's only legislative heartbreak.

The proposed Equal Rights Amendment to the Constitution read, "Equality of rights under the law shall not be denied or abridged by the United States or by any State on account of sex." Considered a done deal when it passed in Congress in 1971,[47] Martha Griffiths, a Detroit representative known as the "mother of the ERA,"[48] predicted in 1973 that "ERA will be part of the Constitution long before the year is out."[49] They needed only thirty-eight states to ratify it, and feminists had convinced many politicians that it would be a bad look not to.

Then along came Phyllis Schlafly, perhaps the most effective political organizer of housewives. She called herself a housewife, but in reality she ran for the U.S. House of Representatives in 1952 on the anti-communist line, winning the primary but losing the election. Head of the Illinois Federation of Republican Women from 1960 to 1964, she became nationally known after selling more than 3 million copies of a self-published 1964 book, *A Choice Not an Echo*, which accused Republicans of succumbing to elites rather than respecting grassroots activism. She would go on to publish a monthly newsletter, starting in 1967, called *The Phyllis Schlafly Report*, which mobilized thousands of housewives to conservative political action.

Schlafly had long ignored feminists, as she was far more focused on the upcoming Strategic Arms Limitation Talks; Nixon was for them and she against. She was hardly paying attention to the ERA when Congress debated it, assuming it was "innocuous and mildly helpful."[50] But after a friend encouraged her to participate in a debate against it, she scrutinized the amendment and decided it was downright dangerous. She founded the National Committee to Stop Taking Our Privileges—(STOP) ERA—and announced in her newsletter that she was opposed.

So were her readers. They worried housewives would be maligned by the legislation or forced to work. They feared they'd be drafted, or more likely to lose their children in custody battles, should they divorce. Schlafly galvanized thousands of those women into action. Her volunteers, she said, were "housewives" who "didn't even know where their state capital was." But Schlafly trained them in (STOP) ERA talking points, which they repeated as they lobbied local representatives. She taught them to send thank-you notes after those meetings and how to dress for television and how to wear their makeup and hair as she did, so they all looked like proper Midwestern housewives.

Another conservative housewife, Beverly LaHaye, organized Concerned Women for America (CWA) and said housewives were "very quickly becoming politically active out of concern for the future of their families."[51] LaHaye wrote to Kansas senator Bob Dole: "I, along with the members of Concerned Women for America, am concerned that the past very visible efforts of pro-ERA groups may have led you to believe that support for this proposed amendment, and other intervention by our government into family affairs, is simply a matter of course. I assure you that it is not." She liked to say "Betty Friedan does not speak for me."[52]

Schlafly knew that most states required a two-thirds vote to ratify the ERA. All she had to do was convince politicians that what was at stake wasn't women's equal pay but the American way of life.

Despite the fact that her own family was not so traditional—she had quite a career, including earning a law degree when she was in her fifties—she advocated for the "traditional" family of the 1950s, the way it had always been and should be. The ERA would have in no way forced women from home to office, but that was irrelevant, as Schlafly had created an army of loyal followers. "What I am defending is the real rights of women," she said. "A woman should have the right to be in the home as a wife and mother."[53]

Other groups followed, including Women Who Want to Be Women (WWWW) and Happiness of Womanhood (HOW).[54] The ERA wasn't a pro-woman piece of legislation, they argued. It was anti-woman. After Schlafly testified before state legislatures in Arkansas, Missouri, Virginia, and Georgia, none ratified the ERA. Only thirty-five states did. (Virginia finally became that thirty-eighth state in 2020, but it was it was too late to amend the Constitution.)[55] Finally, housewives had organized on behalf of themselves, except it was in service of denying women equal rights.

Even with all the cultural change and the legislative shifts, the country stopped short of declaring that women deserved the same rights as men.

Without the ERA, and without childcare or comprehensive paid family leave, women had no way to truly escape the housewife archetype. All they could do was drag it along with them into the next chapter, liberated and tied down, pulled forward and back at the same time.

## CHAPTER 8

# The Dawn of the Supermom

G race was thirty-six when she tied the knot and thirty-seven when she procreated. In theory, that would have given her enough time to establish herself in her career and sock some money away. However, she'd chosen interesting but low-paying jobs, which hadn't fortified her financially.

Grace worked for years in the field of archaeology, often on dig sites—hard physical labor, long days, low pay, lots of fun. But then she had her daughter, and that kind of difficult, time-consuming, and low-wage freelance work was no longer an option. She threw herself into being a wife and mother and figured she'd someday go back to school to study something more family-friendly.

She and her husband had never really discussed the logistics. In the beginning, she felt proprietary about the decision-making regarding their daughter, insisting on breastfeeding all the time instead of pumping, which would have allowed her husband to help with the feeding. She hid how challenging breastfeeding was, not asking for help. He commuted to an office, and in Grace's mind her job was to master all things domestic.

"I wanted to be able to make great meals and have the house clean and do it all," she told me. "He never once said, 'Hey, this house is a mess. We need to have dinner on time.' It was me."

What her husband *really* wanted was for Grace to work, especially after their second daughter was born. Her getting a job mattered more to him than nice dinners or a tidy living room, and he didn't want to be solely responsible for his family's finances.

But that was almost impossible. Grace applied for a job at the local museum; after childcare and travel expenses, she'd be taking home only thirty dollars a week. She would have benefited from paid parental leave when the kids were born—provided by the government, since contractors and freelancers aren't eligible through employers.

In the end, Grace did what many women like her do: She took part-time contract work at a day care, which her kids attended for free. But still her salary was frighteningly low, and she never had a break, from her kids, from any kids. Not only was Grace unable to stay home as she wanted, but she was also continuing to do everything she'd done before getting a job. "I would race home, pick him up at the train station, and then deal with the babies and making dinner." Her husband was willing to help with household chores, but Grace had to remind him, nag, set a basket of laundry before him to encourage him to fold it.

When the kids got bigger and went to school, she took several part-time jobs and tried to make jewelry that she hoped to sell on weekends at flea markets, trying to build skills and contribute financially; it still wasn't enough. "I loved being a mom and having a family and doing all the sweet things, and I love working and making money," Grace said. "And I was unable to do both at the same time."

# SECOND SHIFTING

LIKE ME, GRACE was reared on the Enjoli perfume vision of twenty-four-hour womanhood. We were teens in the '80s, when the romanticized 1950s housewife had long faded amidst the bright glow of the counterculture, and then finally morphed into a new creature: the Career Woman. Domestic and isolated gave way to girl bosses (not that that term existed), normalized with blockbuster '80s movies like *Working Girl* and *9 to 5*.

Entering the workforce had added a second set of responsibilities to women's already full plates, hammering away at the office all day and then returning home to a full load of housework and childcare.[1] Instead of Rosie the Riveter *or* June Cleaver, modern women were supposed to be both. As historian Elaine Tyler May put it, "Most women still faced what their mothers had tried to avoid: overwork, inadequate pay, and extra burdens at home."[2]

These were the early rumblings of what sociologist Arlie Russell Hochschild eventually called, as she titled her book, *The Second Shift*. Women performed some thirty twenty-four-hour days' worth of domestic labor more than men each year, leading to a "leisure gap." They put more hours into childcare after 1985 than they did in 1975 and 1965.[3] In fact, there were infant schools in the early nineteenth century; childcare had been more the rule than the exception.[4]

Eventually, many Gen X women, some the daughters of Women's Movement activists who'd fought for the right to work outside the home (and be paid equally for it), grew up believing they should work full-time and handle all the kid, family, and traditional wife stuff. We believed we were supposed to be able to have and do and be it all. We were expected to be, and expected ourselves to be, Supermom. Which did not exactly lead to the liberation the women's libbers had envisioned. Nor did we realize that this expectation was unreasonable—nay, nearly impossible.

Pressure to be everything—mom, wife, worker—became so intense that in 1984 writer Marjorie Hansen Shaevitz coined the term "Superwoman Syndrome."[5] "I found that, professionally, some women were at the top of their field," Shaevitz told me. But "emotionally and personally, they were a mess." Some studies have found the do-it-all expectation is particularly trying for Black women and contributes to health disparities.[6]

So who should come around to diagnose the problem but Betty Friedan. In her book *The Second Stage*, Friedan argued that 1980s "superwomanhood" had put women in a double bind, oppressing them both at work and at home. Even after so much had changed since she first chronicled housewives' unrest, she argued, feminists must reach the "second stage" of the movement so that both public and private gender roles would shift. Because the cultural change didn't co-occur with the structural change required to improve women's lives, Supermom was an even more oppressive archetype than housewife. Good grief, with each gain women made, expectations—and unhappiness—rose.

Oh, men did more. Let's give credit where credit is due—one estimate said by the end of the twentieth century, they'd tripled their childcare input, although some had started at zero and so could only fall upwards.[7] Their role as caregivers was increasingly normalized so they no longer had to worry about being called sissies just because they took on the dusting. No, there was masculine-enough Michael Keaton in *Mr. Mom* to guide them.

But more wasn't enough. It wasn't half. Study after study found men did less housework, childcare, and emotional labor—the planning and conceiving of it all—than their female partners.[8] Having children younger than six reduced the number hours women could work but had little impact on fathers' hours.[9]

## THE INTENSITY OF MODERN MOTHERING

MANY OF US who were reared in the 1970s remember the era's parenting zeitgeist, which bordered on loving neglect. Shoo the kid out the door in the morning and say "See you at dinner," without knowing their whereabouts or activities throughout the day. Children were neither to be seen nor heard, especially if the parents were doing something fun like, you know, drugs.

Then on May 25, 1979, six-year-old Etan Patz convinced his mother, Julie, who ran a home day care in the family's SoHo loft, to let him walk alone the two blocks to the bus and get himself to school solo for the first time. Nervous Julie consented because she had other kids to tend to. Etan took his tote bag decorated with images of elephants and left. He was never seen again.

Etan's image was splashed across newspapers, his picture perhaps the first to be featured on a milk carton under a "missing child" banner. Though a man who'd worked in a bodega where Etan stopped for a soda was arrested in 2012 for his murder, Etan himself was never found.

In many ways, Etan's disappearance marked the end of the 1970s and its lax parenting, creating the sensation that any, and every, child could be vulnerable to the worst imaginable crimes, anytime, anyplace, by anyone. Children learned about stranger danger. President Reagan declared May 25 National Missing Children's Day.[10] In 1981, six-year-old Adam Walsh disappeared from a Hollywood, Florida, Sears; his severed head was found a week later in a canal over a hundred miles away. Adam's father, John Walsh, became an advocate for missing and murdered children, and went on to host Fox's *America's Most Wanted* in 1988.[11] The potential for parents' worst fears to be realized, broadcast on national TV, was synthesized by families, rendering the worst possibilities omnipresent.

And so, just as the number of women in the workforce increased, so did fear for children's welfare, and the accompanying practice of "intensive mothering."

Suddenly, mothers had to be "constantly watching out for too much junk food, or making sure kids are getting their sunblock, or being careful about what they're watching on TV, or 'stranger-danger,'" said Jodi Vandenberg-Daves, author *Modern Motherhood: An American History*. "All those things crop up right at the moment when women are also more involved professionally. And it helped create that sense that no matter what you're doing as a mother, it's not enough."

Many of us have since become mothers with this overparenting expectation seared into our brains, terrified of our children facing not just real danger, but just about any hardship or pain. Nineteen-seventies lax parenting gave way to 1980s helicopter parenting, and in the twenty-first century that became "snowplow parenting"—not just hovering over our children but clearing any obstacles out of their way, rather than teaching them how to overcome them. Relying on us that much more, our children became less independent. (I've just taken an hour break from writing to help my thirteen-year-old fish an AirPod out of the gutter, but maybe it's too much to expect her to have developed that particular skill on her own.)

In the twenty-first century, Momfluencers and C-suite women began advising mothers to "lean in"—as if it were not too much to sew

Halloween costumes and cook beautiful meals while also presiding over an economic empire. Some of us did lean in, only to tumble into the abyss.

Between 1975 and 2019, the number of employed women with children under three almost doubled.[12] Women now make up slightly more than half the entire workforce. While the United States still spends less than 1 percent of GDP on childcare, parents with low incomes spend more than a third of their income on it.[13] A majority of American families live in "childcare deserts."[14] When women have children later, their prime working and parenting years overlap. How can we have so little affordable childcare, work full-time, and never take our eyes off our kids? The expectations of women, and the expectations we levy on ourselves, have reached, I hope, an apogee.

Grace has been trying to figure this out for well over a decade. Once both her kids were in middle school, she took a full-time, salaried job at a different childcare facility. She now has more money but far less time for the kids. Now that Grace is around less, she worries about her younger daughter's debilitating anxiety, how it affects her socially and academically.

But in addition to accumulating less debt, there's another upside. Grace is still responsible for the bulk of household tasks like keeping the fridge filled, but since his schedule is more flexible, her husband must now do more with the kids. "I don't think it was until lately that he's been realizing how much I did," she told me—the doctor's appointments and soccer games and meals, all those things that she used to take care of. The unexpected outcome is that he appreciates more how hard Grace has worked over these last thirteen years, and he helps her more.

# HAVING IT SOME

LOOK, IT HASN'T all been bad. As more women continued to enter male-dominated professions, the pay gap began to close, especially for non-moms, though women still earn eighty-one cents for every man's dollar, with Black women earning sixty-one cents for every white man's dollar.[15] Girls and women have made incredible achievements in education. They can have credit cards, and marital rape is technically illegal in every state. Lots of businesses have private breast-pumping areas.

But the level of discontent, the lack of structural support—that hasn't changed all that much. Which is why women like Grace and me feel like we're forever stuck in the 1978 bubble bath commercial, in which a mother can't get any support other than a tub full of hot water, and cries, "Calgon, take me away!" Perhaps this is why I spend a disproportionate amount of time in the bath; one can accomplish very little parenting and housework while naked and submerged.

We've been circling around these issues for the last fifty years, finding new ways to say "This is unfair. This is wrong. We need help." Women, mothers, have felt guilty over missing key moments of our children's lives if we work. We've experienced work–life balance as a cruel joke of a phrase, dangled before us like the rabbit before greyhounds, which we've been chasing for decades. And thus—privileged whining warning—we feel exhausted. We feel we'd been sold a lie. And in the twenty-first century, we finally began to talk about it.

In 2012, Anne Marie Slaughter, the first woman to serve as director of policy planning for the U.S. State Department, explained in the *Atlantic* "Why Women Still Can't Have It All." "[T]he feminist beliefs on which I had built my entire career were shifting under my feet," she wrote. "I'd been part, albeit unwittingly, of making millions of women feel that *they* are to blame if they cannot manage to rise up the ladder as fast as men and also have a family and an active home life (and be thin and beautiful to boot)."[16]

Her advice? Synchronize work and school schedules—a policy suggestion I could not agree with more. Why is the bank closed on school holidays, but most other businesses aren't? Try to find work with flexible schedules and work-at-home options. (She wrote this pre-pandemic when such approaches were generally frowned upon in workaholic America.) Marry someone who'll carry at least half, if not more, of the weight. (See chapter 11 for more on this.) Sequence pro-creation right, which means try to have kids as young as you're ready, so you'll still be in your prime when your kids are finishing high school.

Also, close the leadership gap by electing more women to govern-mental office and promoting more women to the C-suite. "Only when women wield power in sufficient numbers will we create a society that genuinely works for all women," Slaughter wrote. "That will be a soci-ety that works for everyone."

"If women were in more positions of leadership and power, we would be able to have traction," C. Nicole Mason, executive director and CEO of the Institute for Women's Policy Research, told me.

I'm less certain about that. After all, a historically high number of women now serve in Congress, though it's still only 24 percent, when women make up slightly more than 50 percent of the population. Some 38 percent of House Democrats and 36 percent of Senate Dem-ocrats are women, but only 8 percent of House Republicans and 15 percent of Senate Republicans are.[17]

A politician's sex doesn't guarantee loyalty to ameliorating the

conditions that affect fellow members of her sex. Not all female politicians will support sane school schedules and universal childcare.
We finally have a woman in the second-highest office in the land. But
structural change? It eludes us still.

The slow pace of policy shift may have something to do with Congress's lack of awareness—or, if we're putting on our cynical lenses,
lack of concern—about women's plight. They may push ideas for the
America they want—or the one they recall from 1950s TV—rather
than the America they have.

But we must make policy based on real people and not fictional
archetypes and stereotypes.

A core issue and the recurring thesis of this book: Americans
wrongly believe moms should and will do it all. "The sense that women
should stay at home and take care of the kids is still underneath a lot
of this," Mason said. According to the Pew Research Center, more
than half of Americans believe that one parent should stay home with
young children.[18]

Slaughter admits her solutions work best for the top tier in which
she travels. Hourly workers in fast food won't have work-from-home
and flexible-schedule options, but affordable, or better yet, free, day
care can help everyone.

## WHINING WOMEN

TOWARD THE END of my editing this book, I met Meg, a twenty-six-
year-old magazine editor, at a gathering one night. TV-gorgeous and
whip smart, with flawless skin and flaxen hair, she told me she had a
four-month-old at home and had returned to her job a month earlier.

"Are you going crazy, trying to figure out how to work and perform perfect motherhood?" I asked her. I assumed Meg was early in the realization that our line of work didn't leave much of a profit margin after childcare expenses, that she'd been tearing her hair out trying to navigate a reasonable path.

I was wrong. Meg told me she was energized, not enervated, by the challenge of figuring out just how much she could accomplish in a single day, how much she could push herself to the limits of efficiency and productivity, and how little childcare she could spring for and still be a good employee. Despite being Catholic, Meg had embraced a Protestant work ethic and loved the feeling of completing a hard day's work. As a "privileged knowledge worker type," her job was so intellectual and sedentary, she welcomed the physicality of having a baby, the way it made her body tired, not just her brain. "My back is tired from carrying him in the baby carrier or from bending down to change diapers ten times a day," she said, with pride and joy rather than lament—not the way I kvetch "Oy, my aching back" on a regular basis. (Maybe if her back is still hurting twenty-five years later, as mine is, the exultation will curdle into complaint.)

"I'm kind of interested in testing myself," Meg told me. "Do I actually have the mettle?" How much could she push herself to be a career woman, mom, and housekeeper? She didn't know the answer yet, but she embraced figuring it out. "I love vacuuming," Meg admitted. Meanwhile, I shared none of these sentiments, right down to the affinity for vacuuming. I feel the same way about it that I do about writing: I'm happy after it's done, but I don't like doing it.

I asked Meg to meet me the following week so I could interview her, the living embodiment of supermom. Though my kids are only about a decade older than her son, I was nearly twice her age, and I wondered if my original supposition about why I seem to struggle so much more than my mother had, despite my having fewer external stressors and obstacles, held up. That is, was it just so much easier because Meg was young and not yet exhausted?

Meg chewed on that idea while nursing her cherubic son and sipping a latte. Her grandmother had given birth to her first child at eighteen, and Meg's mother had given birth to Meg at twenty-one. Her mother-in-law, on the other hand, had given birth to Meg's husband at forty-three, and Meg was able to compare those experiences. "I'd rather do this when I have more energy and flexibility," said Meg. "You can embrace the difficulty when you're twenty-six or you can embrace the difficulty when you're forty and maybe more financially able to afford a nanny." For now, to keep childcare costs down, she had to turn down some enticing work opportunities that didn't have the potential for career growth or the pay to make it worth leaving her son with a sitter.

What Meg didn't want to do was complain. When she described a genre of writing as "wealthy, privileged women doing the pity-party thing," damned if I wasn't at that moment casting doubt on my entire project, since it could very well be shelved at the bookstore in the section where all those titles were corralled into one spot. (She did say later, "Just because people are wealthier and educated doesn't mean their problems or feelings don't matter.")

The main difference between Meg and many people of her educational class was how surprised they seemed at the challenges of working motherhood. How could they *not* expect it to be hard, after all this time? So she had to scrimp some before the baby was born and can't socialize as much. So what? We're too stuck in our scripts about how our life is supposed to go, like college is about partying and our twenties are for having fun, she suggested. "That sets people up possibly for more failure, because then the contrast is really striking to them, as opposed to trying to integrate all these things," Meg said. "There's some hard work and discomfort, but there's also some enjoyment, and you can find joy in some of the difficult things." Meg describes herself as stoic and having a "keep it together, hard-core mentality." Her generation seemed to be fragile, lazy, made soft by low expectations. Life is hard. Buck up, moms.

Meg is a libertarian, and as I explained the thesis of this book—that interdependence is far more a traditional American trait than independence, and that families, the culture, and the government must support women—I realized that she would absolutely hate it. What I'm advocating for bumps up against socialist tenets, anathema to libertarian ideals.

But then I thought, a lot of the people complaining are not privileged. And many societies have these supports with few citizens complaining; their culture prioritizes them. There may be less economic inequality because of them.

Still, I had to admit that some of what Meg said made sense. Many Americans maintain a sense of entitlement, eschew hard work, and run screaming from emotional discomfort. Heck, in this current era of snowplow parenting, many parents have knitted themselves into a panic ball over the fear of their child experiencing a normal range of human emotion. We should stop expecting raising children to be easy.

And at the same time, we can't expect too many people to adopt Meg's steely reserve, her stoic, hyper-realist, tough-guy libertarianism. Most of us want to live in a society where we do feel we owe something to one another, paying in collectively and withdrawing individually as needed. We just haven't figured out what, or how much, or how to fund it.

## THE NEW OPPORTUNITY

OVER THE YEARS, politicians and pundits, academics and activists have imagined many great solutions for the supermom problem, or the tired mom, or the overwhelmed mom, or the mom who tried to do it all and landed on her ass. But not much changed between the end of the '70s, when so many important pieces of legislation fizzled out or didn't have the intended effect, and 2020.

Then the SARS-CoV-2 pandemic shut down schools and businesses. Women outside the laptop class were forced to work despite having nowhere for their kids to go. Women inside that class had to help with schooling while attending to their jobs. Some 80 percent of women said they were overseeing most of the remote learning during high pandemic times, and 70 percent of women were handling most of the housework.[19] During the height of the pandemic, one in four women were pondering leaving or downshifting jobs.[20] Almost 2.2 million women had left or been forced from the workforce.[21] More women than men[22] had left or lost jobs, and the pandemic seemed to be setting mothers back a decade in gender equality gains.[23] Women's primal screams not only were heard around the world, but actually became newsworthy.

We became acutely aware that our economy and our country cannot run without women. Reshma Saujani, founder of the Marshall Plan for Moms (now called Moms First), noted that some 41 percent of mothers are breadwinners. "When they lose their jobs," she said, "their entire family suffers."

Supermom stopped in her tracks, and the world woke up to just how much she'd been keeping things running.

Yet few envisioning the country's economic recovery homed in on women in discussions. "Even though women are being most impacted, [politicians] still frame this around men's experiences," Mason told me.

In some ways, the crisis allowed us to acknowledge the unsustainability of modern motherhood, the way the housewife archetype had been subsumed by the supermom archetype, the improbability of it all. It gave us an opportunity to reexamine—or maybe to look at for the first time—how the ominous shadow of the housewife still hangs over us, woven into relationships, policies, and politics, the subjects of Part II of this book.

Maybe it will also provide us with an opportunity to move toward the light.

# PART II

## CHAPTER 9

# The Displaced Housewife, or: Married, Pregnant, Dependent, Screwed

After her first child was born, Nora, a social worker, found contract work with an agency doing home visits with clients. With flexible hours, she could work when her husband, then training for what would someday be a high-paying job, was home—she didn't have to pay for childcare. "But it also left a lot of liability because if people didn't show up or if they weren't home for their home visits, I couldn't charge anything," she told me. Or, if the baby got sick and she couldn't go, then no pay.

When she had her second child eighteen months later, Nora was making more money than her husband was. But his schedule was unpredictable, and he had no control over when he'd be home or gone for days at a time. Now Nora needed childcare to do her job, which would have zeroed out her earnings.

She tried hiring people, but her hours were scattered, and so were the babysitters. "The first person we hired got arrested on the second day of her job," Nora said. The sitter was jailed for disorderly conduct and couldn't come—which didn't inspire much confidence in Nora that a stranger would do better watching her kids than she would. "It was just this constant struggle with me having to miss appointments because the kids were sick or the childcare didn't show up or the childcare worker's kids were sick or...it was nonstop."

Once they had another kid, it became clear to Nora that piecing together childcare so she could work was no longer viable, and it made sense for one parent with a stable schedule to stay home. As a social worker, she'd never bring in the big bucks, but her husband's job would someday be lucrative. Together they made a clear, conscious decision that Nora would forgo her career for full-time motherhood. It would be tight for a few years, but when the kids got older, and her husband earned more, it would ease up. They had two more children and decided that she would homeschool all four kids. Nora let her social worker registration lapse, even though she knew it would be too time consuming and expensive to get it back later. "It was a clear, cost-benefit analysis," she said.

In many ways, the arrangement worked. While Nora fully supports mothers who want to work full-time and believes we should create a society that allows for that, as someone who had studied child development, she felt that having a parent or caregiver home full-time created a sense of safety for the kids. "And safety is where good development happens," she said. "We should find a way to take care of parents and families if moms decide or dads decide to stay home."

Her husband agreed. Or he acted as if he agreed that Nora's work as their mother and teacher was valuable and viable. He was happy being the breadwinner—that role suited his ego, his sense of self, and the gender dynamics of his family growing up. But her husband also wanted Nora herself to perform a specific part. "I think that he absolutely wanted me to play that 1950s housewife role," she said.

As her husband moved up the ladder, making more money over the years, they—mostly he—also racked up tens of thousands of dollars in debt. The more he made, the more he spent. Still Nora wasn't worried, at least not on the surface. "I did see his money as my money," she said. "I felt very strongly that I was providing for our family in a way that was different from his. My work was just as important as his, and I did see it very much as a job, and I took it seriously." More importantly, the decisions they made at the time were reflective of the expectation of future wealth.

But tensions began to arise. Nora's husband was gone sometimes for five, six days at a time, and she felt that she was working full-time as much as he was. When he was home, she expected him to be an equal partner, looking after the house and the kids. "When you get home, it's an even split. I'm not the maid. I'm not the 1950s housewife."

That didn't go over well, because her husband saw his days at home as his time off, just as she saw his days at home as a respite for her. When he was there, he didn't want to be bothered with the vagaries of daily life. "He wanted me to greet him at the door with an apron on. And to have his beautiful kids around. He didn't want to know the struggles. He didn't want to be involved in the discipline of the kids. And so our struggles came from that, because we were both tired," said Nora. "We were both exhausted. We had four kids I was home-schooling. And in addition, we had the debt."

His salary still was not getting them through. By the end of the month, as they waited for his next paycheck, her card would be declined at the grocery store checkout line. "I kept thinking, well, in the future, it's going to get better because he's going to be making more money. The struggles just all kind of became, I think, too great."

The marriage was crumbling. Nora knew that on some level, but she didn't want to get out and leave herself financially vulnerable. She thought if she could stay long enough, he'd be making good money, and the stress of debt would be alleviated and maybe things would get better.

The proverbial back-breaking straw emerged when she discovered he'd been unfaithful, a lot and ongoing, with many people, on his days away from home. That was the end. He moved out. The negotiations began. "It then became crystal clear how little he valued my role in the family," she said.

At that point, he was just starting to make good money, and in theory, by local law, she was entitled to have half of everything they had. But in addition to the modest house and his income, what they had was massive debt that had to be paid off. That was divided between them, too. The house already had a second mortgage, and the only other assets were the retirement funds. And with two houses to pay for now, the expenses added up.

They could sell the house and split the retirement funds, but this was their kids' home, and Nora could not afford another house with only half the proceeds. So they took money from the retirement funds to pay off the marital debt, including the second mortgage, and she bought the house from her ex-husband while he kept what remained in the retirement account. That left Nora with a stable home for their kids but no savings, including retirement. He still had his retirement fund plus all the money he'd be contributing to it year after year. The minute Nora decided to quit her job and stay home, she said, "I lost his future earnings, and I lost my own future earnings."

## DISLOCATION AND DIVORCE

NORA'S EXPERIENCE IS so common there's a name for it: "displaced homemaker." The term refers to a stay-at-home mom (or dad) who is "no longer financially supported by their spouse," per the New York State Department of Labor.[1] She's recognized as someone who "[p]reviously provided unpaid services to their family" and "[c]urrently is unemployed or underemployed." That is, someone who assumed their job was to stay home but now must find paid work. New York State considers them "dislocated workers" and offers career counseling and computer workshops, which, for someone like Nora, would never be enough to rectify the divorce inequality that has befallen her.

Despite ye ole misogynist proverb "cheaper to keep her," divorce is, on the whole, bad for women financially—unfortunate, since so many forces propel them to marry, from tax breaks to the gender pay gap. The U.S. Government Accountability Office found that women separated or divorced after age fifty saw their income drop by 41 percent, as opposed to 23 percent for men.[2] Their credit scores fell, too. According to the Pew Research Center, husbands earn more than wives in 69 percent of heterosexual marriages; women are in riskier financial positions the minute they're on their own even if they're working.[3] It costs adults an average of almost $10,000 if they leave the workforce for twelve weeks.[4]

We might assume that the problem of the displaced homemaker is less pervasive these days. After all, housewifery hasn't been the norm since the baby boom, and after the sexual revolution and feminist movements, women began to work in greater numbers, thus were more likely to edge toward financial independence. But it's a myth that state laws that split assets evenly keep housewives financially safe.

Sociologist Pamela Smock at the University of Michigan compared cohorts of women marrying and divorcing in different time periods to see if indeed the negative economic consequences of divorce have declined. "The answer was no," she told me. "I don't think things have changed nearly as much as people think."

Generally, the better educated and higher-earning men are, the greater the chance they marry, and some scholars think the same might be true of women, too—more money makes women more attractive spouses.[5] However, other research has found it's harder to get a husband if a woman is a high-earner.[6] There's an "independence effect"—they're less dependent on the economic boost from marriage that women without high earning potential rely on for a class lift.[7] Those women are often left in precarious positions if the source of their income is a philandering, dim-witted asshole who abandons not just marriage but also financial duty—not that I'm talking about anyone in particular.

But the issue here really isn't women becoming wives. It's becoming mothers that makes them vulnerable to economic duress. This is known as "the motherhood penalty"—the financial hit working women take when they have kids.[8] Being the primary caregiver lowers a woman's earning power, and that power is even more threatened if she's not in a privileged position. Per the Bureau of Labor Statistics, the 2017 unemployment rate among women who were "married, spouse present" with young children was 2.6 percent, but increased to 9.9 percent for mothers with other marital statuses, like divorced, widowed, or single.[9] And of course, housewives don't collect Social Security or unemployment—but, as we'll discuss later, they probably should.

Married women, too, become vulnerable because of motherhood, which I became acutely aware of during the pandemic, simply by talking to my childhood friends, most of whom I met when I was eleven. They lived in the same town as my dad, and although I only saw them on weekends, holidays, and summers, we had always been close and never lost touch.

Early in the pandemic, we all began Zooming every weekend. When

I told them about this book, they began to share about how their own lives related to it, especially in terms of employment and motherhood. The first of us to marry—and the first to divorce—is now remarried to a stay-at-home dad, while she's the breadwinner. But the rest of us had found ourselves in the same situation without exactly realizing it: We had all become financially dependent on our husbands once we had kids.

## AT HIS MERCY

NORA'S SITUATION WAS especially precarious because she hadn't had an income for so long. In negotiations over child support, the mediators and her ex-husband kept asking her to predict how much money she could earn so they could adjust the formula. She'd been out of the workforce for fifteen years. And she was still homeschooling the kids. Nora had no idea.

Even if she'd gone back to work full-time, the motherhood penalty would have hit. Hiring managers are less inclined to hire mothers than women without kids and usually offer mothers lower salaries.[10] The Census Bureau revealed that the earnings gap between heterosexual couples doubles a year after the birth of their first child and keeps growing for another nine years.[11] Even if it eventually levels off, the chasm remains. Meanwhile, white-collar men often get a "fatherhood bonus," a salary bump for procreating, while children cost all women. But the motherhood penalty seems to disappear among the very top economic strata of women and increases the lower down on the economic ladder they are.[12]

Right after her divorce, Nora's income was sixty dollars a week, from working six hours in a craft store. Her ex-husband found this unacceptable and insisted she stop homeschooling their kids and work more. Their kids didn't want this, and she rejected it. "I didn't want them to feel any more of a loss than they already felt, because there were so many losses for them," she said.

When he realized the courts wouldn't uphold this demand, he accused Nora of not providing a proper education to avoid having to support her staying home. Then he took a Covid pay cut and asked to reduce his child support payment. When Nora refused, he petitioned the court not just for him to pay less but also for custody of their kids, forcing her to use whatever money she had left to hire a divorce lawyer.

The battle has been going on for six years.

Two of her children are now in college, which her ex-husband refuses to pay for. One is almost finished home schooling. The youngest decided on his own to go to public school. Still, her ex-husband fights her; still Nora pays lawyers to defend herself.

They'd made this decision and crafted this arrangement together, that she would forgo earning her own money and stay home. Nora had rendered herself at his mercy financially, giving up her career based on the understanding that someday he would earn a good income to support her and their children. Knowing that in the future he'd be bringing home his current salary—over $400,000 annually—Nora had withstood the financial hardship of the early years of their marriage and did not press too hard on his overspending. They'd discussed how, when the kids were grown and gone, they'd buy some property, and she'd manage it—someday going back to earning once she was done raising their kids. "That was kind of what I thought of the future. But suddenly, that future was not mine. Not at all." The monthly payments

Nora receives are calculated according to her ex-husband's salary from six years ago; according to her, he makes over 70 percent more than that now.

She entered the negotiations at a financial disadvantage, yet she also went in with a kind of optimism that was soon replaced with dismay. "I guess I thought that if someone behaves like an asshole, that the court is going to see that. And I guess I thought that there would be some kind of morality around the fact that having the affairs is not the moral choice," Nora said. "But that's not actually what the courts are designed to do at all. They're actually designed to strip all of that away. The goal is to clear the courts as quickly as possible. And so the attorneys are really kind of charged with trying to come to a settlement."

So she signed the agreement that they came up with. Maybe it was a mistake not to fight harder, to hold out for his future earnings, especially when she had agreed all those years ago to forgo her own.

Nora was forty-six when they got divorced. She was over fifty when I interviewed her. Getting back on her feet financially wasn't just a problem because of her age and the amount of time she'd been out of the workforce. The long-term effects of unemployment that mothers suffer are extensive— fewer retirement benefits, less accrued interest, slower earnings growth. "It ends up costing a lot more than your salary," Michael Madowitz, an economist at the left-leaning Center for American Progress, told me. He called this phenomenon "unemployment scarring."

"There's just so much loss, financially and in terms of the progression of a person's career and in terms of all of that networking and all of that meeting people," Nora said. "There's so much loss that it's impossible to recover."

Not for her lack of trying. She's taught meditation, started a consulting business, gone back to social work. "I'm still paycheck to paycheck," she said. "And he's making four hundred thousand dollars a year."

## THE LAST HAPPY DAYS

I COULDN'T HELP thinking about two other women who shared similar experiences with me. Christina had met Faraji at summer camp for gifted children when she was a fourteen-year-old camper and he a twenty-one-year-old counselor. Nothing happened that summer, but they'd kept in touch via Facebook.

A few years later, she got into his alma mater, a Southern technical school, where she planned to major in mechanical engineering with a specialty in robotics. They began to chat about what the college and city were like, and then on to their personal lives. It got a little flirty. Two years later, when he returned to see a football game, things changed.

Three months after that, they moved into an apartment paid for by her grandparents, as he waited to take a licensing exam so he could start work, and she continued her studies. She was twenty, the daughter of liberal Southern whites who valued education but also felt that a mother should stay home. He was nearly twenty-seven, a South African immigrant whose parents both worked and valued education. They wanted to get married, but he didn't have a job, and she was on her parents' health insurance. It seemed prudent to wait.

Then, four months later, Christina was pregnant. They decided to keep the baby. Although Faraji passed his exam, he broke his pelvis, badly. She ferried him to physical therapy appointments while she dealt with relentless morning sickness and preeclampsia. Christina thought, *I'm going to take the semester off. I'm going to get through this pregnancy and then I'm going to go back.*

She gave birth to their daughter a month early, in December. Christina ended up taking the next semester off, too. When their daughter was seven months old, they relocated to Washington, D.C., renting a sublet while Faraji looked for work. All of this was funded by Christina's grandparents.

When their daughter was sixteen months old, they married, and she enrolled in his health insurance plan. They decided to try for a second child—better to have them close together, and later she would resume her studies. Christina didn't have any interest in being a lifetime housewife, but it seemed fair now that he was the breadwinner, after her grandparents and she had footed the bills for so long. And they both felt it was important for the kids to have an available parent. Her husband took care of all the finances, and that was fine because Christina trusted him.

He worked long hours, helping with almost none of the childcare, after their son was born. She was quietly resentful, stuck in the closed world of her children. The tension increased, but it felt diaphanous, not acute. Until he announced, when their daughter was six, that he was leaving.

The whole of their relationship, he'd keep his paycheck, depositing money for rent or groceries or kids' clothes—but never enough for anything for her—into a joint account from which she drew. Then he started putting in less and less.

She'd remind him: *We need groceries. We need diapers. There's only twenty dollars in the account.* He would question her about every single transaction. *Oh, you spent thirty-five dollars at CVS? What was this for? Was it all makeup and nail polish?* Christina put on a brave face for the kids, not badmouthing their father, not complaining. She was just kind of existing, trying not to break. The worse her husband treated her, the more shame she felt.

Christina experienced a kind of domestic abuse called financial abuse, which may occur in as many as 99 percent of domestic abuse cases. Through control of the purse strings, the abuser creates an economic dependency that leaves the abused feeling helpless and unable to fend for themselves, both emotionally and financially. This coercive form of power and control is often invisible, and therefore difficult to prosecute, to prove, or even for the victim to recognize.[13]

Christina tried to reclaim her dignity. Exhausted by begging for milk money, she took a job as a nanny so she could bring her infant son to work. The mother who hired her, a partner in a big D.C. law firm, worked sixty to seventy hours a week. Christina loved the baby and the baby's parents; this working mother gave Christina the time to be with her son as well as the financial security that her husband had dangled in front of her only to snatch away.

Eventually, when she told her father about the way she was living, he insisted she and the kids come live with him and Christina's stepmom in North Carolina. There she was able to take classes and save a little money while working at a café. She's still in school.

But Christina and her husband are not yet divorced. She and the kids are still on his health insurance. He comes down for Christmas, and she lets him stay in the house—he doesn't want to spring for a hotel. Though she supported him financially for years, when they divorce, they will divide only what he made after they were married and before they separated, not the big six-figure salary he currently draws, which Christina's housewifery made possible. Because of the income cap on child support, it doesn't matter how much he makes;

only the first $200,000 is considered. But they will divide the marital debt, of which there is more than profit.

With a mind like that—robotics, engineering—Christina had had so much earning potential as a young woman. She trusted the wrong man. But she also trusted that the judicial system would be fair, would consider the needs of the children.

THEN THERE WAS Charlotte. She'd met Martin on Match two weeks before her thirty-fifth birthday, and they hit it off. A year after their first date, they got engaged, and two and a half months later they married. He'd been offered a job in Finland and couldn't bring a girl-friend, only a spouse.

They'd had many long discussions about wanting to be together forever. But Charlotte had never been dependent on a man. She'd been on her own, taking care of herself, and was not very domestically inclined.

Martin told her to trust him and come with him. He'd pay off her credit cards. She was starry-eyed, and she loved adventure.

The day after returning from their honeymoon, they got on a plane and moved. They lived almost two years in Europe. They traveled all over the continent. Martin was always very indulgent of her. He wanted her to be happy.

Then, while Charlotte was pregnant, the economy crashed. About ten months after her son was born, the company transferred her husband back to the States, where they bought a house she loved, a pale blue bungalow with a rambling porch in a neighborhood with good schools. They had a second child, then a third. Charlotte had been home with the children, volunteering at schools, planning playdates, and introducing the children to museums, but finally she took some time for her own reinvention. She enrolled in classes ranging from pre-med requirements to butchering and was full of optimism for their future.

Then came the last happy day. As they were walking home from a party, the sky opened up and drenched them. The kids tore their clothes off and ran to their trampoline. The baby stomped around in her boots. They all were stupidly blissful.

Two weeks later, Martin told her they needed to go out to dinner so they could talk. At a dodgy Indian restaurant, he said, "We're in trouble." Their credit cards were maxed, and Amex was canceling their account because of the unpaid debt. Charlotte didn't even know Amex let anyone carry debt. Her husband hadn't been paying the mortgage, or any bills. They were on the brink of foreclosure.

The world dropped out from beneath her, but at least she could still call up the independent person she'd trained herself to be before coupling. The next day, Charlotte quit all her classes right before tuition was due. A month later, she put the toddler in day care and started a full-time job. Charlotte bailed them out of everything. She paid off every debt. She called everybody.

Martin had a breakdown. She checked him into an inpatient psychiatric facility for two weeks and told no one, not even the children. She arranged with his company for sick leave, but he never really came back from it. On their thirteenth wedding anniversary, Charlotte filed for divorce. Martin hasn't seen his children other than for four hours one summer.

She has advice for women like her. Never change your name and never drop out of the workforce—even if it's just keeping your toe in. Don't romanticize the nuclear family or get married if you don't want to. Embrace extended family. Rely on yourself more, and, at the same time, spread the dependency around so your fate is not resting with one person. Don't imagine for a minute that it's better to have a mother who's staying at home all day, because there's plenty of research about why it's good to have a working mom. Quit acting like the nuclear family is the be-all and end-all—that's bullshit, she told me, adding, "Every stay-at-home mom I know who's had an ounce of education is bored as fuck."

## EQUALLY VALUABLE LABOR

THE LATTER SENTIMENT isn't true (see chapter 12), but women do need good advice when it comes to making themselves less vulnerable due to marriage and motherhood. The problem is not just bad dudes like each of these men—but let me add, it was easy to find these stories, and there were plenty of others I left out. The problem is a society that doesn't value the contributions of a stay-at-home parent.

"Why can't we understand as a culture that kids need to be raised and that the raising of kids is going to cause someone in the couple to have to not work to their fullest potential?" Nora asked. "How can it be legislated that stay-at-home moms have retirement funds? What would be fair is if we had an economic system that allowed people to stay home if it's right for them. And that didn't completely punish them for doing so." Evolutionarily speaking, we're made to couple and reproduce, Nora pointed out, "and we can't figure out how to make people safe in that process and financially secure?"

Sociologist Jaclyn Wong of the University of South Carolina, author of *Equal Partners: How Dual-Professional Couples Make Career, Relationship, and Family Decisions*, told me she'd push back on the idea that we can ever make equal a gendered division of labor where he works and she stays home. Not because it shouldn't be so, but because America is a capitalist society. "Survival under capitalism is having access to valued financial resources," she said. "So if you're the one who's earning, and you leave a relationship, you're fine. If you're not earning, and you leave a relationship or you get left, you are not fine."

Unpaid labor is so undervalued, Wong said, and there is so much economic precariousness in not working (unless you're independently wealthy), "that it seems to be potentially safest for families to have everyone participate in everything because you have no idea what is going to happen." Maybe someday we can get to a place, she said, where paid labor and unpaid labor become equally valuable—if we decouple the tasks from gender.

I get her point. Because we live in a sexist society, the more we redefine "women's work" as "everyone's work"—that is, men's work, too— the more likely we are to value that work and give it meaning. Then maybe we get to a place where there's more support for a parent to stay home regardless of sex. We should create a society where raising children is valued and valuable because, even if we look through a capitalist lens, we need workers. We need kids to grow up and work and pay into Social Security. We need good citizens, and to create good citizens, we need good parents; Republican motherhood, reborn as Republican *parent*hood.

"We want to raise the next generation of kids who can then grow into adults who will support us in our old age and contribute to society in all these different kinds of ways," Wong said.

Perhaps the saddest part of Nora's story—besides how common it is—is the way her ex has treated their kids, and how little value he ascribes to the amount of time she spent raising them, to make sure they're independent and resourceful and kind. He cares more about protecting his finances than he does his children. They had agreed to a division of labor where she was the homemaker and he was the breadwinner, but now he's cut off the bread, seeing no value at all in what she made in the home.

"I have four emotionally healthy, well-rounded kids," she said. To him, that means nothing. To Nora, it means everything.

## CHAPTER 10

# All Work and No Pay: Why the First Lady Has No Salary

They met in passing when she was twelve and he was nineteen, and both were students of an educator named Samuel P. Black in Murfreesboro, Tennessee. But it wasn't until eight years later that Sarah Childress and James K. Polk were formally reunited by Polk's political mentor, Andrew Jackson. Jackson identified Childress as prime wife material because she was "wealthy, pretty, ambitious, and intelligent."[1] In other words, she had the goods for a post she was, in many ways, born and bred for: First Lady.

Though it's unconfirmed, the National First Ladies' Library notes a rumor that Sarah teased James "that they would marry only after he had been elected to political office in his own right." She had political ambitions not for herself but for whomever she would eventually attach herself to. The Polks never had children, possibly owing to James's bladder surgery, thought to have left him sterile, and early in their career they lived on the Polk family estate in North Carolina, where social functions took place at the main house and which James's parents took care of. This left Sarah Polk with a potent combination of education and time, both of which she trained on her husband's political career.

She became his political confidante and sidekick, his backroom operative, facilitating relationships with politicians and judges, handling his correspondence and schedule. She was, without title, his secretary, his image consultant, his press liaison. "None but Sarah knew so intimately my private affairs," James once said.[2] She often worked by his side until the wee hours, worried for his health, hoping to take away some of his strain. Her strategy paid off when James was elected the eleventh president of the United States in 1844. Sarah was, per the library, "seated with prominent visibility at her husband's swearing-in ceremony in a heavy rainstorm."[3]

Her reign as First Lady—and she did reign—was complicated. An Orthodox Christian, Sarah banned alcohol, music, dancing—all the social lubricants one would think necessary for the events she was to be overseeing. But as a political partner, she was constantly involved—so much so that Vice President George Dallas complained, "She is certainly master of herself and I suspect of someone else also." Sarah was the person controlling access to Polk, and she had an outsize influence over him. Many believe she set the stage for modern First Ladies, who, behind the scenes, pulled at least some of the strings.

Or at least, she set the stage for *some* First Ladies. One hundred seventy-two years later, Melania Trump assumed the position, disappeared for weeks at a time, and then reappeared to complain, "I'm working my ass off with the Christmas stuff that, you know, who gives a fuck about Christmas stuff and decorations, but I need to do it, right?"[4]

Though their enthusiasm for their roles could not have been more starkly different, these First Ladies did have something in common. They both worked to serve their husbands' agendas and run households and didn't receive a dime for it—a full roster of responsibilities with no compensation.

Why, as the job—and women's roles—evolved, has the First Lady never been paid?

## THE EVOLVING ROLE

THE FIRST LADY is a truly odd and impossibly difficult position. The White House Historical Association notes that the Constitution provides no parameters for the role, and since it's not outlined there, it's not an official government post.[5] "There's only one job responsibility for the First Lady," Jennie Highfield, former CEO of the National First Ladies' Library, told me over Zoom. "She's the hostess of the White House."

That's because, Highfield said, the American political system was initially modeled after the British monarchy, in which there were social seasons, marked by events like balls and dinners during which powerful people would connect. "It was the wife's duty to make sure that those parties happened," Highfield said. It's a full-time managerial post, as it was with colonial housewives, in service of supporting the family business—in this case, the presidency.

From the beginning, it was a role of contradictions. A First Lady must not be too extravagant, lest she be accused of wasting the people's money. Her wardrobe must have some glamour, but she can't be either too polished or too casual. And she cannot own the clothes she purchases with White House funds, unless she buys them back from the people or pays income tax on them. If a First Lady gets a free designer outfit, she is to wear it but once before either donating or paying for it.

"I was amazed by the sheer number of designer clothes that I was expected to buy," Laura Bush once said.[6] Nancy Reagan was relentlessly criticized for the $1 million in designer outfits she accepted without paying taxes. But she noted that, had she worn street clothes, "Instead of calling me extravagant, the press would have started referring to me as 'dowdy' and 'frumpy.'" (Michelle Obama later drew praise for her J.Crew selections, however.)

A First Lady is meant to be pretty and have good manners and represent the highest embodiment of womanhood in the land—but not in, like, a snooty way. "She needed to be set apart somehow because she couldn't be seen as too royal," said Michelle Gullion, director of collections and research at the library.

The role comes with a long list of requirements and prohibitions. First Ladies can't drive themselves or redecorate more than selected spots in the White House. They aren't allowed to open windows or accept presents from foreign governments (such gifts belong to the people, unless Congress gives her the go-ahead to keep them, which they do if it will offend the giver if she doesn't accept, and then she may have to pay taxes). They're compelled to attend events like the White House Correspondents' Dinner, and they're supposed to oversee the Christmas decorations, even if, like Melania, they think it's baloney.

First Ladies had to figure out for themselves how to create, then walk, this narrow and confusing path. Their ultimate goal, their worth, is that they provide the feminine alternative to what author of *On Behalf of the President: Presidential Spouses and White House Communications Strategy Today* Lauren A. Wright calls "the most hyper masculine post that we have in American politics." The mere presence of the First Lady softens his image, provides a nonpartisan palliative lubricant, someone relatable yet aspirational, and a picture of unwavering support, there to do whatever is needed to make the president more likable and help sell his platform to the public. The real purpose of the First Lady is "filling the male agenda," Highfield said.

The reason they're so helpful to the president is that their approval ratings often soar above their husbands'. Laura Bush and Michelle Obama's ratings often remained in the upper sixties and seventies when their husbands' descended to the forties. Even Melania's were in the high fifties[7] when her husband's sunk to 34 percent.[8] (Perhaps Melania's rejection of the role explains the number of times Donald J. served fast food like McDonald's to visitors.)[9] Thus, they're often dispatched as their husband's better half and surrogate, sent to pacify unruly peons more likely to spar with a politician than his unthreatening wife. Sometimes they make more speeches than presidents and vice presidents. They're the administration's public face and behind-the-scenes mover and shaker, with more presidential access than anyone else.

But it's a job of sacrifice, of putting all others' needs first. Gullion and Highfield told me of the multiple First Ladies who lost children while in the White House, or just before they moved in, or had babies while in office; all were expected to get back to work immediately. For early First Ladies, "[a] woman's place is to be behind her husband at this point, not beside her husband," Highfield said. "It's sincerely a tough job."

Her post is the opposite of a sinecure. "They are the mother of our country," Gullion added. In other words, a First Lady is the ultimate housewife—toiling full-time and unpaid.

## CAUSE CÉLÈBRE

As time went on, First Ladies expanded their roles, from hosting parties and events to creating platforms for their personal agendas— or rather, agendas deemed politically and socially beneficial. "They had a voice, and they wanted to be heard," Highfield told me. Like Sarah Polk, they became more involved in their husband's political ambitions, and some even pushed their husbands to run. However, no matter how much power they wielded behind the curtain, they were always expected to be entirely in a supporting role in public. Theirs was a quiet influence, though at times it got a little louder.

For instance, when her husband was secretary of state, Dolley Madison assumed many First Lady duties to help the widowed Thomas Jefferson, her husband James Madison's boss.[10] She held legendary parties and even helped raise funds for the explorers Lewis and Clark, and all that experience proved tremendously useful when she herself became First Lady. Dolley relished her role, and James relied on her for it. He was shy and didn't like the social aspect of politicking, happy to let Dolley take the lead.

Dolley established the first inaugural ball and knew how to work the crowd, to tease information from politicians and their wives and bend them toward her husband's views and ambitions. She wielded influence over establishing the Easter egg hunt tradition and maintaining D.C. as the capital of the nation. Called by some the "Presidentress" and sometimes "Lady Madison," Dolley was a certifiable First Lady phenom.

She also established the tradition of a First Lady embracing causes. For Dolley it was the founding of an orphanage for girls in Washington, D.C. And perhaps the First Ladies who followed felt some pressure to emulate her success, or to one-up it. "There's nothing to say that a First Lady has to do any of those things," Highfield noted. But the media and the American public expect them to, and many First Ladies did.

Eleanor Roosevelt took up women's equality. For Michelle Obama the cause was childhood obesity and girls' education. Laura Bush chose childhood literacy. Nancy Reagan encouraged us all to say no to drugs. Lady Bird Johnson: beautification of the environment. Melania Trump: cyberbullying (oh, the irony). Be best!

As noble as they may be, the causes First Ladies are most known for are not their biggest contributions. Abigail Adams, the second First Lady, counseled her husband on his appointments. Helen Taft managed to engineer a 1912 workers' protection law. Eleanor Roosevelt took to the radio each week to deliver speeches and advance women's rights. Jackie Kennedy further professionalized the role. She was the first First Lady to have her own press secretary. They've often had real and lasting policy contributions, whether the public knew about them or not. The First Lady has influence, but not power, and of course, no pay.

As women's roles changed over the course of decades, and it became more common for wives of politicians to engage in careers of their own, First Ladies ceded more to accommodate the position. Hillary Clinton resigned as partner from Rose Law Firm, where she earned nearly three times as much as Bill in the early '90s, $110,000 a year.[11] Michelle Obama gave up her job as a hospital executive, for which she'd earned $212,000 a year, and described herself as "mom-in-chief." She had truly done it all—just not all at once.[12] But her new role was likely even more demanding. The First Lady's schedule tends to start about six-thirty a.m., according to Highfield, and often continues until ten or eleven at night.

In many ways, this arrangement mimics the subsidized, contrived, and "typical" American family.[13] Men do less unpaid labor, women do more of it. Paid labor is associated with masculinity, unpaid labor with femininity. Plenty of presidents acknowledged the inequity. "Michelle would point out First Ladies get paid nothing," Obama once joked at a town hall event, where he was discussing equal pay legislation.[14] "So there's clearly not equal pay in the White House when it comes to her and me."[15] Ronald Reagan noted something similar in 1982 when he said, "You know, with the First Lady the government gets an employee free; they have her just about as busy as they have me."[16] And President Harry S. Truman said, "I hope someday someone will take the time to evaluate the true role of the wife of a President and to assess the many burdens she has to bear and contributions she makes."[17]

And not all First Ladies liked it, or knew they were signing up for such a gig when they wed. Lady Bird Johnson, wife of Lyndon B., described the position as "an unpaid public servant elected by one person, her husband." Martha Washington wrote to her niece, "I think I am more like a state prisoner than anything else."[18] Mrs. Truman, Mrs. Roosevelt, Mrs. Trump—not particularly fans of the post. Margaret Taylor, wife of twelfth president Zachary, and Eliza Johnson, wife of seventeenth president Andrew, had such distaste for the role that they abdicated and put their daughters in charge. "Many of them will say, as they're going into it, 'I didn't want to do this,'" Highfield said. "They are going in kicking and screaming."

Others' disdain grew once they inhabited the role because it involves having every single decision you make scrutinized by a vicious public that expects more of you than you can ever be prepared to give. Mary Todd Lincoln was relentlessly criticized for baring her shoulders in a ball gown though others had previously done so. (Mary—who overspent when economic times were tight, and expressed deep emotions and spoke her mind—wasn't a particularly popular First Lady, so neither were her fashion choices.)[19] But when Mamie Eisenhower sported a strapless dress, it was peachy (well, it was actually Mamie pink). "She's married to Ike and everybody likes Ike," Highfield explained, referring to Eisenhower's successful campaign slogan. The critiques never stop. She looks too tired or too old or she's wearing the wrong shoes or she got the wrong haircut or that color is off or her skirt is too short or why is she wearing pants?

A little-known secret about the role of First Lady: It's one of the worst jobs in the White House. "It's excruciating," said Gullion. "And for some of them, it's unbearable."

## DOING FIRST LADY ALL WRONG

WHEN VERMONT DEMOCRAT Howard Dean went from front-runner to caboose in the 2004 presidential election, after what the media deemed a tantrum (but was really just a rallying cry to his supporters that they'd do better in the next state), the question of clothes came up. His wife, Judith Steinberg Dean—Dr. Steinberg at her practice, Mrs. Judy Dean when she was very occasionally beside him at the podium—sat beside Dean in her first ever TV interview, a *60 Minutes* episode, in an attempt to resurrect his image.

"Will the governor's wife become part of a last-minute rescue?" reporter Leslie Stahl asked.[20]

Mrs. Dean wore no makeup, her brown hair plainly stretching to her shoulders, unfussy bordering on mousy—the look can be summed up as "no nonsense."

"She's a lot smarter than I am," Howard said about her.

But that's not what Stahl was after. "Mrs. Dean? Dr. Steinberg—how should I call you?" Stahl asked.

"Judy Dean," she said, but Stahl couldn't quite grasp it. Nor could she grasp how unconventional the couple was. Judy professed to not watch TV. She was staying home while Howard was out on the campaign trail because "I am kind of private. I have a son in Burlington. And I have a practice. My patients are my patients and they depend on me and I love it. If I can help him, I will."

For his part, Howard said, "I do not intend to drag her around because I think I need her as a prop."

But he did pressure Judy somewhat to do the interview, or at least he asked. And because Dean asked, his wife said yes. "This is a no-brainer for me," he said. "All you have in your life is your family. If they're going to have to get to know who I am, they're going to have to know who Judy is."

But Stahl, as proxy for the American public, couldn't square who Judy was with the First Lady role. She was 0 percent glamour. For her fiftieth birthday, Howard bought her a rhododendron, which seemed to shock Stahl. No diamonds? No lavish party? Judy Dean's idea of a good time? A family bike ride. She was a quiet, nerdy, outdoorsy Jewish doctor with no taste for excess—not exactly hostess-of-the-nation material.

Stahl kept asking about the choice between Dean's success and their marriage and family, as if it were impossible for those things to peacefully coexist, noting that being a First Lady meant being picked apart constantly for one's tastes in clothing and hair. "Is that something you want to subject yourself to?" Stahl asked, as if she were trying to save Judy from the mob. Or maybe to save America from a First Lady like Judy Dean.

Judy's answer was downright presidential. "What Howard can do for the country really would override that," she said. "I don't really care that much what I wear, and I'm sure I would be criticized, but it just doesn't bother me that much."

It's a little bit like swearing about the Christmas decorations, but because it came from the mouth of a modest woman instead of a former underwear model, it was unacceptable. We'll never know how a Dr. Steinberg would have handled being First Lady Dean, since the interview did nothing to help Howard bounce back.

We do, of course, have Hillary Clinton's experience as testimony to just how hard it is to mesh First Lady-dom with modern womanhood.

Oh, how they hated Hillary. She got the wrong haircut. She was too pushy, too uppity, too employed, too educated, too powerful, and too disdainful of the female gender role. When Bill ran for president in the early '90s, Hillary was asked about elevating her career ambitions over housewifery, and she was unapologetic about her decisions. "I suppose I could have stayed home and baked cookies and had teas, but what I decided to do was to fulfill my profession, which I entered before my husband was in public life," she told reporters.[21]

How reasonable. She planned her life according to her own education and ambitions and didn't just spend decades waiting to see if her husband might someday attempt to secure a position as leader of the free world. Hillary also quipped, "I'm not sittin' here as some little woman standing by my man like Tammy Wynette."[22]

Oddly enough, that's not how you make friends in Washington or get the women's vote. Her comments caused an uproar. "If I ever entertained the idea of voting for Bill Clinton, the smug bitchiness of his wife's comment has nipped that notion in the bud," a *Time* magazine reader wrote in 1992.[23] Another said, "I resent the implication that those of us who stay at home just bake cookies. We hardly have the time!"

Political handlers swooped in, and soon after, *Family Circle* was holding its first annual Presidential Cookie Poll, where the sitting and challenging First Ladies, including Hillary, submitted cookie recipes, readers tried them and then voted on whose tasted best. (Clinton won.) No one was talking about whether Bill illegally directed clients to Hillary's law firm when he was governor anymore. They were talking about Hillary's use of shortening over butter.

But Hillary wasn't going to be behind her husband, or even beside him. She was going to be the first feminist First Lady, taking up nearly as much space as he did. In 1993, Bill appointed Hillary chair of the President's Task Force on Health Care Reform. This was a sharp turn from the benign causes the First Ladies of the past had embraced, those amorphous self-help signifiers that were easily approved of and non-threatening. Others felt an unpaid unofficial person was playing an official role. It made all kinds of people and politicians uncomfortable that a First Lady would be so directly, instead of tangentially or invisibly, involved in policy-making. This disrupted the gentle purr of the First Lady machine, because Hillary headed the task force and dared to act like an *employee.*

The American Association of Physicians and Surgeons filed a lawsuit against Hillary and then Secretary of Health and Human Services Donna Shalala, aiming to gain access to the information from their private meetings.[24] They initially won but lost on appeal. Nonetheless, the suit established that members of the task force were, on some level, government employees. "That gave Hillary Clinton some institutional standing," Wright said. But it didn't help their recommendations seed into policy, nor did it change the First Lady itself into an official post or come with compensation. Nor did it cause Hillary to be beloved by the public.

Still, even during her darkest First Lady days, Hillary's job approval ratings averaged 64 percent, nine points above her husband.

The question of whether the spouse of the president should be paid, or what the duties of said spouse should be, came up again in the run-up to the 2016 election, when Hillary was running for president herself. "No one expects Bill Clinton to surrender his ambition or his opinions if Hillary Clinton becomes president," opined Connie Schultz in the *New York Times.*[25]

Hillary was asked who would perform the traditional First Lady tasks, should she become president. "Her response, much to the chagrin of many feminists across the nation, was, 'I will still broker deals with China and pick the china,'" said Highfield. "She was trying to say, 'I will be president of the United States and still do the expected female duties.'" She would have done two jobs for the price of one.

Whether Hillary said that because she knew it would be politically unacceptable for a man—especially a former president—to be selecting china patterns or because she epitomized the predicament of the post-feminist working woman, who had to do it all, we'll never know.

## MONEY FOR NOTHING;
## NO MONEY FOR EVERYTHING

AMIDST THESE ENDLESS expectations and nonexistent paychecks, perhaps the oddest thing about the First Lady's outsize role is that every single other person around her gets paid. Since 1978, when the East Wing received federal funding, she has managed a staff that includes speech writers, secretaries, and project directors.[26] Per ABC News, Michelle Obama's press secretary, Joanna Rosholm, made $70,700 in 2014,[27] compared to the president's Josh Earnest, who earned $172,200.[28] According to Wright, the budget is usually somewhere around $2 million a year.

But the salary has increased. Melania's chief of staff, Lindsay Reynolds, earned $179,700.[29] The First Lady's chief of staff also assists the president, attending meetings with White House senior staff. Everybody in the West Wing receives a paycheck. Everybody in the East Wing receives a paycheck. Even White House interns now get paid.[30] The First Lady is the only person in the White House working more than full-time for no salary at all.

In earlier times, before upper-class wives had (paid) careers of their own, they were expected to share their husband's salaries, and it would make sense not to pay them for their labor (kind of). But now their roles carry clear expectations and traditions, and today's First Ladies are likely to vacate high-paying and hard-fought positions to attend to their housewifely First Lady duties—Jill Biden maintaining her academic career aside.

Several journalists have tried to calculate what First Ladies might earn were they hired for similar responsibilities for, well, any other job in the world. In 2016, Money.com ran the numbers. By one measure, they compared her duties to being a COO—event planning, legal compliance, managing people—and estimated her labor was worth $287,000 a year.[31]

So why not behave like, say, a university, and see the wife as a spousal hire? There are both simple and complicated reasons. "The institutional answer is [First Ladies] are not mentioned anywhere in the Constitution," said Wright. "It's not an official or appointed government role, and they're not paid for that reason."

Okay, simple enough. There's no line in the budget for you, no precedent, no Founding Fathers' vision to fulfill. But the political reasons for not paying a woman who is expected to work more than full-time are more complex. First Ladies, said Wright, are perceived as apolitical. That's part of what indemnifies them against the stain of their husbands' partisanship. Wright describes their role as "benevolent volunteers" who have a special relationship with the president. It's a role that must remain unsullied. And nothing would sully it more than paying her, which would stink of nepotism (even though nepotism is how most ambassadors get their posts).

Were the First Lady paid, she would lose her elusive armor and outsider status. As an employee, she would be inculcated. Implicated. The role of First Lady is too valuable to expend this free public relations boost by tarnishing it with payment. I guess in the end she's more useful to the president as his volunteer than his employee. And ultimately her value to him is greater than what she might be paid—and depends on her not being paid.

Perhaps compensating the First Lady hasn't happened, and will never happen, because, as Highfield said, "It's the woman's duty to support her husband and secure the house. And why should we pay for her to do that?" She's parroting an opinion not her own but that still circulates beneath the foundation of our society: The First Lady is doing what we expect her to do—housewife of the nation—because she's a woman, and nobody gets a salary simply for performing her gender role.

Gullion noted how similar the role is to stay-at-home mom—one that requires tremendous labor with no remuneration. "We don't value the role and work that women do," she said. And maybe it's better to leave the position unpaid; the scrutiny that can crush a First Lady's spirit would only increase if she were compensated. "It would just be one more burden," Gullion said.

It is that age-old tension, the feminine catch-22. Women matter because of their unpaid labor, and their value hinges on being devalued. They occupy the role we've drawn for them, and then we demean them for it.

Should the First Lady be paid? Yes. But, said Highfield, "I think society is not in a place to accept it." Perhaps, if someday there is a First Gentleman, the issue will be addressed again. Maybe then the role will become optional, and a paid employee can take over the duties that seem ceremonial but are actually political. Maybe then First Ladies can determine what, if any, role they want to play.

For now a First Lady's importance remains ephemeral and tied to her husband. After John F. Kennedy was murdered, Jackie Kennedy stayed in the White House with her children for only two weeks. She sent the new president, Lyndon B. Johnson, a letter promising to ske-daddle as fast as she could. "It mustn't be very much help to you your first day in office—to hear children on the lawn at recess. It is just one more example of your kindness that you let them stay—I promise—they will soon be gone."[32]

Rumor has it she returned only one other time, to stand before her late husband's portrait.

## CHAPTER 11

# Let's Get Divorced! And Other Paths to Egalitarian Marriage

The problem was all in her lower back. That's how the writer Maya Shanbhag Lang felt for years. Nothing she did seemed to assuage the rumbling pain.

Nothing, that is, until she realized the problem wasn't her back at all. Rather, the rest of her muscles weren't strong enough to support her back, to take the pressure off. This metaphor became extremely important to Lang as she extricated herself from her marriage.

Lang was living in New York when her husband got his dream job as a lawyer for a video game company in Seattle. She'd just finished her PhD in comparative literature and planned to teach, but soon after they moved, she got pregnant. She ran the numbers and understood quickly that even a tenure-track assistant professorship, if she were lucky enough to be offered one, would cost the family money after factoring in childcare. She decided to be a stay-at-home parent. Her affable and laid-back husband was surprised but not unmoored.

After taking care of their daughter all day, Lang would go to a cafe at night to write. "I was just frying myself as a human being, burning the candle at both ends," she said. She felt as if she was tiptoeing around his job, arranging everything to protect it, but the urge to type overtook her.

Then something unexpected and wonderful happened. Lang sold her novel, *The Sixteenth of June*, and suddenly a new career began. A less remunerative career than her husband's, yes, but one with incredibly high job satisfaction and potential for an upward trajectory both financially and emotionally. The uneven split of labor was not going to work anymore.

Her husband was unfazed by that, too. "I think he thought of himself as an equal partner. He really wanted to be a great dad, and fatherhood was deeply important to him," Lang said. But he couldn't seem to grasp what an egalitarian split would entail. "He was a great dad because he would cut the grapes in half when our daughter was a toddler or because he would run the vacuum occasionally," she said. "But it was a fraction of what I was doing."

Still, it was hard for Lang to recognize exactly what was wrong. After all, her father had been abusive and emotionally distant. By comparison, this man was a peach.

The rumble of her dissatisfaction grew louder when the editor sent the final proof of her novel; Lang had one last chance to read the whole thing through and make changes. She asked her husband to take charge for twenty-four hours, and he agreed. But a few hours later, she got a call from the preschool. Her daughter had a fever.

"Can you call my husband?" Lang asked the teacher. The teacher told her that she'd already called him, and he'd said he was at work and to call her instead. "I remember just having this moment of fury, you know, like all I asked for here was *one day.*"

Later, they talked it out, and he apologized. But Lang became increasingly aware of the inequity, its spectral presence hovering. Supposedly they were fifty-fifty parents, but she dropped off and picked up their daughter at preschool every day. She also did the cooking, the cleaning, the menial labor, the mental labor. Lang was exhausted and unhappy.

But she always had interpreted this feeling as something wrong with *her*, some test she was failing, some level of modern motherhood she couldn't attain. "I internalized so much blame," Lang said. "I was constantly thinking like, maybe if I read that article or download that app or wake up thirty minutes earlier or have an extra cup of coffee... I was always thinking there was a way to optimize myself."

Only after she submitted a draft of her memoir, *What We Carry*, to her editor did Lang begin to tap into the truth she'd blinded herself to. Her editor noted that although Lang had described her husband as caring and wonderful, her memoir had no scenes illustrating that. "I remember kind of being internally like: 'Huh. He's not in it with me. I'm in this all by myself,'" she said.

What finally helped?

"I didn't really get the co-parent that I wanted and needed until my divorce," she said.

When they finally split, Lang suddenly had days to herself to work. When their daughter was with her ex-husband, whatever happened— a fever at school, a forgotten notebook—was on him to figure out. After navigating a long learning curve, he eventually arrived, and their co-parenting became fifty-fifty after all. The other muscles were now supporting her metaphorical lower back.

"So often as women, I think when we feel strained, when we feel fried, when we feel exhausted, we think, *Oh, it's because I'm not strong enough, and it's because I'm weak, and it's because I need to do better.* And it's actually that we don't have the support systems that we need." The whole body fares better, she said, when all of the muscles are strong, so the lower back should not feel guilty about getting those muscles to literally pull their weight.

So what's the whole body in marriage? Sure, it's all the structural, societal supports, like universal childcare and paid family leave and community institutions and a zeitgeist that elevates the benefits of interdependence. That's the macro. But on a micro level, having an equal partner, Lang said, is like having those other muscle systems kick in. "That's what makes lower back pain go away."

What if you want an egalitarian division of labor—without getting divorced?

## THE CONSISTENT COMPROMISERS

ASSISTANT PROFESSOR OF sociology at the University of South Carolina Jaclyn Wong found out what an egalitarian marriage looks like— at least, for a particular class of people.

For six years, Wong studied the relationships of twenty-one "dual career" couples. These were professional folks, doctor and lawyer types with advanced degrees and pedigrees. People with options. She wanted to know, though, when they got married and had kids and choices had to be made, what their decisions looked like. If they entered the relationship on equal footing, where were they standing later?

Wong divided the couples into three pathways based on their espoused values and how they lived: consistent compromisers who aim to be egalitarian, autonomous actors who make decisions almost independently as if they don't have a relationship to account for, and tending traditional couples who embraced more traditional gender roles.

Among the tending traditionals, some of the women worked, some didn't, but either way, the men's careers were considered paramount. They'd do whatever needed to be done to protect his career. It wasn't about money—they both had plenty of earning potential and were among the lucky few in this country who could survive on a single income. But sometimes they'd pretend it was about money if they needed to do that to fit their narrative.

"People would cherry-pick opportunities to bring up economic justifications for her not working or for her having the secondary career," Wong said. They'd invoke the gender pay gap—she'd never earn as much as him anyway—to make sense of her subjugated career trajectory.

But Wong said couples would throw that reasoning away when men experienced unemployment while their wives worked. Even if she was making bank, they might move across the country to a place where he had more opportunity, forfeiting her job. "It's his identity as a bread-winner that kind of drives the way these couples make career decisions," she said—even when it didn't make economic sense.

Consistent compromisers, however, began their relationships with the question "How do both of us pursue these careers that we've spent time getting these degrees for and that we're really passionate about and are really kind of central to our identities?" said Wong. "How do we not let each other lose that part of ourselves?"

They expected, at all times, men and women to be responsible for and participate in home life—household chores and childcare. But they did not expect equal participation. Rather, for both of them to pursue those careers, they had to have *equitable* participation.

"They cannot escape the fact that gender inequality is built into the workplace," Wong said. "They recognized that her workplace is stacked against women. And so she needs to have her full energy and attention devoted there in order to reach the same sort of career success that he reaches without these additional burdens."

For instance: Women endure more workplace harassment than men (per the Pew Research Center, 69 percent of women who've experienced sexual harassment said it happened at work)[1] and have slower career growth, even when they tend to do the same sorts of jobs.[2] And women may be penalized for doing the things that make them good mothers, like taking time off when a child is sick. Women in Wong's study were anxious about taking parental leave, fearing it would affect how their teammates saw them. They worried their bosses would find them having a hard stop at four-thirty for day care pickup anathema to success.

"Men, on the other hand, are kind of cheered on at work for being great dads and being so involved at home and their careers," Wong said. "They don't take a hit from participating at home." Women endure a motherhood penalty, but some dads—high earners—may partake of that fatherhood bonus. Fatherhood conjures up the responsible, stable, committed authoritarian of yore, which translates into leadership skills—no matter what the dad is *actually* like.

Because women often experience the opposite trajectory, to achieve not just equality but equity, "men become more responsible for domestic things so that women can simply keep up with men on the professional front," Wong said. In the egalitarian relationships she studied, men had to prioritize their wives' careers over their own and take on *more* than half of domestic duties. If there were options on the table—a job in a new city, for instance—that would imperil their wives' career trajectories in some way, the men said no.

In other words, the way to have fairer heterosexual marriage in America is for men to do way the hell more. Of *everything*. Men's gender roles must change, and this particular class of men—complimented for being good dads for the same behavior that gets women chastised for being bad workers—can afford to do so, Wong said, both financially and politically.

By the end of Wong's study, the consistent compromisers had more parity not just in their marriages but in their salaries. The tending traditional couples had the biggest gender pay gaps, because many women had opted out, or been pushed out, of their careers, or worked part-time or consulted in small gigs—they had little opportunity to achieve parity. Nor was that important to them. In couples with traditional values, those values manifested in a traditional gender inequality. But if the couples valued egalitarianism, that manifested in salary parity.

## UNEQUALLY HAPPY

You'd think that since both kinds of couples were living their values, they'd be equally happy. But Wong found that the consistent compromisers had the highest relationship quality. The autonomous actors and the tending traditionals were more likely to be in couple's counseling and more likely to divorce. "None of the consistent compromisers ever talked about running into marital troubles," Wong said.

A lot of sociological research concludes that perceptions of equality correlate to perceptions of marital happiness, and the likelihood of divorce increases with perceptions of inequality.[3] One study found that for middle-class, different-sex couples (who can't just pay for someone to make up the differences), the perception of inequality was the biggest predictor of strife.[4]

Amanda Pollitt, assistant professor of health sciences at Northern Arizona University, wrote that "women who believe women and men *should* share equal power in relationships report less relationship satisfaction than women who believe power should be divided based on sex (i.e., that men should hold more power in relationships)." The emphasis is mine on the almighty "should." Yet, oddly, tending traditionals were still more dissatisfied.

Those of us tethered to an endless rope of martyrdom and complaints about the inequities of our situations (hand raised)—the privileged whiners—should aim for equity, while also understanding that part of our anger stems from our sense that things *should* be different.

## HARD WORK, ALL THE TIME

So who is at peace? Who believes in equity *and* has it? When I put a call out for married people who felt they were actually in egalitarian marriages, I heard from few Gen Xers, but some Millennials and younger couples raised their hands. And what I learned from them reinforced what Wong had found: To be egalitarian is constant work.

One who responded was Irina Gonzalez. She met her husband shortly after they both turned thirty when she moved back to her hometown in Florida, after twelve years of living in New York City. Both her husband and Gonzalez, the daughter of a Russian immigrant mother and a Cuban immigrant father, had grown up with working mothers. But other than that, the arrangements were pretty standard: Her mom did all the organizing, planning, and caretaking. Her dad expected that his time on the weekends would be filled with his favorite hobby, fishing—while her mom did all of the cooking, cleaning, and childcare.

This was not the arrangement Gonzalez sought. "I really wanted a partner who believed in having an equal marriage as much as possible," she said. And that sounded all well and good to her eventual husband, but he'd been reared in a culture in which "feminist" was a dirty word. So from the beginning, they had a lot of discussions about how to divide chores and responsibilities and money—and why they should. "We really worked hard to understand each other's strengths and weaknesses and interests," Gonzalez said. "If someone really hates something much more than the other person, that's going to be your task." She does the cooking because he both hates it and is bad at it. And she likes it and is good at it.

That puts Gonzalez in charge of everything food-related for the family, which now includes a three-year-old son. But, as she likes to remind him, being head of provisions is actually several jobs: meal planning, shopping, cooking, keeping a running tally of preferences. And while cooking may be a classically feminine job, her husband handles much of the cleaning—he likes laundry and vacuuming—as well as some of the more traditionally masculine stuff like taking care of the cars and insurance.

The idea, Gonzalez said, is to demonstrate for their son what an ungendered division of labor looks like, one that is divided by skills and interests rather than sex, even if gendered expectations likely had some kind of influence on the development of certain skills and interests. "We are equitable partners," she said.

At the start of their relationship, her husband made more money than she did—and she only bridged the gap after seven years together. In the beginning, they agreed that each puts a percentage of their paycheck into a mutual account, and from that pot they pay the bills. Whatever was left from their paychecks was their own. But she did not feel a sense of financial dependency during the years when he was the bigger donor, since she was the one managing their budget. "I don't think my husband really could afford his life on his own either," she said. Eventually, they merged bank accounts and she became the CFO of their household.

To keep this kind of egalitarianism requires vigilance, especially when kids enter the picture. Childcare needs shift with age. When Gonzalez was breastfeeding their son, she'd be up with him during the night, but her husband would take care of as much of the day shift as he could so she could sleep. Once their son went to day care, they had to renegotiate, and they've done so over and over again. As she said, "It's very much an ongoing and difficult conversation."

## ON BENDED KNEE

SO WHY AREN'T more marriages like that (apart from the fact that you have to be a serious adult to be that communicative, responsive, and responsible)? Why aren't more couples, aware of gender gaps in the workplace, working harder to overcome them at home? Why is it that, as a 2013 paper called "The Second Shift: Why It Is Diminishing but Still an Issue" puts it, "modern men do not adjust the amount of time they dedicate to housework based on their wives' employment status any more than their predecessors would have"?[5]

Why do I know so many women who espouse feminist philosophy and fully expected egalitarian marriages, yet didn't end up in them? How come there are so many ladies wearing tight black T-shirts with "Feminist" in metallic serif script doing Pilates at the Y after they drop off the kids at school, while their husbands trot off to the office—women with degrees in French literature or accounting? Sure, I'm homing in on a particular demographic—mine, or at least the one I live next to—but, bottom line, the expectation of egalitarianism seems to far outshine the reality of it.

Perhaps, surmised Ellen Lamont, associate professor of sociology at Appalachian State University and author of *The Mating Game: How Gender Still Shapes How We Date*, that's because of a pattern that gets set in motion as the early wheels of the relationship turn. Lamont studies how gender shapes the way we date and has written about the relationship between courtships and gender balances in marriages. She found among Gen X and Millennial different-sex couples that the expectations created during courtship impacted the division of labor in marriage—no matter what the women, or the men for that matter, said they wanted. If women waited passively for a bended knee and a ring, they'd often find themselves later with an uneven load.

"On the one hand, you had all these narratives about wanting egalitarian relationships and women power and feminism," Lamont told me. "And at the same time, we also had these romance narratives that were premised on men as the initiators and women as the reactors."

Why would people say they wanted an egalitarian relationship but engage in activities that undermined that goal?

Some women chalked it up to tradition. Letting the man propose was just what a person did. Other women may have felt that there was so much equality in other parts of their lives, or perhaps so much expected of them now that was once the domain of men (at least in American myth), courtship was a place for a little allowable femininity at no cost to their reputation as a kick-ass babe. And there was an element of status in the traditional proposal: being so desired that a man would get down on bended knee and request your hand. "It's almost like having your cake and eating it, too," Lamont said. "*I want to be treated in this special way, and I also in this other realm want to be seen as an equal.*"

Still other women harbored anxiety that men are commitment-phobes (not true, said Lamont, and possibly the opposite) who'd be scared away by a woman requesting partnership in eternity. Therefore, they take the back seat and leave room for him to lead, hoping he'd feel more amenable to the whole marriage thing that way.

"Women didn't want to seem desperate," Lamont said. They were playing by *The Rules*, which said to withhold, to reserve, to not emasculate men by splitting the check or requesting their hand in marriage. But they never thought doing so would impact the marriage itself.

They were wrong. "The same narrative that we see during courtship pops up again in marriage," Lamont said. "Even if you think this pattern is an exception to the way you want to live, you still are establishing a pattern of some kind."

In marriages that had begun with traditional proposals, women were more likely to get up in the middle of the night with kids or to do more of the housework. And that's likely because, whatever they told themselves about why they'd waited to be properly proposed to, some kind of underlying belief about men and women probably powered that desire. Maybe upholding that one idea about what is a man's versus a woman's role leaked into other aspects of the marriage, and as long as she'd *chosen* to assume the bulk of childcare and mental labor, then it wasn't about gender itself—in her mind, anyway. Or maybe a woman who maintained traditional ideas about proposals was just *entertaining* ideas she didn't actually embrace, for the look, the fashion of it. Maybe she wasn't really a feminist.

But there was perhaps another reason that these inequities permeated relationships. These women, my Enjoli sisters, were raised with the expectation of doing it all, and wanted it all, including making their own money, which ultimately mattered more to them than egalitarianism, or perhaps which *felt* like egalitarianism. "It was like, 'Oh, as long as I'm kind of *allowed* or supported in my career, we're equal,'" Lamont said. "'I have my own resources.'" If they were going to achieve equality in one place in their lives, it would be at the office, or in the bank account.

Perhaps Gen X just didn't have enough distance yet from the gender-role stranglehold of the 1950s to reinvent themselves. One study found that breadwinning women do a disproportionate amount of housework as a kind of "deviance neutralization" to establish the femininity their high income might threaten.[6] Another found that non-breadwinning husbands might do less housework because they already feel so emasculated.[7] (Come *on*, fellas.)

Many of the people in Lamont's study had been told by their mothers—some of them hailing from the problem-that-has-no-name era—"Don't sacrifice your career for a man; you'll end up trapped." "They got a lot of advice about emphasizing those career aspects," Lamont said. "And that that would be a way out if their marriage was unhappy." While putting them at a disadvantage, the unevenness was a kind of insurance policy.

These women wanted the power associated with a career, the freedom associated with egalitarian marriage, and the status of being treated the way women "should be" treated in some traditional way. Maybe they weren't quite old enough to know that they'd get to equity faster if their husbands shouldered more of the traditionally feminine burden, because few societal shifts have actually enabled and facilitated having it all.

The men, Lamont said, wanted it both ways, too. They wanted the women to pick up the domestic tab but to also contribute financially. Conclusion: Gen X is a mess.

According to the Pew Research Center, Millennials like Gonzalez seem to have a better grasp on this stuff.[8] Almost three-quarters of Millennials prefer egalitarian marriage and are more likely to have grown up with some version of it, with fathers participating in cooking, cleaning, and childcare. But the preference wasn't equally distributed; 78 percent of women were looking for equity, and only 67 percent of men were. Per an article in the *New York Post*, "Millennial Men Want 1950s Housewives after They Have Kids."[9]

## NINETEENTH-CENTURY EQUAL MARRIAGE

IF YOU WANT to bake equality into your marriage from the beginning, I suggest a model from 1855.

When Lucy Stone was born on August 13, 1818, on a farm in rural western Massachusetts, her mother said, "I'm sorry it is a girl. A woman's life is so hard." But Lucy was determined to make women's lives easier than her own mother's had been. At the age of sixteen, Lucy started teaching school for a dollar a week, and it took her nine years to earn enough money to attend college.

Her goal was not just to be educated for her own sake, but to correct the moral ills of the world into which she was born, including slavery. Stone wrote to her mother, "I expect to plead not for the slave only, but for suffering humanity everywhere. Especially do I mean to labor for the elevation of my sex."

Eventually, she made her way to Oberlin College, where girls were allowed to earn a degree but were barred from public speaking. Though Stone was invited to write a commencement speech, she declined, as it would have had to have been read by a man.[10] She read in a college textbook the words "women are more sunk by marriage than men," and became determined never to marry.

After college, Stone made sure her voice was heard, writing—and delivering—speeches for William Lloyd Garrison's American Anti-Slavery Society. She was an outspoken abolitionist and suffragist, but she also railed against the sexist institution of marriage, which she compared to slavery, for it required women to give up their rights and submit to a husband's demands. Two years after the 1848 Seneca Falls Women's Rights Convention, Stone organized the first national women's rights convention in Massachusetts, delivering a speech that was syndicated even in international publications. Hers was an example of the liberated life a woman could live if she fought for her rights and defied expectations.

There was one problem. Stone fell deeply in love with a man named Henry Blackwell, who wanted to marry her and vowed to "repudiate the supremacy of either man or woman in marriage."[11] He was the brother of Elizabeth Blackwell—the country's first woman to earn a medical degree—and she and sister Emily, also a doctor, convinced Stone to marry him, insisting that egalitarian marriage was possible.

When she finally caved to Blackwell's request, sobbing through the ceremony on May 1, 1855, the minister who married them, Thomas Higginson, said, "I never perform the marriage ceremony without a renewed sense of the inequity of a system by which man and wife are one, and that one is the husband."

Their marriage was a protest of sorts, in which they vowed to love and honor but renounced the word "obey," and refused to utter it. They published a pamphlet explaining their resistance to the institution of marriage, even as they entered into it.

They wrote:

> While acknowledging our mutual affection by publicly assuming the relationship of husband and wife, yet in justice to ourselves and a great principle, we deem it our duty to declare that this act on our part implies no sanction of, nor promise of voluntary obedience to such of the present laws of marriage as

refuse to recognize the wife as an independent rational being, while they confer upon the husband an injurious and unnatural superiority, investing him with legal powers which no honorable man would exercise, and which no man should possess.[12]

Early women's rights activist Elizabeth Cady Stanton described Lucy Stone as "the first woman in the nation to protest against the marriage laws at the altar, and to manifest sufficient self-respect to keep her own name, to represent her individual existence through life."[13] The couple had two children, though only daughter Alice Stone Blackwell survived, herself growing up to become a feminist and abolitionist.

All the while, Stone continued her civil rights and women's suffrage activism, never giving up her work to tend to house and home, always sharing domestic work with her husband.

## LGB FAMILIES

How much of this relentless inequity that Stone fought, and which couples are still negotiating today, is about the expectations we attach to biological sex—our ideas of masculinity and femininity—as opposed to other confounding factors? One way to find out is to look at same-sex families, which made up more than a million households in 2019 (as compared to almost 70 million opposite-sex married and unmarried partner households).[14] Some 191,000 children live with same-sex parents.

The general assumption is that same-sex partnerships are more egalitarian than those of different-sex couples, and some studies do suggest as much.[15] Because lesbian, gay, and bisexual people are less gender conforming than heterosexual people—homosexuality itself is a gender nonconforming trait—and gender nonconformity is related to perceptions of power-sharing, this all adds up. Disparities would be lesser when there's no difference in sex. In theory.

But once again perception and reality have a complicated relationship. First of all, gender dynamics seem to differ in gay partnerships and lesbian ones. Some research shows that the more gender-conforming partners in *male* couples were—the more they enacted traditional masculinity—the stronger their sense of shared power. But in couples where one man was more feminine than the other, trouble brewed. The partner "who does not meet masculine ideals of paid labor is expected to conduct more 'feminine' tasks at home, and couples struggle to reconcile these divisions as equal and fair," Pollitt wrote. Gay men "may be constrained by masculine norms and the devaluation of femininity." Devaluation of feminine traits, it turns out, is a problem for people regardless of sex. Men who take on most of the domestic labor—those activities that are viewed societally as feminine—might feel they hold less power in the relationship.

Gender conformity in women, on the other hand, doesn't seem to affect the perception of shared power. Women in same-sex couples tend to be more flexible about power-sharing, less aggrieved when they have to take on traditionally feminine work, perhaps because there's no man around to compare themselves to. Breadwinner and caretaker aren't readily thought of as gendered roles, or the duties may be more evenly distributed. That doesn't mean lesbians are more likely to achieve marital bliss; a recent study found that they're more than twice as likely as gay men to divorce.[16]

One study asserted that in Black lesbian stepfamilies, biological mothers of the kids did more household work than non-biological mothers, perhaps based on the assumption that the biological mother *should* do more. Sometimes gender roles are layered over a partnership based on who earns more, with the low-earner being expected to take on the "feminine, unpaid labor at home."

In his book *No Place Like Home: Relationships and Family Life Among Lesbians and Gay Men*, sociologist Christopher Carrington described egalitarian "lesbigay" marriages as a myth. Of the families he studied, only 25 percent achieved some hazy manifestation of parity in their division of labor. They used chore charts or other measures to make sure each person understood their obligations, while the wealthier families outsourced labor like cleaning and cooking. But many of them *described* their families as egalitarian, even though Carrington's recording of their familial goings-on revealed they weren't living that way.

He suggested that lesbigay families feel more pressure to appear equitable, so as not to mimic the sexist architecture of heterosexual families, especially because they are quite new in American society. They want to appear high-functioning "to provide a respectable image of ourselves in a society often bent on devaluing and marginalizing us," he wrote.[17] In other words, they are just as prone to being affected by the "shoulds" as different-sex couples.

If a couple named Steph and Kimber are representative at all, the fact that they were both women increased Kim's resentment at the traditional breadwinner/homemaker split. They had been together since they were in their early twenties, each helping support the other as they took turns going through graduate school. But then, after Steph became a lawyer and they adopted two children, Kim decided she wanted to stay home, and they could almost, kind of, afford it. Still, Kim found herself relentlessly enraged about the division of labor. Despite the fact that Steph sometimes worked sixty hours a week, Kim expected a fifty-fifty split on parenting and household tasks. Steph tried her best, but eventually the hailstorm of resentment became too much, and she filed for divorce. Steph said she thinks part of the problem was that Kim couldn't let go of gendered expectations. They were both women, so they should both do women's work.

Kim apparently wasn't hip to the trends. Some researchers have found that gay families are getting increasingly inequitable, becoming more traditional after gaining the right to marry. "The same norms start to then play into those relationships," said Lamont. Marriage can have a "conservatizing influence."

## TRANSITIONING TO HOUSEWIFE

How DOES GENDER transition affect roles? The short answer is: in any number of ways. Some trans women become more sympathetic to the way society imposes the housewife expectation onto modern women. That eventually happened to Dawn Ennis, a former ABC news producer who'd married and had three children before coming out as a trans woman in 2013, then retransitioning briefly to male, claiming she'd had amnesia. Her transition had sparked a news frenzy, she told me, and she'd been unable to handle being the subject of tabloid gossip. Though she and her wife, Wendy, never divorced, they separated after Ennis transitioned. At first they co-parented, but eventually Ennis relocated to Los Angeles for work while Wendy stayed behind in Connecticut with their kids.[18]

Then, in 2016, Wendy died of cancer, leaving Ennis as their kids' primary caretaker—not *their* mom, Ennis told me, but *a* mom, and a single mom at that. Ennis quit her job, and the family lived off the insurance money. In the documentary about her, *Before Dawn, After*

*Don*, Ennis laments the pain she caused her wife, whom she called "the love of my life." "I cheated this woman out of the last ten years of her marriage," she tells a friend. (The friend replies: "That's why you marry someone for better or for worse," and notes that people get divorced for all kinds of reasons.)[19]

Later, standing in a kitchen strewn with dirty dishes, Ennis realizes the sheer amount of physical and emotional labor associated with being the mom. She thought she'd been living the life of a woman but now realizes that vision edged out so much of the reality of the female gender role.

"As I come into my momhood, for lack of a better word, I feel like I'm pissed off," she says in the film. "I'm pissed off that I didn't step up more before. That I didn't share in the cooking, because I love cooking, and I could have made this much more of an equal partnership. I knew already that I wasn't doing enough around the house in terms of scrubbing toilets, in terms of doing the laundry, in terms of keeping the house clean. These were things that Wendy just did because she did, and it's completely unfair that this all falls to the woman." Having lived as a man and then transitioning enabled Ennis to be more empathetic, but sadly not before her wife died.

"Being a mom, being a housewife, was something that I never sought, let alone considered," Ennis told me over the phone. That was not her vision of what womanhood entailed. But after seven years of the cooking and cleaning and the raising her kids as a single parent, she calls it the "hardest job I'd ever loved." If only, she said, "I had learned this lesson when it could have counted." She called her new role "domestic engineer," and said, "I think the job is totally underrated."

But not all trans women become more sensitive to female gender roles, or take them on, once they transition. I also spoke to several women who refer to themselves as "trans widows." They'd married men, not realizing those men harbored secret feelings that they were or should be women, and things went downhill after their husbands transitioned; the women they now identified as bore little resemblance to the lived experience of most women.

When Madison first met her husband, Will, for instance, he rekindled her faith in men, in marriage. He was solicitous, gentle and kind, and good with her tween daughter. "After the first date, I knew he was the one," she said.

For the first few years in their small Southern city, it was bliss. "When other people would talk about their relationships and the words that they would say to each other like, 'Fuck you' or 'Shut the fuck up'—he would never have said that to me. Ever. And we hardly ever fought. It would be like one fight a year." He was her safe place: helpful around the house, an equal partner in the life they'd created.

But slowly, Will let it be known that he wanted to wear women's clothes and underwear during sex, to make up his face. Madison works in healthcare, often leading workshops about sex positivity, on everything from safe sex to BDSM—bondage, discipline, dominance/submission, and sadomasochism: erotic preferences and practices, including roleplaying, that often involve contracts and consent. It was important to her to have a healthy sex life and a clear communication channel, and so she supported him. She took Will to drag shows, which was risky in their conservative, Southern part of the country, and her daughter even taught him to do his makeup better when he occasionally "dressed," as he called it.

But the more he wanted to live full-time in the identity he was exploring, the more his behavior curdled. When she'd ask him to help out around the house or go grocery shopping, as he always had, he'd grumble or yell or insult her. Once she asked him to load the dishwasher, and he stomped outside with the plates, scraping them against the brick sides of their house.

The more he lived "as a woman," the less compassion he seemed to have for women's actual lives, for the uneven emotional and physical labor that characterizes our existence. "He went from being a very compassionate, generous, loving, doting husband to a verbally abusive wife."

Debbie Hayton, a physics teacher in the U.K., transitioned in 2011, but realizes now that she was terrible to her wife during most of her transition, self-absorbed and unable to co-parent. "[My wife would] be talking about something the kids have been doing: 'We've got this problem about trying to ferry one child from A to B when the other one needs to be ferried from B to A. Have you got a solution for this?' And I'd say, 'Maybe I think I need to bring my transition day forward from March through to December. What do you think about that?'" Hayton recalled.

Her wife tried to be patient, Hayton said, but she couldn't square the person Hayton was becoming with any reality of womanhood she knew. "She would say that being a woman was doing more than your fair share of the housework, looking after the kids, responding first, you know, taking the initiative here, there, and everywhere," Hayton said. In many ways, it was the exact opposite of the self-absorbed person Hayton was turning into. "All I could think about was myself," Hayton said. And the self she thought of was an extremely traditionally and stereotypically feminine woman, with little resemblance to Hayton's wife. That is, when she decided to transition to womanhood, never did the vision involve the actual gender role most women inhabit. It temporarily made her less sympathetic to her wife's daily life.

If even queer marriages can be infected by inegalitarianism, what should we do to walk us all closer to fairness?

## WOMEN'S WORK IS MEN'S WORK

PERHAPS ONE SOLUTION is to associate what has been perceived as "women's work" with men. "Anything that breaks down this belief that men are this way and women are a different way, anything that addresses that and helps us break that down and kind of challenge that idea," said Lamont.

In one of Wong's tending traditional couples, both people ended up working for companies with generous paid parental leave, and when their child was born, they took time off concomitantly. Though they'd imagined that she'd take on more of the diaper-changing and the swaddling and the stroller pushing, the fact that they were both there at the same time meant they got into a parenting rhythm of parity. "This couple actually reported attitude changes," Wong said. They no longer viewed housework or childcare as within her purview, and they shifted from tending traditional to egalitarian. That's the potential power of policy to change attitudes and behavior.

"If we as a society can put down some rules that say everybody is responsible for everything, I think that we can see a little bit more change at the individual level, which will then feed back into broader societal level changes," Wong said.

## THE LOWER BACK

WE'VE BEEN TRYING to pass comprehensive family-friendly laws since the dawn of the women's movement, and we haven't made it very far. And that puts non-rich folks in a constant position of having to compensate for where policy fails. I myself have maintained the feeling that because I earn less, I must do more, even if I am working nearly as many hours. After all, without my husband's job, we cannot pay the rent. Without mine, we won't land on the street, but we can't enjoy extras like takeout and vacation. He would prefer that I work and make good money, but the latter part has so far eluded me, even though he takes on more housework and childcare with each passing year. Around and around I go, navigating the muddy terrain of competing ambitions of career and motherhood, wanting to be a good parent and a successful (or at least well-paid) writer. What are those of us in this all-too-common situation—working, but also exhausted, confused, angry, and guilty—supposed to take from studies of egalitarian, well-off folks?

If you have any wiggle room at all in the budget, then you take money out of the equation, and you prioritize equity. And if you don't? You make decisions according to how to maximize family profit, whoever is more likely to generate it, and then you divvy the rest so it feels fair. If one person makes the bulk of the money, you ask how the rest of the tasks will be divided. The thing you don't do is assume that the woman will do most of it.

Also: Learn to act more like happily divorced people.

Wong's egalitarian families have a level of privilege that few of us can reach, and what she uncovered is not possible for single parents without an ex-partner or co-parent to help. They must rely on family and friends, or, if they don't have them, the anemic government options for day care, and resign themselves to doing everything. Most of the people I talked to who'd achieved this fairness had both money and time, while many people have little of either, or have to choose between the two. Egalitarian marriage without the consideration of monetary contributions is only for the wealthy.

For Irina Gonzalez, one thing that helped was making a physical list of who does what and how much time and labor each task takes. This exercise reduced any resentment that had built up because she saw that his responsibilities—finding insurance, taking care of the car—required mental labor, too, even if they were very different kinds of tasks that might take a long time even if they weren't completed as often. Things were more balanced than she'd sometimes made them in her mind.

It was hard for Maya Shanbhag Lang to let go when she and her husband first split, to trust that he could take care of whatever came up. She wasn't there to make sure he bought the right shampoo or arranged their daughter's room the right way. "I used to kind of secretly love being the person who was indispensable," she said. "There's a dark, twisted pleasure in being the lower back and being the person who does everything. The first person she wants is mommy, and that can be gratifying." But she learned to let go and to savor her time alone.

Let's hope we don't all have to get divorced to emulate that.

# CHAPTER 12

# It Takes Two to Tradwife

When Alena Kate Pettitt was a child in England during the 1990s—when Spice Girls and Girl Power and *Sex and the City* permeated popular culture—her teachers always asked the girls what they wanted to be when they grew up. Her friends' answers garnered approval: scientist, maybe, or interior designer. They set their sights on careers, and never mentioned marriage or family.

But Pettitt had always harbored a specific aspiration. "I wanted to be a housewife and a mum," she said on an episode of the British TV show *Roundtable*.[1] "And I was shamed for it constantly." Other girls idolized Xena: Warrior Princess, but Pettitt's role model was Doris Day. So after a successful run as a marketing executive, Pettitt got married, had a child, and gave up her career to do what she'd always wanted: stay home.

Pettitt and her husband perform the traditional gender roles of homemaker and breadwinner, but it's more than a lifestyle choice. Pettitt calls herself a "tradwife," short for traditional housewife, a movement of modern women who take 1950s housewives as their patron saints and live accordingly—and, I think it's fair to say, happily.

Pettitt does all the housework and receives an allowance for household supplies and for the occasional personal indulgence—her caramel-colored hair that ombres into blond past her shoulders doesn't come cheap, after all. And her husband earns the money and makes the decisions. He is not just Mr. Moneybags but head-of-household. Trad-wives talk up submission—not subjugation or subservience, they clarify, but rather a hierarchy that places the decision-maker—hubby—on top, with wife's priority being his happiness and satisfaction.

Pettitt cottoned to this existence so much that she started a company called the Darling Academy to proselytize about it. It "celebrates the role of the housewife, traditional family dynamics, great home-making, and shares the beauty of what makes 'being at home' truly worthwhile." She authored two books, *Ladies Like Us* and *English Etiquette*,[2] and calls the world she's creating "The New Stepford" (perhaps forgetting that in the old Stepford, the women were murdered and replaced by robot versions of themselves—sex dolls who shopped for groceries).[3]

Like many tradwives, Pettitt readily shares her ideas and advice about what women should do and be. "A traditional woman's place is not under a man's feet, but under his wing, by his side. A traditional housewife chooses her husband based on his ability to care for people, provide for their children, and most importantly upon his integrity and values," writes Pettitt on the Darling Academy website. "Having such a partner enables you to take pleasure in traditional domestic duties while promoting feminine submissiveness, domesticity, and wife-hood." A wife serves her husband, she wrote, "preparing food, clothing and other personal needs." A mother cares for children's needs, including education. But, "[a]s a housekeeper you run the show."

Tradwives present motherhood and housewifery as satisfying alternatives to the 1980s archetype of career womanhood any of us who watched *9 to 5* assumed was our rightful path. That entering data into spreadsheets is more fulfilling than raising children "is the biggest con we're ever told," Pettitt said. "It was all, 'Let's fight the boys and go out and be independent and break glass ceilings,' but I just feel like I was born to be a mother and a wife."

Tradwives are not forced into this arrangement. They choose to submit, obey, and look good for their husbands, and often identify this as a feminist choice. They love to opine about tradwifery's virtues, on blogs, TV shows, Instagram.

As the "president of the family," as my husband calls me, I can understand the lure of this arrangement, since I am regularly dragging from decision fatigue and our lopsided distribution of labor. But tradwives get a heap of hate from some feminists who accuse them of rolling back sixty years of progress and point at the extreme politics of a few tradwives as misrepresenting the rest of the movement.

What's funny—or sad—is that Pettitt is still shamed for her choice constantly.

## WHAT TRADWIVES WANT

I SPENT AN afternoon consuming videos and Instagram posts of deliriously happy, submissive, and yet somehow tremendously assertive tradwives. Though the phenomenon is mostly centered in England and the United States, other Western countries have their own movements. In Russia, "womanhood schools" train women in how to be passive and make polite conversation, in service of attaining "harmony, money, and a man."[4]

American CEO-turned-tradwife Rebecca Barrett created a video called "How I Went from Raging Feminist to Feminine Traditional Wife."[5] Barrett grew up with a homemaker mom and breadwinner dad, and her mother taught her how to perform the woman's role. At a young age, she learned to cook and clean, take care of her siblings, and—importantly—not trust men. "And that's kind of what shaped me and molded me into becoming more of a feminist," she says, sitting on a white couch, every hair in her neat black bob in place.

For the longest time, Barrett's goal was independence. "I didn't want to rely on a man's income," she said. So she majored in mechanical engineering with a robotics minor, became an oil and gas engineer and eventually a CEO, all of it requiring a constant production of what she called her "masculine energy."

"I had to be one of the boys," she said. And that left her unhappy and resentful, combative and competitive. And it made her hate men.

Then Barrett met a different kind of man and underwent a kind of conversion experience—or maybe a reversion experience—in which the world she came from beckoned so much more than the world she'd made for herself. She read Jordan Peterson's *12 Rules for Life*. She and her fiancé attended premarital counseling, where they discussed the roles of wife and husband. Barrett decided to submit to her husband, learned to lean on him, and trust in his decision-making. "I'm his co-pilot," she insists, but "at the end of the day, he makes the final decision." They complement each other, but they don't compete.

When I Zoomed with Barrett a few weeks after watching her video, she told me, "I went from being a very miserable person to be around to just...I felt like myself again, like bubbly. I just, I feel lighter. I feel refreshed. I feel invigorated." Indeed, Barrett was smiling, relaxed, her nine-month-old daughter bouncing on her lap. She said most of her friends and family were supportive because of her profound personality change; she called it a "transition." The once blue-haired, grumbling feminist transformed into a fount of positivity. Barrett has no problem with feminists, no problem with women working. She just wants other women who were as unhappy as she was to know that there's another path.

The thing that most people bristle at, Barrett said, is the word "submit." "I submit to my husband the decisions that he makes for the family—unless he's making decisions that are completely like, hey, let's rob a bank," she said. "That's the traditional aspect of our marriage. And the other traditional aspect of our marriage is that I am home." She'd been home since they married, not just once their daughter was born.

Among tradwives, submission is seen as a sign of strength because it's a choice, and a direct path to happiness. "I'm a submissive wife, and I love my life," reads an Instagram post by a user called tradwife-original, whose bio educates us that "Tradwife stands for educated women who prefer a role of feminine and respectful submission in a loving relationship."[6] In another post, tradwifeoriginal explains how to be a good tradwife: nurturance, sweetness, supportiveness, modesty, empathy, passivity…you catch the drift.[7] A woman who embodies such traits will be more feminine, and thus, more desirable.[8]

There's quite a bit of overlap here both with the nineteenth century's Cult of Domesticity and the 1950s women's magazines that were filled with messages for former Rosie the Riveters about giving up all ambition outside their own families and excelling at housewifery. The difference is that these messages are not coming from the media or men but from Millennial women—not just to draft others into the lifestyle, I'd say, but to normalize the experience they've been told not to want.

After all this research, I obviously believe that housewives with breadwinner husbands are not the norm, and that we were actually cut out to live much more communally and divide some chores as much by skill as by sex. But I also know that traditionally, marriage *was* about complementary skills, not true love or equality. Husband

and wife came together (or husband took on wife) because each had something to offer and did their part to create the working machine of the family. This tradwife version of marriage echoes that in some ways.

## WHITE SUPREMACIST TRADWIVES

IN 2021, CYNTHIA Loewen splashed her happiness all over the press, declaring that spending her days cleaning house and tending to kids was far more fulfilling than what she had been doing: training to become a doctor.[9]

Like Pettitt, Loewen's goal is to take the shame out of housewifery—because for a generation of women supposedly emancipated from traditional gender roles, it can be incredibly confusing, if sometimes liberating, to embrace them. As noted in chapter 8, Gen X was the first generation in which all women—not just poor women—were raised with the expectation of working full-time *and* raising a family in a society without policies like paid leave or universal childcare. The paradox contributed to a state of misery for many of those women, and some Millennials saw that path and decided not to walk down it.[10]

It makes perfect sense to me that some daughters of Gen X mothers would reject do-it-all motherhood and retreat to the simplicity of strict gender roles, nixing the office to concentrate on the kitchen and bedroom instead. Since gender norms crest and fall in generational waves, I understood that looking upon the lot of harried Gen X moms and saying "No thank you" was both a natural zeitgeist shift and a reasonable choice.

While some tradwives are apolitical or don't mention religion, Christianity plays a key role in how others organize their lives—and why.

Wifely submission, after all, is what the Bible decrees:[11] "Wives, submit to your own husbands, as to the Lord," goes Ephesians 5:22–24. "For the husband is the head of the wife even as Christ is the head of the church, his body, and is himself its Savior" (New International Version).

On the British show *Stacey Dooley Sleeps Over*—in which reporter Dooley spends seventy-two hours with a wide variety of British families to understand and showcase the diversity of their lives—young, nonprocreating Dooley spends the weekend with tradwife and tradhusband Lilian and Philippe.[12] She's Chinese American, he's Guatemalan American, but they're both living in the U.K. (and are friends with Pettitt and her husband).

"I would have identified myself as a feminist before getting married," Lilian, bearer of two master's degrees, claims. But then she agreed to this arrangement in which Philippe is in charge of everything outside the home, and she's responsible for everything in it, including homeschooling their three children and daily Bible study. Now she feels the liberating power of submission and of placing unbridled faith in her husband and in God. "I think the world would be a better place if more women were willing to back down and say, 'Okay, I trust you,'" Lilian says. They are creating a Christian, pro-life, loving two-parent home. Nothing wrong with that.

Some tradwives go beyond "traditional" values, descending into downright bigotry. That is, some have connected old-fashioned gender roles to a Trump-style MAGA nostalgia for a whiter America. In a *New York Times* opinion essay, writer Annie Kelly asserts that the tradwife resurgence is not a reaction to the relentless burdens of post–women's movement motherhood but a kind of "mommy-vlogging" with "a virulent strain of white nationalism."

A PoliticalResearch.org article states that between their posting on fashion and memes, tradwives "fantasize explicitly about the mythical post-war Americana of the mid-twentieth century, which they envision as full of Aryan nuclear families and blonde, Tupperware-touting women who are submissive to their husbands."

Indeed, such women exist. A tradwife called "Wife with a Purpose" proposed "the white baby challenge" as a fix for declining white birth rates in the West. "I've made six!" she wrote about white babies. "Match or beat me!"[13] In her Instagram bio, typical.tradwife described herself as "Alt Right, Believer in Traditional living and European Culture."[14]

Yet I think these extreme voices are the minority. Many in the movement extolled the virtues of a simplified lifestyle, promoting it to push back against the shame they'd been taught to feel about their preference for it. Most wanted women to know that it was okay to participate in a relationship like this, to embrace what has been painted as anathema to liberation and happiness, when in fact for these women it was the most direct path to those things.

Some critics seem unable to separate the embracing of traditional 1950s gender roles with whatever other injustices befell that era, as if Jim Crow, hourglass dresses, and mushroom casserole were inextricably linked. When I searched for research or scholars to contextualize the movement—perhaps as a zeitgeist shift in reaction to the intense unhappiness of so many overworked and under-supported Gen X moms—I mostly found articles about racist tradwives like "From Swiffers to Swastikas: How the #Tradwife Movement of Conventional Gender Roles Became Synonymous with White Supremacy."[15] This, despite the fact that one of the most visible tradwives is a Chinese American woman married to a Guatemalan American man.

Rebecca Barrett is the first-generation daughter of Brazilian immigrant parents, and her husband is half Black and half Puerto Rican. Though rejecting the notion that tradwifing itself has anything to do with white supremacy and the white birth rate, she does realize that her message has been embraced by the notoriously misogynistic Red Pill and Manosphere communities. Barrett doesn't agree with them on many things, but they happen to align over traditional gender roles.

Tradwives—educated, mostly white, upper middle class—are now the exception to the new rule of stay-at-home moms. A third of stay-at-home moms are poor, and they're more likely to be immigrants. On the other hand, the history of housewives is deeply entwined with whiteness, and concern about white women's behavior is deeply entwined with moral panics about declining birth rates. The "traditional values" they promote do have some morally murky history.

What the media and tradwives themselves seem to forget is that less than a decade before this current fad, left-wingers with social work degrees spoiling their husbands with massages and their children with attention were called "feminist housewives" in a *New York* magazine article.[16] It was meant to cause a double take, an assumption that the moniker was an oxymoron. As if the only kind of person who would choose this role must have internalized so much misogyny that she couldn't see that she'd been duped. But I read the description and almost coveted their existence. I wanted that a little bit, but I wanted to want that a lot.

But that was before the kind of social justice ideology that has permeated much of American culture due to Trump, social media, the pandemic, and the murder of George Floyd. Our analysis of and contempt for "the patriarchy," that power blob that links all men with Darth Vader, because they are the greatest beneficiaries of societal inequities and stand to gain the most by inoculating themselves against its abuses, has led to a recent cultural vilification of straight white dudes. If man-hating feminists have poisoned traditional marriage, well then, tradwives will resurrect not only the benefit of traditional marriage but also the idea that Father Knows Best. Because it's okay to be a "real man," they believe that returning men to where they belong, at the head of the household, is what's in fact good for them.

This thread emerges at a time when some, even on the left, have begun to question the value of the cultural focus on toxic masculinity, worried it shames men for traditionally and stereotypically masculine traits—one can be masculine without being toxic, they remind us.[17] So as much as this movement stems from women protecting and asserting their right to be traditionally feminine, it also reclaims the right for men to be "manly."

## TRADWIFE BACKLASH

THOUGH THE PUBLIC rebuke to tradwives sometimes centers around its abominable intersection with race, that's not critics', especially feminist critics', sole objection. The *Guardian* article "'Tradwives': The New Trend for Submissive Women Has a Dark Heart and History" noted "this is about women fighting against their own insecurities about their lives. And because of these insecurities, they then insist they are the oppressed ones, the brave speakers of truth." The assumption: Tradwifery is an expression of internalized misogyny and twisted, martyred logic. No way it could be feminist.

Sometimes, people are just mean to tradwives, especially working moms. In 2020, an Australian mother named Brooke Smith shared her daily routine with a Facebook group called Mum's who organise, clean, cook and chat.[18] "I always make sure I don,t [*sic*] go to bed until everyone's lunches are packed, their clothes are set out for the next day including my husband's and the house is clean dishwasher is on and load of washing is on sometimes it means I get to bed at 9 sometimes that means I get to bed at midnight but I always get up early (430 with husband to make his breakfast and coffee )" read the first part of it.

That part of the post was picked up by various media outlets, including Australia's *The Today Show*. In a segment called "Back to the '50s," the hosts audibly groaned as they quoted her.[19] "Go, Brooke. Whatever," said one female host. They wondered at how this could possibly happen. Has the husband hypnotized her? Is he disabled? Does she just really like him a lot?

They noted tangentially that husband and wife own a mixed martial arts gym, breed bulldogs, and have four children under the age of six. But instead of awe, or asking for tips, they belittled and berated her. "You're making the rest of us look bad," one said.

What they didn't do is share the rest of her original post. In it, there is no period after "I always get up early (430 with husband to make his breakfast and coffee )." Rather, Smith says that she gets up so early "to make time for me have a hot coffee and do my hair get a little peace and quiet meditation/exercise in and do my face for the day happy mum equals happy household do it even when you feel like not doing it because you'll be happy for it the next day." [*sic*]

In other words, the host ignored that Smith is not solely dedicated to serving others, and that she's actually incredibly capable and organized, putting her own oxygen mask on first. I wake up at four-thirty many days, too, but mostly because I have perimenopausal insomnia, and I read the *New York Times* and play word games for an hour, instead of doing housework, work-work, meditation, or exercise, all of which would be better for me.

So yeah, go, Brooke. No "whatever" from me, at all. Just props.

An Australian YouTuber and freelance writer named Daisy Cousens dissected this episode in a video called "Tradwives Make Feminists JEALOUS."[20] She noted the "decidedly cruel tone of the hosts" and that what Smith described was, on the one hand, a fairly normal domestic arrangement, and on the other, the work of "a woman whose extraordinary organization allows her to not only keep an efficient household but gives herself time to regroup, refresh, and remain healthy and happy." Smith and her husband "very clearly have equal but different roles." She stays home with their four kids, and helps with the gym and the dogs, and he goes out to work. What is so objectionable about that?

Cousens has some theories. "There is nobody quite so good at tearing down women as other women," she says. "We're always jockeying for status within the pack." This kind of reaction—jealousy, shame, a sense of being threatened—is what some tradwives reject about feminism.

Maybe it's just my own tiny knot of jealousy, my own conflict about not being more domestically present, but I believe that some women looking down on tradwives know that housewifery is actually both more challenging and sometimes more rewarding than the tedium of a retail job (or, for me, the back pain from having to stand on my feet, watching the clock) or the exhaustion of something more intellectually demanding and corporate.

After all, there is some evidence that, as tradwifeoriginal boasts, "Traditional women who live in a patriarchal family are happier and healthier than other women."[21]

According to a 2014 Pew Research Center report—admittedly pre-pandemic—some women fare better emotionally as stay-at-home moms and housewives, getting more leisure time and sleep. After dropping during the career-woman-driven '80s, the number of stay-at-home mothers has been steadily increasing since the turn of the twenty-first century. Pew also reports that 60 percent of Americans believe that "children are better off when a parent stays home to focus on the family." Around 70 percent of women work, but only 35 percent of Americans say kids fare well with that arrangement.[22]

Then again, the "we're happier than the working moms" trope isn't always accurate. A 2011 report by the American Psychological Association reported, "Mothers with jobs tend to be healthier and happier than moms who stay at home during their children's infancy and pre-school years."

## TRADWIFE AS SEXUALITY

ONE OF THE first things that pushed me to explore the concept of housewives was the way I felt Trump was fetishizing them—that's the language I used. In his campaign speeches and tweets, he was putting the white, middle-class, 1950s housewife on a pedestal, holding up an archetype of how women should be that was basically not available to most of us and kind of sucked for women when it was.

I did not mean fetishizing literally, though—I meant idealizing or romanticizing. But it turns out that plenty of people *do* literally fetishize housewives, as a perfunctory perusal of the fetish website FetLife reveals. Who knew that so many people loved to bake cookies in the buff, save for an apron and high heels?

I found a woman who goes by CrinkleCrackleCrunch on Reddit who is in a "Total Power Exchange" (TPE) relationship. "He's my Master and I'm his slave. He's my owner and I'm his property," she wrote to me. TPE refers to a twenty-four/seven expression of BDSM, or bondage, discipline, dominance and submission, and sadomasochism.[23]

With multiple kids at home, Crinkle and her husband sought an outward expression of their relationship that passed as respectable. "As fun as him forcing me to be naked and led around on a leash 24/7 sounds? It's just not possible when he's got the business to run, and I'm herding our brood of munchkins all day," she wrote. How could they, as she put it, "take kink out of the bedroom, and into our daily lives?" With "Happy Cliche 1950s Housewife Play," which would allow them to "keep the dynamic 24/7 without outwardly presenting as freaky weirdos and not scarring our kids."

In other words, the kind of real-life, boring vanilla corollary to dominant/submissive or master/slave is breadwinner/housewife. That means, she said, "Traditional Gender Roles within as many aspects of our marriage as possible—this helps us keep the dynamic alive as much as possible, seeing our family/non-kinky-friends/ public at large, thinks nothing (kink-wise) of a very happily married couple who just lean super noticeably traditional within the bounds of their marriage. He's a badass businessdude who goes out and slays dragons, and he's super successful at that. I'm a happy homemaker who's his 'kept woman,' who's super submissive and obedient to her husband, and is very happy kept perpetually barefoot, pregnant and in the kitchen." Or at least, she wears dresses in the kitchen and yoga pants for exercise.

Crinkle is not an oppressed housewife. She has willingly entered a relationship in which she finds comfort by forsaking any say over her life; she gave consent to give up consent. "It sounds counterintu- itive as hell, but doing that, committing to that POV on a permanent basis? It was (and is!) so liberating to me," Crinkle wrote. It's as if "you captured 'ecstatically on Cloud 900000' into a drug, and permanently hooked me to a mainline of it."

# MAKING A CAREER OUT OF NOT HAVING A CAREER

Unlike the many other critics of tradwifery, I'm troubled by only one thing in addition to the minority of overt racists and the obvious exclusion of same-sex couples (though some can and do enact traditional gender roles, just not according to sex): the economic angle. Having talked to so many women who hitched their fortunes to a man with the reasonable yet unfulfilled expectation that his financial success would be hers, too, only to find themselves unexpectedly impecunious, I worry about tradwives.

And I'm not alone. Sometimes a tradwife appears on a TV roundtable show, pitted against a feminist scholar. Generally the feminist says something like "I respect your right to choose this path, but I worry about the economically vulnerable place you're putting yourself in."

Without some kind of homemaker credit or guaranteed income, tradwives remain financially dependent when they trust in and submit to their husbands. They may Instagram their homemade baby food, but if the men become violent or abusive or neglectful, or tighten the purse strings, they have little recourse. Tradwifery only works if the tradhusband is truly a reliable guy, whose responsibilities are largely outside the home.

One of the tradwife movement's ironies, however, is that some have created full-time jobs, or at least certified influencer status, out of not having jobs. Rebecca Barrett told me that some of her videos have gotten more than a million views. "How much do you make for that?" I asked, and she said, "Not much." (Mint suggests $5 per 1,000 views, so that's $5,000. Not much was right.)[24] But when you have enough of those videos as well as sponsors, it adds up.

However, such success remains elusive for most women. In fact, Barrett day trades in the morning while her baby naps. And doing that work, she told me, doesn't make her any less of a tradwife.

Barrett's not promoting complete financial dependency or lack of agency or identity. She's preaching a flexible schedule that puts her child, husband, and home first; then she can earn "fun money" on the side. She's advocating for a life where roles are clear. And she seems very, very content. The day I spoke to Barrett by Zoom, I was hours from a work deadline, anxious, begging my kids to give me space. She was relaxed, cuddling her daughter.

What few have pointed out is that some tradwives are building careers by marketing their ideas about how women shouldn't have marketing careers. They advertise their happiness as currency, then convert it into literal currency via videos, books, and merch. They are selling the image of the housewife, but the work it takes to sell lies outside of housewifery. In reality, many tradwives are more entrepreneurs than Stepford wives, evoking the Beechers or Louisa Knapp.

Pettitt was a marketing expert before she gave it up to market the idea of traditional homemaking. When you Google her, she is described not as a homemaker or even a tradwife but as an author.[25] If it's so fulfilling being "just a housewife," then why invest so much time building your online empire promoting the idea of being "just a housewife" while you are essentially an entrepreneur?

I would have loved for Pettitt to answer that question, but she didn't respond to my queries. Neither did any of the tradwives I reached out to besides Barrett. I suspect most tradwives have endured so much bashing by my fellow feminists that they assumed my goal was to expose them as fraudulent anti-woman lionesses determined to corner other women in domestic cages.

Yet I see absolutely nothing wrong with their selection of this neo-traditional path. Rather I see something wrong with a world that judges women for choosing that path, and that also makes either choice so hard, each vision so difficult to manifest.

I didn't want to ask tradwives why they chose this path—that much was entirely clear to me. I wanted to ask them if they had prepared for the possibility that their husbands might leave them, and if so, how had they indemnified themselves financially. Did they sign contracts, make financial plans, or otherwise ensure that, should this arrangement end for any reason, they and their offspring would be cared for?

Perhaps that's why so many tradwives rock these side hustles, making money lecturing women on how to not make money, kind of anti–Suze Ormans. Maybe somewhere inside themselves, they feel just how vulnerable their choices have rendered them. Barrett has full faith in her husband, but she also has a money-making hobby, and plenty of skills to make real money if she needs to.

Or perhaps they recognize that they've built their futures on a romanticized past, a time before women were corrupted by unrealistic expectations and no structural way to achieve them. In Pettitt's mind this time is the 1950s and '60s. She harks back to the era "when you could leave your front door open." After finding inspiration in *I Dream of Jeannie* and *Bewitched*, like the fictional women who starred in those shows, she found a man to look after her, despite her own considerable powers.

But Pettitt and her ilk may miss what those '50s and '60s depictions of housewifery were really about. Jeannie had the power to literally move mountains but could be sent back to the bottle at any moment when the major growled. Samantha of *Bewitched* had the full arsenal of witchcraft at her disposal but subverted her own power to please her man, or to tidy the living room. The message of those shows was that if a woman has power, she should direct it away from effecting change that benefits her, or society, and toward her husband and children, turning it on only in the domestic sphere. They depicted powerful women caged without bars—choosing to cage themselves, choosing to submit—in a lovely home. But, yes, they seemed pretty happy about it. It was fiction, and the problem that had no name did not exist in those invented worlds.

And what of Doris Day, Pettitt's original patron saint? Despite playing retiring, chaste, virginal, and domestic goddesses, she herself was no housewife. A powerful woman, Doris Day's personal life bore no resemblance to the fictional personas she inhabited. The actress and singer, who survived four sour marriages to abusive, controlling men, herself described the idea that she was like her characters as "more make-believe than any film part I ever played."[26]

So Pettitt's patron saint wasn't actually Doris Day but the fictionalized archetypes of femininity she inhabited on-screen. Thus, some tradwives are assuming not just a social role but almost a caricature of womanhood, as Doris Day did.

And what of the 1950s housewives that tradwives often evoke? As noted in chapter 5, the "traditional" American housewife didn't appear until the middle of the twentieth century. Before then, colonial housewifery was tremendously valuable and demanding physical labor or a complicated managerial role for wealthier women. When that image of the traditional housewife did emerge, it appeared in advertising to lure women back to the home after their taste of full-time work. And then some of them got so depressed they revolted.

So when tradwifeoriginal claims that feminism "destroyed the Traditional gender roles and the nuclear happy family," she overlooks that 1960s feminism didn't destroy 1950s housewife purity, and that traditional gender roles did not automatically result in happy nuclear families. Those traditions changed based on circumstances and zeitgeist shifts, on cultural actions and reactions. And perhaps most importantly, those traditions weren't traditional at all, but an anomaly caused by demographic shifts and economic forces and government subsidies. Perhaps what we're really nostalgic for is investment in the family, infrastructure, and education—things the government helped finance in the 1940s and '50s, for some social categories, and which we should prioritize again, for all social categories.

Still, maybe it doesn't matter if Pettitt missed the anti-feminist messages of the shows and movies she admired, and that the archetypes she modeled herself after were inventions. What she found was that living a life that echoed those depictions brought her happiness. "It's almost like the fairytale came true," she said.

## I AM TRADWIFE, HEAR ME ROAR

AFTER ALL THIS research, I decided to spend a week experiencing the tradwives' lifestyle to determine which version of life brought me more happiness. That meant taking over the cooking from my husband, who'd assumed the position of family chef during the pandemic, and cleaning way more than I normally would.

My first day of tradwifery did not work out as planned. There had been a massive snowstorm and the drain on the roof of our building had frozen, causing the melted snow to flow straight into my younger daughter's room. With quite a bit of housework to be done, I stopped watching videos of women polishing their silver until it shone like the top of the Chrysler building and got cracking dragging the soggy bits from her room so it could be repaired. All her toys, clothes, and stuffies lined our narrow hallway for an entire week.

No matter how much I tidied, nothing got any cleaner. I was Sisyphus vacuuming, the crumbs and dust just resettling. I cleaned out the fridge while talking to a reporter from Reuters for an hour and a half because the more time I spent away from my computer, my work, the more it tugged at me. I tried to ignore it. Cleaning the fridge *was* my work, I reminded myself, and it was incredibly satisfying. The fridge looked so much better, and I felt saner and more on top of things.

At first, I decided not to tell my husband what I was up to. I would just wow him with my ultra-capability, having dinner on the table, the refrigerator organized, the laundry put away instead of leaning in Pisa-style towers atop the dressers. I hoped he would see the organized cabinets, the properly plumped-up pillows, the lint-free carpet, and extol my virtues.

If he noticed, he didn't say anything.

When it was time to make dinner, I had to retrieve my daughter from a playdate, so my husband went ahead and made sweet potato lentil curry while I trucked through the sludge to get her. We ate dinner, and I would have cleaned up, but the printer was broken, and my daughter needed it to complete a school project, and I'm the tech support in our household, so I spent a full hour trying to fix it. (I semi-fixed it.) Hmm, I thought, the division of labor is more pronounced than I'd thought, and it is not particularly traditional. Then I passed out at nine-thirty because Covid had gotten its grips on me and wouldn't let go, even three weeks later.

The next day, I awoke at dawn from a NyQuil haze and stepped carefully over my daughter, sprawled on a futon on the floor because her room was unusable. My older daughter gets up at six-thirty for school, but I decided to do a six-fifteen workout online. If I'm tradwifing, one of my jobs is to look good for my husband even if his idea of hot is more Sporty Spice than Posh Spice—he loves a ponytail and sweatpants, which was already my pandemic uniform. Anyway, I did squats while he got her up.

But then while I was exercising, I threw my back out. So my husband made her breakfast while I hobbled down the hallway to wake the little one. Then there was the icing and heating and trying to heal my back, all while attempting to make my apartment look good and take notes.

Later, as my husband loaded the dishwasher—my back hurt too much—I asked, "Did you notice how clean and organized the fridge is?" He hadn't. Nor had he noticed that I'd emptied the cabinets, cleaned them, and returned everything neatly. My husband doesn't care about that kind of stuff. He's unbothered by the chaos of our tiny, dilapidated kitchen, whereas I perceive the peeling paint and doors falling off the cabinets as a personal, professional, and financial failure. It's a constant reminder that I'll never have the experience I dreamed of, cooking with my kids around a large kitchen island, because we literally have five square feet of counter space, and it's just an incredibly unpleasant space to be in. I can't get anything about my life to look like Instagram, and it infuriates me.

But my husband isn't on Instagram and feels no pressure to perform fatherhood, or even adulthood, in any specific way. He likes to cook, and as far as he's concerned, our kitchen is fine, and because it's so small, when he cooks he has the kitchen to himself. In other words, if my husband's cooking, I'm parenting, which prevents him from getting nagged—the most traditionally wifely thing about me is my nagging.

So I explained what a tradwife was, and how I was writing about them and trying to be one, and what that entailed.

"But I have to work," he protested.

"Yes," I said. "That's the point. You'll work and make money, and I'll cook and clean and do all the childcare."

"Oh, you mean I have to be the *husband*," he said, his nose crinkling as if an unpleasant smell had wafted into the room.

"Yes, I'm the tradwife. You're the trad*husband*."

He thought I'd been suggesting that he don an apron and spend the week scrubbing the tub and making homemade pasta—totally his idea of a good time. He seemed disappointed at the idea of me, the submissive one, and him, Mr. Dominant. He eschewed tradwifery—unless *he* was the tradwife.

If I learned anything through this experiment, it's that our division of labor makes sense for who we are and what we're good at. And, yes, it's unfair. But not as unfair as it used to be.

I submitted to Rebecca Barrett that perhaps there was something particular about Gen X men that made them less amenable to this arrangement. After all, some of their mothers were women's movement types who ventured into the workforce without a change in the role of fathers yet. These men married Gen X women, the first to try (and fail) to do it all, and the men's roles didn't evolve as quickly. Thus, some of our marriages seemed to be marked by a relentless stream of wives' criticism of their husbands. (Or maybe it's just me?)

"The thing I hear from a lot of women is like, oh, I can't trust my husband to do anything," Barrett said. "Like, the man can't even put the underwear in the laundry basket. But if we don't relinquish that control for ourselves and encourage them to be better and do better, we're going to be mad."

That's where the submission comes in, she said. Women are good at inspiring, and whether they're cooking or day trading, we have to make men feel confident. Women have to "let go a little bit of our control and say, okay, this might not get handled exactly the way that I wanted it to be handled. I'm going to have to bite the bullet and have courage and lift up my husband to take on this responsibility." In other words: Stop nagging. Start encouraging. (A friend pointed out that this sounds a lot like parenting.)

Pettitt's husband himself rarely seems to speak. He's simply described as "a 48-year-old software programmer," and other than saying a few words in one video, I found very little on him. Meanwhile, the Russian tradwives may be ready for a traditional relationship, but apparently alcoholism is such a problem among Russian men that the women have trouble finding one sober enough to be a tradhusband.[27]

In fact, the past few years have seen a robust discourse on a crisis among men who have lost power and position in society while women made tremendous gains. It's nearly impossible to get a Mrs. degree these days, when women comprise 60 percent of the student body on college campuses.[28] Some men want women who submit but also bring home the bacon. It's gotta be hard to find these Marlboro men of the moment who want to live this way, and then finding one who also makes enough money to support his family on a single income? Harder still. If we've encouraged men to feel shame for their impulses and proclivities, maybe tradhusbands have an opportunity to do a little marketing of their own and teach other men how to be better at holding up their end of the bargain, whatever that end may be. Maybe they need to train more men to assume the best parts of "traditional" 1950s dads.

Methinks a solid tradhusband is hard to find, but that's the secret of tradwifery. It cannot work without a man who can be trusted to do what's best for his family. It takes two to tradwife.

## CHAPTER 13

# The Devalued Housewife, the Dismissed Househusband

This was not the life that Monique—or her parents or siblings or cousins or aunts or uncles, or even her husband—imagined for herself.

A British citizen from the Caribbean island of Dominica, Monique said her family expected her to go into business or become an engineer, doctor, or lawyer like her siblings. Her mother was a nurse, and her grandmothers worked close to home as seamstresses, managing to raise kids and tend the land. In West Indian families, education is number one.

But at college in Toronto, nothing took. Monique was always interested in the arts, but she knew her parents would never pay for a degree in painting or writing or acting or dance. Instead she studied economics and business management, in which she had no interest whatsoever. Eventually noticing that she was floundering, her family suggested Monique take a year off.

She went to New York City. Office work, retail, catering management...Monique was good at everything, but nothing satisfied her. In 2000, she met a man in a club, and seven months later they were married. That solved her working permit problem but not the floundering.

But that didn't matter so much because her husband was on a steep upward trajectory himself, a Black man in tech taking the world of online streaming by storm. So Monique followed him from job to job, city to city—San Francisco, Atlanta, New York—working at this and that to contribute to the rent. Although she finished her degree, she continued to toss in the wind. Her husband didn't push her. He assumed Monique would find something.

After they'd been married for eight years, he said, "Okay, let's try for a baby." They'd traveled and had adventures. Monique agreed that it was time to settle down.

And that's when the passion finally kicked in. Monique had thought she would be the kind of person who would earn a business degree, a powerhouse on a magazine cover, *and* manage a home with lots of kids. But it didn't turn out that way. As soon as Monique brought home her son, she couldn't conceive of leaving him—for what? To cater? Work in an office? Stand at the counter of a clothing store all day? Why do that when she was married to someone who made enough money for them all to live on?

But she was nervous. Few Black women in America don't work unless they are on some kind of public assistance. Her husband didn't marry her thinking she wouldn't contribute financially. His family came north during the Great Migration, and all the women worked.

Plus, Monique didn't like that word "housewife." Only one woman in her family stayed home with her child, and that's because the child was sick. Her mom had always said to her that it was important for women to work and have their own money—money gives you a voice in your household.

On the other hand, her working mom friends would tell Monique how jealous they were, how lucky she was. She watched their struggles, their guilt, their tears. The way they worked full-time *and* took care of everything on the domestic front. It was so stressful, so complex.

Still, for the longest while, Monique suffered a lot of anxiety over how she looked as a Black woman who didn't work, even though staying home brought her the most joy.

## JUST A HOUSEWIFE

REMEMBER THAT *DONNA Reed Show* episode "Just a Housewife," in which women with anthropology degrees sported pearls and heels to the supermarket, where a radio announcer, and then their husbands, flatter then belittle them, impugn their contributions, and put them back in their place? We no longer engage in that same overt denigration of traditional femininity to that degree. Nonetheless, women who choose to stay home—even women with the resources to make that choice—often feel judged. The difference is how often those tacit incriminations now come from the women themselves.

The entrenched cultural devaluation of housewifery, of women's work, is centuries old, no matter how segments of our society require housewifery from women or uphold it as the ideal.

Because the U.S. Census didn't list homemakers as gainful workers, the Association for the Advancement of Women implored the agency in 1878 to "make provision for the more careful and just enumeration of women as laborers and producers." Later, in 1976, social scientists objected to the use of the term "head of household." Why should the leader be the person who works outside of the home, as opposed to the person running all the systems inside it?[1]

A woman named Poppy found out just how much our culture

devalues femininity in a surprising and disheartening way. When they had kids, Poppy and her husband decided together that he'd stick to their business, and she'd cook, do the bulk of domestic activities, and be the primary caregiver.

Poppy had grown up in Maine with a working-class single mom, often under financial hardship. "I didn't have one of those *Leave It to Beaver* parent/family situations," she said. "I didn't have any expectation that there were going to be cookies waiting for me when I got home from school." She recalls being at home sick with no one to watch or help her. "I remember just sitting in the bathroom, staring out the window, waiting for my mom to come home on her lunch break."

During Poppy's first year in college, her mother died, and she was effectively alone in the world. She wanted her children to experience what she never did: a stable presence they could rely on. "I didn't have any consistent help and I don't have much family," she said. "I wanted to be home with them." And she was lucky; her family could afford for her to do that.

When her son struggled with learning difficulties, Poppy spent hours in the library with him, working on reading strategies, searching for books about topics he might cotton to. She devoted herself to finding good programs for him. But she never said to her son, "Boy, aren't you lucky—I grew up with none of this." Understanding she had been privileged enough to make this choice, Poppy didn't want her son to see her as a martyr or someone who sacrificed.

But a strange thing happened. Her son didn't feel lucky or privileged. He didn't feel grateful. During adolescence, he became deeply interested in economics, and the more he learned about finance, the less he valued her contribution, critiquing Poppy for not earning money. He could not understand that her labor—feeding and watching the children—undergirded her husband's ability to earn their living.

"At some point in his adolescence, my not working outside of the home equaled my husband having such a higher status than me," Poppy said. "It doesn't matter—the volunteering, the running big events, showing up to read to the class." Being on the board of an important local nonprofit, or even teaching dance classes—Poppy's son saw it all as wasting time because her activities earned so little actual cash.

Never mind that his mother effectively taught him to read, which she couldn't have done as readily had she held a paying job. Her son's lack of respect for her choices was palpable and hurtful and nicked away at her self-esteem. "I would never have predicted back when I made the decisions that I made that this would be the impact," she told me. She began to wonder if he'd respect her more if she, like Grace from chapter 8, worked in childcare and was paid to tend to other people's kids.

The oddest part was how little her husband agreed with their son. He'd often tell Poppy that her work was more difficult, and she was harder to replace than he was. If something happened to him, she could get a job, but if something happened to Poppy, it would be incredibly difficult for him to perform her duties—not just the cooking but also the scheduling, the nurturing, the attention. He valued the split in their duties and loved coming back from work to a home-cooked meal. Their son couldn't see that this system, this division of labor, powered their family.

To critique and debase her, to value money above all else, even her—maybe it was her son's way of rebelling, she thought. But it stung. It made Poppy question her choices, her own self-worth, her achievements, her offerings. But mostly it made her aware that, despite the values she tried to instill in her son, he had internalized a message from our society she had not realized had such a strong hold; her son had absorbed by cultural osmosis a completely different worldview. "How much has it seeped in," Poppy asked, "that what I've done isn't something that is recognized or valued in our culture at all?"

Poppy's story surprised me, because she had improved her financial situation through marriage so much, and when I peered in on her life, it seemed she was living the one I had envisioned for myself. She was always cooking something delicious with lentils and crafting something beautiful out of felt, still playing instruments that I used to play. These were parts of me that I had shed when I became a parent—the person who cooked, crafted, had hobbies other than watching TV, who had not been subsumed by bottomless fatigue.

I felt at times like an octopus or mayfly, some kind of creature that dies upon procreation. Some parts of me just couldn't hang on. After molting my artistic self, only writer and mother—admittedly, perhaps the two most key parts—remained. So at least I retained the skill I needed to cobble together a living. I had a lot of excuses as to why I had transformed into someone whose many other artistic talents receded and who struggled to meaningfully contribute financially to my household. Unlike so many women in my neighborhood, I didn't have a full-time nanny. My apartment was unkempt and cluttered all the time because I lived in a fourth-floor walkup and didn't have, like, a basement to store the piles of crap that apparently come with procreation.

But a lot of it was also that even as I was working full-time as a freelancer, I also was the primary caregiver of two kids. As time went on, I earned less and less money, not just because child-rearing intensified, but because my industry imploded, and I had to work harder for less. The shame I felt at my piddling income was deep and relentless. I felt constantly disappointed in myself and my situation, both my motherhood and my work. Certain that the issue was where I lived and the dynamic I had with my husband, sometimes I was unable to see that the problem was so much bigger than that. No matter how similar or different their situations, these women and I—even those of us who got almost everything we wanted—were wrestling with the illusory archetype of the housewife.

## REINVENTING THE HOUSEWIFE

How do we turn this around? How do we make housewife, homemaker, stay-at-home mom, full-time mom—whatever you want to call it—a respected, viable, but never compulsory option for as many women as possible?

During the pandemic, founder of Girls Who Code Reshma Saujani created the Marshall Plan for Moms—now known as Moms First—which she described as "a historic investment in women's economic recovery and empowerment" and "a national movement to center mothers in our economic recovery and value their labor."[2] Observing that she herself, a successful businesswoman, was struggling during the pandemic, she tried to envision a path to help. "Someone's got to have a plan to support mothers," she told me. "The whole world had collapsed underneath [mothers] and we needed some big, bold ideas."

Saujani penned an op-ed in the *Hill*. "Each day, about 45 million women in this country show up to a job where they regularly work overtime, are paid nothing, and get no time off," she wrote. "Their job title is mother. It's time to compensate them for their labor."[3] The goal, she said, is "[t]ransforming our culture to make motherhood respected, valued, and compensated."

I think we need to talk more about what it means to be "compensated." What if we actually put our money where our mouths are in this respect? One idea that seems to have garnered bipartisan support is paying mothers to stay home. This has some unique appeal because more than half of mothers want to stay home with young kids.[4]

Pre-pandemic, about 20 percent of parents stayed home full-time; 80 percent of them were mothers.[5]

Some economists and politicians floated the idea of a "caregiver credit."[6] Maybe it would be in the form of a tax credit for a non-working parent. Or, like disability insurance, it could be a fund that working people minimally pay into and draw upon if needed, perhaps something they could get back later if never used. Or some kind of universal basic income. Saujani suggested monthly compensation of $2,400 for a mother's unpaid labor of raising children who will be our future workers and caretakers. She points out that if American women earned even minimum wage for their unpaid caregiving work, they'd have garnered $1.5 trillion in 2019. A caregiver tax credit, or a retirement fund for stay-at-home parents, is a nice place to start.

These ideas may appeal to some feminists because they reflect an appreciation of women's unpaid labor, and may help reduce the gender pay gap, allow women more choices, and make them less dependent on men. Some conservatives may like them because they make it financially easier and more socially acceptable for women to stay home. On the other hand, feminists are generally resistant to policies that keep women in the kitchen, and conservatives don't like big government. So these ideas are still floating about in committees—so far.

Tax cuts for the rich aside, Americans tend to quibble relentlessly over who should get government assistance and in what form. Programs like Aid to Families with Dependent Children (AFDC), created in 1935 as part of the Social Security Act, offered cash payments to families of children with an absent or incapacitated parent due to unemployment, sickness, or death. On some level, public assistance—welfare—can help a parent stay home or bail a mother out of poverty.

But it was gutted by Bill Clinton by way of the Personal Responsibility and Work Opportunity Reconciliation Act of 1996 and assorted other policy shifts that both limited the amount of time parents could collect financial assistance and added work requirements. The government shifted to a block grant program called Temporary Assistance for Needy Families (TANF)—note the use of the word "temporary"— in order "to provide assistance to needy families so that children can be cared for at home; to end the dependence of needy parents on government benefits by promoting job preparation, work and marriage; to prevent and reduce the incidence of out-of-wedlock pregnancies; and to encourage the formation and maintenance of two-parent families."[7]

You hear echoes of the Moynihan report here with its emphasis on the traditional nuclear family, the faint pulse of judgment about interdependence, and the idea that only the poor need economic assistance. There's no acknowledgment that our society needs families, traditional or not, and those families need support, thus our society— including our government—should support them. Instead, welfare carries a stigma and comes with stipulations that, ironically, can keep women in poverty; if they earn too much—that is, a living wage, and enough to feed kids but not much else—they'll lose the government assistance.

When I asked Meg, the libertarian supermom from chapter 8, about these ideas, she suggested that the government shouldn't reward people, through tax cuts or compensation, for getting married or having kids, any more than it should reward them for not doing so. That's putting money on individual moral choices, valuing one over another. I understood that point of view, too.

Here's an example of something that at least *sounds* good and fair. Malaysia drafted legislation called the Housewife Social Security Scheme (HSSS), which "provides cover for domestic disasters such as accidents, illness or death, and is open to all housewives, estimated at 2.99 million people," per an article in *New Straits Times*.[8] That would include 150,000 housewives living in poverty. The legislation was created "as part of the social security agenda for housewives who do not have any protection if they are involved in a domestic disaster or suffer a disability. Their contribution has economic value in the development of family institutions, also known as the care economy," said Human Resource Minister Datuk Seri M. Saravanan.

It sounds like something we could use here, and perhaps this progressive legislation sprung from the acknowledgment of a regressive word. By using the word "housewife," they're being honest about the vulnerability of women who are taking care of their children and not able to earn their own money. But it'll be a long time before we know how successful HSSS is; the scheme was only implemented in December 2022.

Nonetheless, these are the kinds of policies that can ease the burdens of lower-income women who've never had the luxury of housewife dissatisfaction, for whom staying at home was never an option, or for whom work is so low-paid that it makes no sense to leave their children to do it. Think of these policies as antidotes or additions to the Personal Responsibility Act: the Collective Responsibility Act.

Here's another recurring theme in this book, and another idea for how to support women who want to raise their kids full-time, and not just policy change but cultural shift. You want to make stay-at-home motherhood a respected option?

Make stay-at-home fatherhood a respected option, too.

## ENTER THE MEN

WHEN CHARLIE WAS a kid, his parents taught him how to iron and set the table. They snookered him into washing dishes by praising him, saying he was so good at it. He and his brother did their own laundry from the age of five and cleaned their rooms every Saturday. In the kitchen, their parents taught them to separate egg yolks. They didn't make a big deal out of training their boys in the domestic arts. But Charlie's grandmother had been a "D.C. badass" in women's and consumer rights. Working women were the norm, as were helpful men.

Growing up in this environment made Charlie particularly equipped to participate in equitable marriage and parenthood. When he and his wife got together, they evenly split household chores. They maintained similar standards of cleanliness and didn't need to nag each other.

When their son was born, Charlie did as much as was biologically possible, and bottle-fed the baby breast milk whenever he could. He handled the sleep training. His wife cooked, and he washed the dishes. He hates vacuuming but is fine cleaning the bathroom. He had no complaints. In fact, he and his wife both felt a little guilty, as if each of them wasn't doing enough. They kept checking in with each other, but each felt supported and included and not overburdened. Later, they took turns with school pickup and drop-off.

When his son was seven and his wife was traveling often for work, Charlie quit his job to pursue a startup, which left him with a flexible schedule. He became the primary parent. He set up the doctor's appointments, picked up and dropped off at school, and took their son to his weekend activities.

But no one at the doctor's office or school or weekend activity places could wrap their minds around the fact that he was in charge. Every Saturday, he'd drop his son off at gymnastics, then get a coffee around the corner while he waited for him to finish. On the last Saturday of the semester, when he returned to pick him up, the receptionist said, "You weren't here to see him get his trophy."

"Oh, weird," Charlie said. "I never got an email about that. What email do you have on the account?"

Well, they had both his wife's and his addresses, but they'd only been emailing hers, even though Charlie handled all that kind of correspondence. In fact, he'd told them multiple times to call or email him if only one parent would be contacted. What if their son had fallen and hit his head or broken his arm, and they'd called his wife in a meeting on the other side of the country? Charlie was livid. This was beyond just *Oh, my feelings are a little hurt that I missed this moment in my son's life*. There could have been serious consequences.

The same thing kept happening. The school nurse never called him first, even though Charlie was the one who would pick their child up if he was sick. If there was an issue, she kept calling his wife until his wife called him. He'd explain to the nurse over and over that she should call him. The nurse would say it was a paperwork issue or they were working on it, but it never changed.

The people doing this to Charlie were always women, and it felt like they believed dads were morons who couldn't be trusted. It made him feel like an interloper in the world of parenthood, which infuriated Charlie, because his son was doing quite well with Dad in charge, thank you very much. On the other hand, he was one of only two dads at the PTA meetings in his western mountain state.

It's up to the men, too.

Charlie is not looking for affirmation or recognition. He's looking for fathers as primary parents to be normalized. He's read multiple accounts of a dad going to the grocery store with his kid, only to have a woman say, "Oh my God, look at you, you're so good as a parent." His unspoken response is "Fuck you. I'm his dad. I'm not a babysitter." (Let me interject here to say that I have heard women describe their husbands as babysitting when they stayed home with their own kids while the wives went out in the evening, but they didn't apply that term to themselves when the opposite occurred.)

What bothers Charlie are the assumptions people make that fathers don't do enough. He knows other stay-at-home dads who bust their asses. He knows their experiences are unusual, but everything about this situation is just so rooted in our culture, so intractable, so inescapable. The assumption is not just that women should do the domestic and familial work; the myth is that men *can't*.

In Charlie's experience, women perpetuate this notion, but the assumption that mom is the primary parent or that all men are bad dads lets fathers off the hook. "Once you just assume that the mother knows best and the dad's an idiot, then there's further abdication of his responsibilities," he said. "It doesn't help." Charlie thinks about the portrayal of, say, Homer Simpson and the incompetent father trope. "It's kind of like the white dad is the last like PC butt of jokes," he said. "But what I think is really insidious about that is that it is actually sexist against women." He thinks expectations of dads need to be raised—individually and culturally.

When Charlie reads an article about a woman wanting more help around the house or with the kids, it always seems to be that the woman wants things done a particular way and is furious at the man if he doesn't comply with her exact desires. And part of it, he thinks, is that Gen X has popularized some idea that we must project-manage our children. That we and they must always be doing something, injecting ourselves every step of the way to make our presence known so our kids know that they're loved. It's the fallout from intensive mothering—or, as Charlie would call it, intensive parenting—and sets up fathers for failure, too. One book even refers to them as "throwaway dads."[9]

The parenting double standard shows itself in all kinds of situations. I thought about a woman in Kansas I'd talked to. Every year, Madeline told me, her kids' elementary school kicks off a program to encourage "school-based father-involvement" and support education and safety. The dads wear matching T-shirts with the program's logo on it and take time off work to volunteer for a day or two in the school. In return, they are feted over the loudspeaker and presented with a pizza party to celebrate their presence, however fleeting.

Madeline seethes at this. Just about every *day*—not once a year—there's a mom volunteering in a classroom, and is there a party? No. Pizza? T-shirts? No. Nobody does anything for the moms who volunteer for the PTA and the bake sale and the field trips. It feels like 1956 some days.

There was one family—a mom, a dad, two kids. When the mom left her family, moving to a new city for a job, the whole school rallied to support this single dad, railing about the mother's abandonment, demonizing her, valorizing him, casseroles, childcare, sympathy. No one rallied to help the dozens of single mothers in the school working and taking full-time care of their kids. Assuming that not having a mom is a travesty and that the single dad needs help, they fail to examine the many biases wrapped up in those assumptions, the assumptions within the assumptions. The main one being, Madeline told me, "You can't be nurturing if you don't have a vagina."

Charlie thinks we need to send different messages to dads as part of the necessary cultural shift. He counsels new dads that they have parental instincts, too. "Don't fucking buy into the gender stereotype of *oh, the mother knows best because of hormones*," he said. "Learn to trust your gut."

The cultural solution, he thinks, is to rear children more the way he was reared: shop and home ec for boys *and* girls. That way, when those boys grow up to be fathers, there's more flexibility in who does what. If a wife is better suited to work in construction and a husband is better suited to stay home, that will be normalized. According to Charlie, what's not normal is the idea that one person needs to do it all. He's seen his wife's guilt at having a job she loves because she's away from home for a few days at a time, and he rarely sees men struggling like that.

Another thing that might create a hard reset is compelling men to take paternity leave. Generic parental leave isn't enough, and gender blindness won't work. To center dads and create more parental equity, Charlie thinks, you have to go a step further.

## EXPECTING BETTER

A WOMAN NAMED Nina agrees that some of the blame lies with the stay-at-home moms themselves. There's an entire culture, she said, of women dissing their husbands, a familiar trope that everybody rallies around. (And of which I have been terribly guilty myself, though in my defense, for many years we had a very lopsided division of labor that put the onus on me to rebalance, and I'm also full of compliments for my kind and hilarious husband.)

Nina has always felt that she didn't belong in that club. She'd grown up in a household with some traditional gender role expectations between her white dad and Mexican American mom, sure, but her father did the grocery shopping and the cooking, and her mother worked. And though her husband didn't have those kinds of models, he'd already been in two long-term relationships where he was used to pulling his weight. He came to their marriage trained, having previously owned a home and knowing how to take care of things.

They never had a big discussion about it. They didn't go to premarital counseling or engage in a huge amount of negotiation to figure out who would do what. It was just sort of a given. "He's a domestic partner in the best sense of both words," she said: a homebody who has always worked from home and was emotionally and physically present for their children.

When the kids were babies, Nina and her husband had a fairly traditional split of responsibilities; she stayed home, and he worked. As an adjunct professor, Nina didn't earn enough to keep working once she had kids. Her husband was fine with her staying home and was helpful. He would wake up in the middle of the night with her, change diapers, help the babies get back to sleep. When the kids were older, she resumed her career, which is now quite strong. He was able to help their daughter with her anxiety, to be calm when doors were slammed during the teen years. The kids trusted their father and sought his counsel.

Disappointed in their own husbands' level of participation, some women Nina knew would concede that their husbands were pretty good at the physical labor of parenting. They'd be fine with the laundry, the running around after the kids…But the emotional stuff? The mental load? Mostly not.

As the culture of complaining continued around her, Nina wondered—was she really lucky? Was her husband a unicorn? Or was there something wrong with those other men? The wives would say their husbands would get lost in the grocery store—as if they were children! Nina didn't understand it. Why had they married men like that? Was something wrong with those women? She didn't mean to be judgmental. She just couldn't understand what was happening in those relationships, and why their persistent dissatisfaction was so palpable.

Nina began to think this was a language between women, especially those staying home with their kids. It was a way of connecting, bonding, making themselves into victims even though they were all living fairly comfortable lives. For the most part, these women had opted into their situations, and yet there seemed to be some cachet in the complaining, some kind of status rooted in announcing the ways they had been slighted. Maybe on some level they were afraid to be happy. Maybe the complaining was a cover for their guilt. Maybe, instead of an embarrassment of riches, they were embarrassed *by* their riches. Maybe they'd created a subculture where the whining was the hazing required to belong, as well as penitence for their privilege.

Is it possible that some of the unhappy housewives are unable to see what they have? Is it possible that some of the men are being permitted—perhaps even encouraged—to misbehave?

Nina's advice to these women: Expect more.

And yet sometimes women fare better when expecting less—not of men, but of themselves or society. I talked to a woman named Sam, who'd given up a career as an art teacher to stay home with her two kids. Her pilot husband had an unpredictable travel schedule, and she didn't make much money anyway. Now, with her kids finally all in school, Sam was just starting to earn money here and there by assisting an artist. The vast majority of artist's assistants were ambitious twentysomethings trying to get into the studio to schmooze or build a portfolio. But for Sam the job was easy, fun, and put some grocery money in her pocket. Staying home with her kids, she told me, "just made me not care anymore. I don't care what anybody thinks. I don't care about having a career that sounds cool, or impresses people. It's no longer part of my identity. I feel free."

She reminded me again how my ambition complicates my life. If I desired less—less success, less money, less ego-feeding, less physical comfort—I might concentrate on wanting what I have, instead of chasing what I want.

## ROCK 'N' ROLL HOUSEWIFE

WHEN I MET Velma, she confirmed this for me. All her life, Velma had subscribed to a feminist doctrine: She must earn as much or more money than her husband, and never depend financially or emotionally on a man. "It was like a mind virus that had gotten into my head at an early age, and kind of propagated and grew into this worldview that I need to make a lot of money and men are the enemy," she told me.

She'd been a liberal, save-the-earth warrior, pursuing a science career with a fervor that left her with both an autoimmune disease and a bad back after years of hovering over the bench and staring into a microscope. It also left her with debilitating anxiety and depression. "I was constantly falling on my face, trying to get my career going," she said, "and I just never really made that much money in my life."

Velma had met her husband, also a scientist, when they both played in bands, and together they ran a small farm. However, she had to move to another state to pursue her master's, and her colleagues and advisor convinced her that she needed a PhD to become successful and financially independent. They were suspicious that he didn't move with Velma, even though she explained that he'd stayed at their home to tend to the animals and farm, that their careers and choices had temporarily placed them apart.

She sought out a therapist who helped her develop skills to manage these difficult emotions and situations. But something unexpected happened. The more fortified she felt, the less she aligned with that feminist, left-leaning worldview. "A lot of those views started crashing into my ability to be happy," Velma said. "Instead of being proud of my husband and finding another way to be in that partnership fifty-fifty other than money—because it's not all about money, but for some reason I had it in my head that that mattered a lot—I was starting to become jealous of him and started to see him as the enemy. And it was causing a lot of friction in my relationship that was unnecessary, because he was just kind of waiting for me to just trust him and accept the love he was offering." He never did anything wrong, she said, but still, "I treated him as though he was an abuser just because of the ideas that feminism had put into my head."

Velma realized eventually that she wanted to quit working and become a housewife. Her husband earned enough and supported her choice. She no longer wanted to discuss politics—not with her friends in the science field or with her therapist.

But in the wake of Trump's election, her therapist had changed, too. He insisted on discussing politics, often invoking the very ideologies that Velma sought refuge from, blaming her husband—white, Christian, straight—for both society's ills and Velma's personal struggles. He wanted Velma to see her husband as a tool of the patriarchy and herself as patriarchy's victim. Rather than framing her choice to be a housewife as a feminist and healthy one, she should feel guilty for having the privilege to make it.

When Velma switched to another therapist, that one outright encouraged her to get divorced, insisting it was cheap and easy to do online as if that would make her other issues evaporate. "The last thing that I needed was for someone, when I'm in a vulnerable state, to tell me that my husband is really the enemy," she said.

The therapists were both acting deeply unprofessionally, but they were also reflecting the left-wing zeitgeist that instilled guilt in Velma and made it hard for her to follow her true desire. She could quit her job, but what about other women with mental and physical illnesses who weren't lucky enough to have husbands who could support them? "And I had to just be like, 'You know what? It is unfair and I need to take care of myself because I'm going to die,'" she said. "The stress was starting to break my body."

So Velma ignored them all—therapists, colleagues, the voices in her head. "I quit my career and I don't miss it at all, and I think I was torturing myself for nothing. My marriage is super happy now," she said. At forty-two, she hopes to adopt a child. "Life is great."

Still, she struggled to explain her choice to her feminist former colleagues. "I feel like being a stay-at-home mom today, at least in my social circle, is probably as rebellious as working was in the sixties for women at that time, because everyone I know is obsessed with their careers," Velma said. Going to parties, having to say what she does for a living—it terrifies her. "I have to work on not apologizing for myself and acting like I'm trying to hide the fact that I don't work."

On the other hand, Velma sees herself as a kind of subversive, rebelling against a system that judges women for pursuing a life that some have deemed unacceptable. And then she wants to say: "I'm going to be a stay-at-home mom and you can suck it." In Velma's mind, she's a rock 'n' roll housewife, a badass homesteader who contributes to the family budget by harvesting food on their land, controlling the amount of money going out, and making it easier for her husband to bring money in.

One of the things that feminism teaches girls, Velma said, "is that your career and your self-worth are linked. And that's toxic, and it has to stop." She thinks we need to teach women to believe in themselves. Not just their careers as their salvation, but that they're strong people who can be resourceful.

And should Velma suffer the same fate as Nora and other women who gave up careers to stay at home, only for their husbands to unexpectedly and royally screw them over financially—she knows she has skills. "I would find a way to survive," she said. "I know I would because I always have."

## FALLING INTO PLACE

DURING HIS SENIOR year of high school, Poppy's son had a bit of an awakening. She began to share with him how painful the way he treated her was, and that planted a small seed in his brain. It blossomed when he started seeing a new girlfriend and hanging out with her group of friends. They seemed to have no supervision at home, no boundaries nor rhythms nor routines they could rely on, all things she'd provided for him but that he'd never appreciated. By the time her son left for college, he'd become more grateful, but Poppy still couldn't shake the shame, the sense that what she did was not enough. She wondered: What if we *didn't* devalue child-rearing and domestic work? What if we didn't assume it was more important to earn money than to raise healthy kids?

Monique's husband and kids never disrespected her, but as much as she loved staying home, she never fully wriggled free of the sensation that she *should* be doing something more. Monique remembered her mother being in charge of so much more than her dad, and coming home wasn't about relaxing for her but hitting the ground running. Then her mom, who had worked throughout each of her pregnancies, told Monique: *Stay home with your kids if you can, because I wish I had.* Although they had a comfortable, middle-class life, her mother felt she should have been there more, physically and emotionally, for her kids.

Monique had another child. She knew that she was putting a lot of trust in her husband to take care of them all financially; she'd seen women left penniless by uncaring husbands. She made sure they had good life insurance, her own retirement, and access to all their accounts. And her mother told her, "You have your education and you're not stupid. So if something ever happens, you know that you can go out there and hopefully get things together."

She made peace with her situation, but her creative desires still bubbled at the surface. Her friend told her, "Don't worry—you will see things fall into place. You will get where you want to get, just do what you have to do now, relax, take care of your kids. It's an opportunity. You have to relish this opportunity."

Her friend was right. Monique had been taking her kids to the library and the bookstore, trying to find books with kids of color, wondering why she had to search like crazy for books that represented her child and her family, that showed Black motherhood and happy, comfortable Black families. She realized she would have to write her own.

And that's what she did. She wrote a picture book about a Black stay-at-home mother, which was published in 2023.

# CHAPTER 14

# The Declaration of Interdependence

Before the pandemic, Maria worked multiple jobs, trying to pay the rent on time and raise her two daughters. She'd worked as a dental assistant, but it didn't pay enough to get ahead of her debt, so she tried to save enough to study computer science at community college. She had begun to work as a housecleaner in her small Nebraska city. Some nights Maria went to school, and others to AA meetings, to maintain her long stretch of sobriety.

Her eight-year-old daughter had been diagnosed with dyslexia, and Maria had spent a lot of time advocating for her to get her an Individualized Education Plan and academic support. Her ten-year-old daughter had been born with a combination of physical and mental health problems, including chromosomal abnormalities and developmental delays. She was nonverbal and still wore Pull-Ups, needing ferrying to various therapies and appointments throughout the day. Their father was in and out of the picture—but mostly not present.

Maria struggled to find work that paid more than the cost of childcare. It was exhausting but, on some level, working. Her family had a routine and some support. She could make it to the end of each day without going mad.

Maria was about to start a better-paying job, cleaning for a hotel, when the pandemic hit. The job disappeared, her younger daughter's school closed, her older daughter's therapies were canceled. She had to quit working and going to school. To be her older daughter's aide and help both girls with their schoolwork, Maria had to quit her dreams for a better life. Watching her younger daughter struggle without knowing how to help her, she grieved for the support she'd lost. And she had to keep sober with no in-person meetings; what's hardest for alcoholics is isolation. Some days Maria thought, *I just can't do it. I don't know what to do.*

But she white-knuckled it and scraped by. Maria fed her children with donations from food pantries. She paid the rent with emergency unemployment and the federal government stimulus check, somehow navigating the labyrinthine processes to get them, thanks to her knack for computers and enough patience to push through limitless bureaucracy. A local nonprofit offered Maria steady part-time work from home, processing applications and helping others struggling to remain in their homes. The organization taught her budgeting skills, which she was able to teach others through what she learned. She miraculously was able to remain in her own apartment with a paltry income. At least her children had that one shred of consistency left.

She proved to be very good at her job, which required the kind of computer skills she had hoped to go to school to learn. Maria moved up to full-time work with benefits, earning a real living wage for the first time in her life. School reopened, and her daughters got the help they needed. And through it all, Maria stayed sober. She got through the worst of it.

The combination of her own grit and determination and community help—both from the government and from nonprofits—kept Maria from becoming homeless, unemployed, and unable to feed her kids. Her friends in recovery kept her sane during the chaos. Someone in her circumstances, Maria said, can't make it unless community assistance is seen as a necessity for the greater good, instead of the need for it reflecting someone's flaws.

## CHILDCARE RESISTANCE

I TRULY BELIEVE that the tracks beneath the train to sanity are made of structural solutions, even as I understand that we as individuals have responsibilities, too.

If a more humane and functional society is our goal, the most important problem to solve is childcare, which can cost more than college tuition.[1] Childcare is considered affordable if it's less than 7 percent of one's salary.[2] Meanwhile, childcare workers earn shockingly low wages. Thus, any post-pandemic job-creation and motherhood support plans should have incorporated childcare. Executive director and CEO of the Institute for Women's Policy Research C. Nicole Mason calls this "national childcare infrastructure." Just as we have public education for K–12 students, we need free, ubiquitous childcare that anyone who wants or needs to can opt into.

How to pay for it? In 2019, Senator Elizabeth Warren suggested that the federal government "would partner with sponsors—states, counties, cities, school districts, tribal organizations, or other nonprofit community entities—to administer the program in a way that prioritizes local community needs and coheres early childhood systems."[3] These can't be seen as frivolous expenses, but as the cost of running the economy, the basic investment in human lives, in the future of our country.

This kind of policy tends to play out in the tax code, which makes debating it hard for the average non-wonk. But basically, the bulk of American families already receive some kind of child or dependent credit. Under the pre-pandemic system, some 23 million families received only partial credit, or none, because they earned *too little*.[4] Yet another example of a tax system that penalizes the poor.

Then the Biden administration extended the child tax credit to low- or no-income families through what's called "refundability," which directly lowered the number of children living in poverty. Families could then use their credit for basics like food and rent, temporarily lifting 3.7 million children out of poverty.[5] In January 2022, when the credit expired, child poverty rose 41 percent.[6] Polling reveals that 56 percent of all voters overall—74 percent of Democrats, 85 percent of Black voters, and 70 percent of Latinos—want to bring back the tax credit and make refundability permanent.[7]

Some start-ups are trying to match stay-at-home moms with working moms—the sharing economy for parents—but that's really not a nationwide solution. Nor has anybody tried Eleanor Roosevelt's idea of matching mothers whose kids are grown and gone with young moms who need help. A friend who works at an art gallery brought her baby to work for the first few years, and when other employees later procreated, they were allowed to do the same. That's a very rarefied space—pretty good for toddlers (if no delicate sculptures sit atop wobbly pedestals) and an elite job that allows a divided focus. But it kept childcare costs low, which was also good for the business's bottom line.

Still, there's a uniquely American resistance to universal childcare based both on the fallacious ideal of independence and the modern

238 | LISA SELIN DAVIS

notion that, in an era of overpopulation, it's selfish to procreate—as opposed to one's moral and patriotic duty as it was considered more commonly in the past. And because it's seen as a "choice" (I write these words just as *Roe v. Wade* has been overturned), those who make it should be solely responsible for figuring out how to navigate the world as a parent.

That's also the attitude of many a policymaker—that women must fulfill their housewifely duty, not that the government should create situations in which mothers have support and choices. As Republican Wisconsin senator Ron Johnson said in early 2022, "Well, people decide to have families and become parents. That's something they need to consider when they make that choice. I've never really felt it was society's responsibility to take care of other people's children."[8] Perhaps Johnson had never heard of, say, public schools, or libraries, or taxes, or any of the various "socialist" institutions that already exist in our society to help care for other people's children.

"America has decided that child care is an individual or a family responsibility, which reads as a woman's responsibility, and is not a collective problem that we all have to solve," said Elliot Haspel, author of *Crawling Behind: America's Child Care Crisis and How to Fix It.*

How do we get Americans to see that creating an environment in which parents can do a good job raising children is patriotic, as we did during the era of Republican Motherhood and, for a blip, during World War II? The childcare crisis must be framed as a societal issue, not just because of economics but because we want to live in a decent world where children are raised properly. That's why, said Haspel, "there needs to be some really intentional narrative change work."

Motherhood, said Reshma Saujani of Moms First, needs a perception makeover. "I just think it's deeply rooted in America, the way that we treat mothers. It's in our films, it's in our books. It's everywhere. So you just need really a cultural shift."

That means not only portraying mothers in pop culture differently, but also providing for them differently in the private sector and convincing them to advocate for themselves with the same fervor with which they advocate for others, especially their own children. It means acknowledging the fallacy of "having it all," and shifting the culture toward "making it all possible." It means shared responsibility, and, as Saujani wrote, it means "[m]aking workplaces work for moms by working with moms and companies to reimagine a better, more equitable future of work."

To have future voters and leaders, we need people to procreate. We don't want to live in a gerontocracy, which tends to have economic slowdowns (see Japan).[9] So parents must become an organized constituency and demand more. If we shift public opinion, policy may follow. And we need to make it about choice, for that, too, is an American ideal—choice about whether to work or stay home, with either option valid.

In 1977, almost 70 percent of Americans thought children suffered if a mother worked outside the home. That was halved by 2012.[10] While some studies showed that the children of women with unusual work hours seemed to fare worse on cognitive tests, most studies show kids of working moms fared *better* in many aspects of their lives.[11] There is no one way to raise kids, but we can create a society in which multiple ways are valued, in which parents aren't punished for what they choose.

## LEAVING FAMILIES WHOLE

WHEN ANH WAS pregnant with her first child in 2017, she fantasized about the time she'd spend cuddling her newborn, the bliss of bonding. But she hadn't really prepared for it logistically. "I had no idea what to expect," she told me. "I just thought, 'I'll take time off,' and three months was the standard that I knew of."

As a pharmacist for a health care corporation with more than fifty employees, Anh was eligible for the Family and Medical Leave Act (FMLA), which allows parents to take up to twelve weeks of leave without jeopardizing their jobs. But it's unpaid leave—something that Anh, like many women, didn't consider until she was pregnant, and that the vast majority of women can't afford.

In many ways, Anh was lucky. She'd saved up four weeks of sick and vacation days, took two weeks of extended leave, and was eligible for four weeks of short-term disability at 50 percent of her salary. Anh had been smart enough to *get* disability insurance before she got pregnant, because pregnancy is considered a preexisting condition. Few of us, especially freelancers with no parental leave, would think to get disability insurance in anticipation of getting pregnant someday—but hot tip: We should. After that, Anh took two additional weeks unpaid, and her job was still waiting for her, even if her income took a mild hit. The problem: She had no more paid vacation or sick leave days to use later if her child became ill. And of course, many women who freelance or perform wage labor have no paid days off to save up.

Anh was okay in part because her husband works in IT. The nonprofit Just Capital, which tracks large corporations' performance on social issues, found that among other industries, tech companies, which are often overwhelmingly male, offer some of the best family leave.[12] In 2022, Alphabet, Google's parent company, was 30 percent female and offered eighteen weeks. Facebook, which was 37 percent female, offered sixteen weeks. Twitter, a little more equitable at 42 percent female, offered twenty weeks (though who knows after the Elon Musk takeover?).[13] Ironic—or smart PR—considering men on average take much less parental leave than women do.

While he didn't have such generous expanses of time off, Anh's husband did receive his full salary for the days he was out. "He was able to get two weeks off fully paid, not using any sick leave or PTO [paid time off], not worrying about where his paycheck was coming from," she said. "It was very mind-boggling to me that a major health care organization didn't have a more progressive maternity leave policy."

Mind-boggling, indeed. The United States is the only developed country in the world without national paid parental leave.[14] (Generally, paternity leave is paltry compared to maternity leave, which in itself can range from middling to nonexistent.) Because of this dispiriting fact, as many as one in four working mothers return to work within two weeks of giving birth.[15] In the relentlessly upsetting documentary *Zero Weeks*, we see that some mothers go back even sooner.[16]

Meanwhile, FMLA covers only 56 percent of U.S. employees, and only a fraction of those eligible for FMLA use it.[17] For one thing, you have to be able to afford to take unpaid leave. For another, you have to know that this option, and your company's other family leave policies, exist. Just Capital found that only 28 percent of the country's 875 biggest publicly traded companies disclose detailed paid parental leave policies to their employees. Lack of awareness is a big barrier.

Some lucky parents live in one of the ten states with statewide paid family and medical leave, which offers eligible workers a portion of their salaries.[18] Because we have no comprehensive national policy, each person must navigate the system, trying to figure out what their company or city or state offers, and not always realizing that such policies do or should be equally applied to both sexes.

"One of the things women most need is for men to share the care," said Ellen Bravo, director of Family Values @ Work, which advocates for paid sick days and paid family leave. "There are a lot more men who want to be good fathers, husbands, and sons, but they can't because they get punished for it at work." That is, not all fellas unlock the elusive fatherhood bonus.

One way to push for this kind of equity is to promote paternity leave. Sweden did this in the 1970s when they hired weightlifter Lennart "Hoa-Hoa" Dahlgren for a campaign. His freckled musculature packed

BARNLEDIG PAPPA!

into a skintight blue-and-gold short-sleeved shirt, Dahlgren appears with a nude infant smiling in his arms, assuring men everywhere that taking care of your child is a perfectly manly activity.

The cultural campaign didn't persuade all dads to stay home for diaper duty, so Sweden eventually backed it up with a humane, parity-producing policy. The government offers parents 480 days of paid leave when parents have or adopt a child, 240 for each if there are two parents; single parents get all 480. Fathers still only use about 30 percent of parental leave,[19] but enough of them have opted in to create a surge in what the media deemed "latte dads," out strolling with their bundled babies and sipping coffee.[20] In America, men are far more likely than women to use vacation time instead of parental leave; perhaps it's just not deemed manly to do so.[21]

To get more men to use family leave, one tack is to make them feel an investment in their kids is a masculine trait—if they get competitive about fathering, they'll know the best thing is to take time off.

"Making sure fathers are taking parental leave is really important," said Ellen Lamont, associate professor of sociology at Appalachian State University. "The research on paternity leave shows that if you get men involved in primary care of babies really early right off the bat, it breaks down that stereotype that only women can be nurturing." Higher rates of paternity leave are associated with higher rates of paternal involvement.[22]

We might guarantee everybody the same decent amount of paid parental leave via legislation, and then create a culture in which parents actually take it, regardless of sex. "Companies should offer gender-neutral family leave," said Bravo. That is, we should conceive of this not as maternity or paternity leave, but new child leave and, even broader, family leave, which would allow workers to care for sick parents and other loved ones, as well as kids. "It's not just women who are parents and it's not just new kids who need care." In fact, women make up around 67 percent of caregivers for parents and older adults.

Let's face it: To get more states to pass paid family leave and more companies to improve their offerings, we have to talk more about economic benefit as well as the kind of society we could and, in my estimation, should have. It's well documented that returning to work too soon is bad for parents' physical and mental health, which hurts efficiency and company bottom lines.[23] Unsurprisingly, paid leave is good for kids, too, and reduces chances of infant mortality and head trauma, in part by reducing parents' stress.[24]

"We want to revalue caregiving and get people to see that this work that makes all other work possible has to be recognized and compensated," said Bravo. "We have to have leave that's comprehensive and inclusive and affordable and break through the ideological partisanship."

The Center for American Progress has an exhaustive list of

suggestions for policies to create more equity, less stress, a healthier economy: expanding unemployment benefits, bailing out the child-care industry—and subsidizing it going forward, creating living-wage jobs, and closing the gender wage gap and the maternity pay gap, among many other suggestions. To have two-parent households in which one parent electively stays home to care for children means massively increasing blue-collar wages, dramatically hiking up the minimum wage, and taxing the pantaloons off the rich. It requires bringing back unions so they can collectively bargain for better pay.

I'd suggest that we also create affordable, multigenerational housing and family-friendly school calendars—why are there so many half-days for students but not parents? Why are school days already several hours shorter than the adult workday? Why is there rarely affordable childcare to cover the gap? Why are there so few options for year-round school?

Then brand all these initiatives under the banner of "Strengthening the American Family" to make these otherwise socialist-sounding initiatives appeal to the majority of Americans, regardless of party affiliation. Most of us can probably agree that we want children to thrive and their parents not to suffer, so we must find ways to package these policies so that even those who subscribe to the myth of American individualism can support them.

Saujani advocates for both public and private sector changes to "expand choices for women and to remove barriers to equality." Women were told to break glass ceilings, she noted, but were largely sitting in the shards of glass. She suggested a task force headed by a caregiving czar.

The Marshall Plan for Moms collected some polling data and found tremendous bipartisan support for these ideas.[25] Half of those surveyed expressed that childcare expenses were too great for mothers to return to work. More than two-thirds of women polled believed the government didn't do a good enough job supporting mothers—80 percent of liberal women and 73 percent of conservative women. Eighty-three percent of mothers polled supported the Marshall Plan.

In 2021, Representative Grace Meng of New York introduced the Marshall Plan for Moms as a "bold and sweeping piece of legislation seeking to revitalize and restore mothers in the workforce."[26] The goal: save the childcare industry and work toward universal childcare, invest in education and broadband, expand the child tax credit and earned income tax credit, maintain benefits like Supplemental Nutrition Assistance Program (SNAP), and increase the minimum wage.

Good stuff, all of it, and also what most people in Scandinavian countries can expect just by paying taxes. Alas, despite bipartisan support, the bill sat in subcommittees for well over a year. (Congresswoman Meng and Senator Amy Klobuchar plan to reintroduce the bill again.)

Biden's American Families Plan aimed to do much of the same, combining $1 trillion in spending and $800 billion in tax credits for childcare, pre-K, paid leave, free community college, health care, and refundability in the child tax credit. It was a social democracy cornucopia of reasonable offerings from one of the world's richest countries. It, too, largely withered.

Saujani doesn't think we should leave it up to the government to fix our societal ills. She outlines several ways businesses and communities can help, without waiting for governmental red tape to untangle: flexible hours, which can include job-sharing, compressed workweeks, or remote work; supporting childcare, which can include offering subsidies or on-site childcare; shaping gender dynamics at home, which can include paid leave for parents of both sexes, or having men take more paternity leave to signal to other men that it's okay; paid time off for illness, whether that's tending to someone else's or your own; getting rid of the motherhood penalty, which can include management tracks for working moms or not letting career breaks affect hiring; ample parental leave; and strong re-entry strategies, including coaching for returning moms and recruiting moms back to the workforce.

Businesses can implement these policies now. Journalists can write about them. Visionaries can make plans based on them. Filmmakers and TV producers can create narratives that normalize them. This can be manifested in the culture first, which can then push the government to follow.

# WONK THIS WAY

IN THIS BOOK, I wanted to detail what's being done to craft a bold new vision for post-pandemic America, incorporating all that we learned about the integrality of working mothers to our society and economy during the two-plus years of shutdowns. I wanted to catalog how we'd rejiggered our values to prize interdependence over independence and understood the former not as a weakness or a failing but as the most essential building block of society, community, and democracy.

Alas, that didn't happen, despite the fact that more than 64 percent of U.S. mothers are co- or primary breadwinners; that's 84.3 percent for Black mothers. Thus, the economy can't function without them.[27] And mothers not in the workforce need to have economic security, too. Even after the pandemic imposed on upper-middle and middle-class women the experience that those with fewer resources have always endured, the powers that be did not become more sensitive to the need for a social safety net. Although we acknowledged the contributions of women and mothers, we didn't accept that interdependence is paramount to improving our economic reality.

This anti-interdependence problem is, well, ahistorical, since, as shown in chapter 3, this country was founded upon it. And we're still helped by the government in all kinds of ways, from mortgage interest deductions to tax breaks. Yet, as historian Stephanie Coontz writes, "[L]egislators remain wedded to the notion that subsidies to banks and corporations create jobs while subsidies to families create only laziness."[28]

We've bailed out banks. We've bailed out automobile industries. We've bailed out burger chains and private clubs. But our government, our culture, our industries have not focused on bailing out moms by creating a sustainable and reasonable system in which they can work. We need to enact policies that allow women to be housewives yet build a society in which no woman *has* to be one.

We don't actually need a bold new vision. We can reenact older visions or adapt blueprints from nations where interdependence is woven into the cultural fabric and is not political football. During prime pandemic times, parents of quarantined children in France were paid to stay home.[29] Denmark offered a year of paid time off to parents whose children took sick. Ireland footed the bill for three months of childcare. Japan arranged paid family leave for parents when day cares closed.[30]

Still, it's just so easy to sweep these perfectly reasonable ideas under the rug by trotting out the fearmongering flag of socialism. But there are reasonable critiques, too. Meg, the libertarian new mom, described tax breaks for married folks or parents as weaving social values into the tax codes. "Government should be as neutral as possible," she said. Rather than government-funded childcare, she'd prefer to simplify the tax code. "I would just like for people to have a little bit more money in their pockets to be able to make the specific individualized childcare decisions and schooling decisions that work best for them."

Meg posited that childcare was so expensive because of the arcane and overstepping government workplace regulations. Deregulate it, she said, so that we can pay childcare workers less. On the one hand, she laments the cultural devaluing of caregiving, but on the other, she proposes paying less for it so we don't have cause to continue the privileged complaining. I did not find myself converted to libertarianism after this conversation; some institutions must prioritize people above profit.

I could go on, but here's the thing: We're not really lacking for money or ideas; we're lacking political *will*. In the 1940s, the government funded the socialist-ish utopia ("ish" because it was privately owned) Vanport City, which provided subsidized childcare, free public transit, and affordable housing to working mothers. Of course, they didn't do it for women; they did it to win a war. The point is, there was a will, and thus there was a way.

Honestly, the specifics of *how* to do it almost don't matter for this discussion. If we could wrangle entire single-mother utopias to fight the Nazis—or to avenge ourselves after Pearl Harbor—we could create these family-supporting policies and market them in ways that appealed to many different swaths of society. To conservatives, we could say: Here's what will fortify the nuclear family and allow women to stay home, and strengthen the economy. To liberals we could say: Here's how we can provide women with choices and make sure their basic needs are met in the workplace. To libertarians we could say: This is actually the American way. You might not like it, but it's the right thing to do. (It's okay—they're used to not getting their way.)

The most important thing, C. Nicole Mason said, is to *not* get "back to normal." The important thing is to make life better for mothers, working outside the home and not, than it was.

## CONCLUSION

# It's Up to the Women—
# But It Shouldn't Have to Be

A church carnival. That was thirteen-year-old Cari Lightner's destination on May 3, 1980, when she was struck and killed by a drunk driver, Clarence Busch, who'd been arrested for another hit-and-run not even a week before. Cari's mother, Candy, discovered that drunk driving was rarely prosecuted or punished. Had there had been good laws, good policies, good policing, Busch would have already been locked up or had his license revoked. Her daughter would still be alive.

Hell hath no fury like a mother who's lost her child, and Candy channeled her grief and rage into activism. She carried her child's photo with her as she pressed California lawmakers, and then the nation's policymakers, to hold drunk drivers accountable and create safer streets. The organization she founded, Mothers Against Drunk Drivers (later changed to Mothers Against Drunk Driving) became one of the country's most effective lobbyist organizations. They invented and popularized the concept of the designated driver, got roads named after drunk driving victims, and organized victim advocacy panels and trainings. And they got laws passed. By 2013, there had been a 55 percent drop in drunk driving deaths.[1]

The lesson: Moms get shit done.

Now what would happen if we took moms' fury, ferocity, determination, indignation, brilliance, competence, drive, and vision, and trained it on...better options for moms?

Sadly, the last time we had something called a "mothers' movement," it involved several far-right isolationist women's groups, including the National League of Mothers of America in California. Just after the start of World War II, white, educated, middle-class Christian women fought to keep the U.S. from entering the war. Many were pro-fascist and eventually charged in the Great Sedition Trial of 1944. These mothers failed to effect change—but in that case, it was a good thing.

Today, we do need a real mothers' movement to advocate not just for others but also to rally on our own behalf.

How do we do it? A Million Moms March, perhaps? We assembled on Washington when Trump was elected, but not when we were pried from the workforce. "You didn't have millions of moms showing up in Washington to say, 'Let's get this done,'" Moms First founder Reshma Saujani told me. After all, we were busy homeschooling.

What could moms achieve if we used our powers for self-advocacy?

Help. Not just for ourselves but help educating our society overall on what is appropriate, safe, humane, and realistic to help us raise kind, responsible children who can take care of themselves and others and contribute to the world—or, if nothing else, who can contribute to Social Security. Moms aren't united, thus we can't strike—though a mothers' union isn't a bad idea.

Admittedly, it's hard to imagine a bunch of moms leaving their kids in day care to march on Washington to demand universal childcare;

those optics aren't good. The moms' movement shouldn't just have moms, anyway. Dads should rally in support of mothers, too, in support of equitable families—and policies that can make them possible.

The cultural messages of the 1950s told women that they must protect children from moral depravity like homosexuality, communism, and juvenile delinquency, and their husbands from sexual deviancy. They told women that a stain on a shirt was a moral deficiency. In the '80s, they told women that they must keep eyes on their children constantly, lest they be kidnapped or succumb to the suboptimal environment of day care. They must work and be financially independent *and* be the mistress of the domestic domain. Now we're supposed to create a series of Instagram-ready Momfluencer moments while shuffling the kids to Lego Robotics and music lessons and get a promotion and get good grades and put in overtime and oversee the homework and make up for two years of pandemic learning loss and swim team and gymnastics and tutoring and...Enough.

Mothers need personal zeitgeist shifts, to collectively reject the present expectations—and set new ones. As tribal animals, not many of us have the fortitude to cast off these contradictory cultural expectations and say "Screw it, *I'm* going to decide how to raise my kids, how to spend my time, and what works for me." And those who are strong enough to resist the cosmic rays of the shame machine need to have enough money to forge their own path.

But we must give ourselves cultural and personal permission to do that. If we believe that we *deserve* these structural changes—perhaps the tallest hurdle of all—maybe, maybe, something in the post-pandemic twenty-first century will give.

On the other hand, Eleanor Roosevelt was onto something when she said "It's up to the women." I think we need to move away from privileged whining, and to remember, as Meg, the beautiful and bootstrapping libertarian, told me, that raising kids is not supposed to be easy. We seem to be under the erroneous impression that life shouldn't be hard, rather than toughening ourselves enough to navigate its inevitable difficulties.

As I was working on this final chapter, women in Iran were throwing off their hijabs to protest a militant, violent regime. A friend pointed out that some of women's and mothers' lingering unhappiness in this country is a luxury; we're not in danger of being burned at the stake like Indian widows or viciously brutalized and murdered by morality police. If we widened our lens, perhaps we'd recognize that those of us who have a place to call home and enough money to eat are in fact doing better than the vast majority of the world, and that if we didn't allow ourselves to feel inferior, as Eleanor Roosevelt suggested, maybe we'd have more gratitude.

There are small things we can do within our own families and neighborhoods to create more community-oriented lives for ourselves. Find families to engage in meal-sharing with—I'll feed your kids Tuesday, you feed mine on Thursday. Carpool. Have childcare swaps. Expect dads to do more and don't give them hell when they don't do it your way. (That'll be my first assignment.) Feel less pressure for your toddlers to master Mozart. Ask for help when you need it, and readily offer help to others whenever you can.

A STRANGE AND unexpected thing happened in my marriage while I was working on this book. We of the laptop class were relatively lucky during the pandemic. My husband was furloughed one day a week but kept his job and became a work-from-home dad. Until then, I had done a lot of the parenting grunt work (not to say that it wasn't at times joyful): the shlepping to and from school, the cooking and cleaning, figuring out the schedule and activities. I'd also done the heavy lifting of deciphering what our kids needed and how to meet those needs, researching everything from sports to sleep training (which we failed at pretty horribly). What I most wanted help with was the big-picture stuff—the character-shaping stuff, the what-are-we-doing-with-our-lives stuff. As a person who had dealt with a lot of mental health issues for most of my life and who still didn't know how to cobble together a good living, I didn't think I had the skills to shepherd my children into functional adulthood. I was often angry at my husband because of our familial inequities, but because he paid the bulk of the rent, it was really important to me to protect his job, and so I had to do more.

But during pandemania, as I came to call it, he was just *around* more. He took on the cooking and afterward cleaned the kitchen. Though he made more deep-dish pizza than the veggie curry I desired, and didn't always clean the kitchen as I preferred it to be cleaned, I slowly learned to support him in healthier ways. That is, I criticized him less and delegated properly. My husband took over a lot of that grunt work. It wasn't the help I thought I wanted or needed, but it did free up space in my mind and in my schedule.

I admit it was hard to get used to. One evening, I spent an hour stretched out in the bath reading a book on colonial housewives while he cranked out homemade pasta and roasted cauliflower. I felt like I was slacking, but what I actually was doing was using the space he'd created for me to do my work. And he liked cooking, which I had lost my appetite for (not for eating, just cooking), and schlepping never bothered him.

The more my husband took control of his own duties within the family project, the more involved he got in other aspects, like the kids' schooling and sports. It was as if giving him space to master his own domain—the domestic one—in his own way (that is, without me nagging about how I want him to do it) helped him develop a sense of himself, of his place within our family. Before the pandemic, I'd been sucking up all the air in the home and was perpetually pissed about it. He'll never be much of a scheduler, and I'm really good at planning. I'm still handling big-picture stuff. Even though we weren't consciously trying to, we found ways for me to back off and for him to step up. It only took thirteen and a half years!

And like tradwife Rebecca Barrett, I felt lighter, refreshed, and invigorated. Except that I felt that way because he'd gone deeper into tradwifery than I had.

Recently I asked him, "Do you feel like things are more balanced, in terms of the distribution of labor?" I was worried he'd say no. After all, I was standing there with computer in hand while he chopped onions.

But he said, "Yes. I really do."

"Do you...like it?"

"Yes," he said. "I really do." If we could afford it, he'd gladly be a full-time househusband.

It's not that I'm not still aching over what I should be doing, what I miss, that I don't find it both weird and a little sad how infrequently I've baked cookies with my kids. But in post-pandemania, I've learned to shift expectations. My kids are okay (knock on wood), and after the insanity of the last few years, okay is the new great. I feel so much better about life when I cook and clean, when my domicile is organized. Not working, and concentrating on domesticity, leaves me more contented. But it also leaves me less fulfilled, and the urge to write, investigate, interview people, and work through ideas cannot be contained.

That elusive thing called happiness must be some combination of those seemingly contradictory desires, but I'll never achieve an even split. The only thing to do, nearly fourteen years in, was to make peace with the imperfection (easy for me to say, because I am 0 percent perfectionist). I thought of that Japanese phrase *wabi sabi*, the beauty of imperfection. That's what I would embrace: wabi sabi motherhood.

THIS IS NOT to indemnify the politicians, the institutions, the businesses, the designers of school calendars.

On the first day of a housing class I took in college, the professor wrote a quote on the board. To paraphrase: Homelessness in communist and socialist countries is a sign of governmental failure, but in capitalist countries, it's a sign of personal failure. I'm certainly not a communist, but I do believe that in exchange for paid taxes, the government should help citizens meet basic needs, and that when Warren Buffett pays a lower percentage of his income in taxes than his secretary, we have a problem. Crappy policies, not just personal moral failings, exacerbate inequality. My point is we should see the dire situation women find themselves in as a societal and governmental failure. Our society was founded on interdependence. That truly is the American way. We should normalize interdependence. Sing its praises. And demand it.

Interdependence looks like paid family leave and universal childcare. To achieve that, we need the same political will that led both to the creation of entire cities that supported working mothers, and later the suburban expansion that cut them off from everything non-domestic. But I think the reason we lack this political will, even after the pandemic exposed the urgent need for these changes, comes down to an old joke that my mother once told me:

Question: "Why does it take a woman so long to have an orgasm?"

Answer: "Meh, who cares?" (My mom likes dirty jokes.)

Though I despise when complex social, economic, and psychological problems are simplistically attributed to bigotry or hatred, I do suspect that this general dismissal of women's experiences—meh, who cares?—is part of how we ended up in our current predicament. We have to care deeply. And I'm so sorry to start wrapping things up on this sour note, but I think most people really just don't care about "women's issues." And we're also so incredibly polarized, so busy hating on those across the aisle that we haven't dedicated resources to figuring out where we overlap.

So along with policy shifts, we need to abandon the archetype of woman-as-housewife that still pulses beneath our personal expectations and public policies. Staying home with your kids is a fine option. Putting them in day care and going to work: also fine. Prioritizing the nuclear family? Go for it. Wanting a more communal experience? Also good. Pluralism is difficult to harden into policy, but it certainly can be woven into a culture.

From writing this book, I learned that women evolved to be domestic, in the way we understand it today. While some reproductive behaviors and maternal instincts are innate, the hunter/gatherer binary that developed in part because of ecological changes and eventually a kind of Western understanding of gender isn't a corollary to the breadwinner/homemaker binary.

Meanwhile, the latter was itself also a construction, part of a concerted effort by the government to get men back to work and keep women at home. I learned that what we think of as a housewife has conjured different ideas and ideals throughout decades and over the course of centuries. I also learned that whatever cultural changes occurred, women often ended up unhappier, stirring the pots with the short ends of the stick, with more freedoms generating greater expectations at each turn. Mostly I learned that we seem willing to subsidize almost every facet of modern life but motherhood.

If there's one thing researching the history of housewives has taught me, it's that quitting my job to dote on my children may not be what's best for them, or for society—but society should support me if that's what I chose to do. Wired for clans, humans are social creatures who were never intended to live alone in these nuclear families. "It takes a village" is such a cliché because it's true!

What's best for my own children, I've come to believe, is to be part of a caring, loving, extended community in which many adults look out for them and in which they're emotionally connected to many different children from diverse families, while at the same time their father and I have strong boundaries, morals, values, and endless wells of love for them. (These are our goals—I'm not saying we regularly meet them, beyond the endless well of love.) Housewives are not the answer to the ills many American families face; good parenting within thriving communities—supported by childcare, well-funded schools, and social programming—is.

To fix this mess, it's not just a matter of men doing more, but obviously that's an important place to begin. It's also a matter of changing our relationship to government and to community. It's a matter of lengthening our cultural memory to account for what historian Stephanie Coontz said: "Depending on support beyond the family has been the rule rather than the exception in American history."[2]

If there's one piece of information I can give you to empower yourself, it's this:

You were never meant to do this alone.

# ACKNOWLEDGMENTS

To my darling tradwife-ish husband, Alex: Thank you so much for your support, encouragement, enthusiasm, pushback, and meal-making, and for giving me time to write. Thank you to my beautiful, wonderful daughters, for understanding when I said, "Please, can you go ask Daddy instead?" 117 times over the course of the last year. To my four parents, Helaine Selin, Bob Rakoff, Beverly Davis, and Peter Davis: Thank you for spending so much time with the girls so I could work. They loved every minute of it. To my mother-in-law, Susan Sherwin, and my late father-in-law, Marty Sherwin: endless gratitude for your support, advice, and help paying for summer camp. I may not live in a family-friendly country, but I'm so grateful to have such a friendly family.

To my editors, Sofia Quintero and Krishan Trotman: Thank you so much for the marvelous notes, for the queries and suggestions, for making this a much, much better book than it was when I handed in the first draft. The whole team at Legacy Lit, including Amina Iro, Anjuli Johnson, Tara Kennedy, and Maya Lewis (sorry to those I may have left out!), has been wonderful. And to my agent, Eve Attermann:

Thank you for staying with me on this book-writing journey. May it continue for a long time!

To Aruni Kashyap, Adrienne Day, and Mary Bergstrom: Thank you for all the feedback, the calming-down, the pep talks. Thanks to Gretchen Aguiar for the Cult of Domesticity tips, and Dana Dillon for the long and very helpful text exchanges about these issues. Thank you Dave Mizner and Miri Navasky, for letting me hole up in your home for some solo editing time.

To Amy Knippenberg, Katie Capelli, Kristin Brenner, and Rachel Kieserman: Thank you for being my wonderful and supportive friends. In the words of Kelly Clarkson: My life would suck without you.

To all the women, and men, who shared their stories with me—I won't name you since I've protected some of your identities, but I am honored that you entrusted me with your thoughts and histories. And to all the scholars and thinkers whose brains I picked, who educated me about the complex history of housewives: I'm so grateful.

And finally, to my own once-single mom, master of knitting and cooking and grammar and hiking and hard things, and to all my single mom friends: I don't know how you do it, but I hope someday we make it easier on you.

# CITATIONS

## INTRODUCTION

1 Alana Joblin Ain, "Poet's Guide to Home Repairs" (*Rattle*, September 2023).
2 Anne Helen Petersen, "Other Countries Have Social Safety Nets. The U.S. Has Women," Substack newsletter, *Culture Study* (blog), November 11, 2020, https://annehelen.substack.com/p/other-countries-have -social-safety.
3 "Enjoli Commercial 1978—YouTube." Accessed September 19, 2022, https://www.youtube.com/watch?v=xRoGbiOGC54.
4 Philip H. Dougherty, "Secrets of Selling to Women | Advertising," *New York Times*, October 31, 1979. Accessed September 22, 2022, https://www.nytimes.com/1979/10/31/archives/advertising-secrets -of-selling-to-women.html.
5 "Employed Moms Say Working Is the Best Option," *Bizwomen: The Business Journals*, September 17, 2019. Accessed December 8, 2020, https://www.bizjournals.com/bizwomen/news/latest-news/2019/09 /employed-moms-say-working-is-best-option.html.
6 "An Unequal Division of Labor," *Center for American Progress* (blog), May 18, 2018. Accessed September 22, 2022, https://www.american progress.org/article/unequal-division-labor/.
7 Lara Bazelon, *Ambitious Like a Mother: Why Prioritizing Your Career Is Good for Your Kids* (New York: Spark, 2022), xiii.

8 Betty Friedan, *The Feminine Mystique* (New York: Norton, 2013).

9 Jeanine Santucci, "Trump to Women at Rally: 'We're Getting Your Husbands Back to Work,'" *USA Today,* October 27, 2020. Accessed November 9, 2020, https://www.usatoday.com/story/news/politics/2020/10/27/president-trump-rally-women-were-getting-your-husbands-back-work/3755175001/.

10 Sarah Jane Glynn, "Breadwinning Mothers Continue to Be the U.S. Norm," Center for American Progress, Mahy 10, 2019. Accessed September 15, 2022, https://www.americanprogress.org/article/breadwinning-mothers-continue-u-s-norm/.

11 Soo Youn, "Quitting Was Her Only Option. She Is One of 865,000 Women to Leave the Workforce Last Month," The Lily, October 7, 2020. Accessed February 1, 2023, https://www.thelily.com/quitting-was-her-only-option-she-is-one-of-865000-women-to-leave-the-workforce-last-month/.

12 "Employment Characteristics of Families–2022," https://www.bls.gov/news.release/pdf/famee.pdf.

13 Graeme Massie, "Donald Trump Claims Women Love Being Called 'Housewives' as He Begged for Their Support," *Independent*, October 15, 2020, https://www.independent.co.uk/news/world/americas/us-election-2020/trump-election-2020-suburban-women-support-b1055522.html.

14 Jason Lemon, "Trump Says 'Suburban Housewives' Support Him but Poll Shows Majority 'Strongly Disapprove,'" *Newsweek*, August 12, 2020, https://www.newsweek.com/trump-says-suburban-housewives-support-him-poll-shows-majority-strongly-disapprove-1524615.

15 Donald Trump (@realdonaldtrump), Twitter. Accessed September 15, 2022, https://twitter.com/realdonaldtrump/status/1286372175117791236.

16 D'Vera Cohn and Andrea Caumont, "7 Key Findings about Stay-at-Home Moms," Pew Research Center, April 8, 2014. Accessed September 15, 2022, https://www.pewresearch.org/fact-tank/2014/04/08/7-key-findings-about-stay-at-home-moms/.

17 Gretchen Livingston, "About 1 in 5 U.S. Moms and Dads Are

Stay-at-Home Parents," Pew Research Center, September 24, 2018. Accessed September 15, 2022, https://www.pewresearch.org/fact -tank/2018/09/24/stay-at-home-moms-and-dads-account-for -about-one-in-five-u-s-parents/.

## CHAPTER 1

1 Hailey Eber, "The Surprising Origin Story of Bravo's 'Real House-wives,'" *New York Post*, October 19, 2021. Accessed September 20, 2022, https://nypost.com/2021/10/19/the-surprising-origin-story-of -bravos-real-housewives/.

2 Kathryn VanArendonk, "Housewives: How TV Changed Our Defi-nition of the Word," Vulture, January 17, 2018. Accessed September 20, 2022, https://www.vulture.com/2018/01/what-does-housewife -mean-anymore.html.

3 "Philip G. Monzon Obituary (1940–2022) *Arizona Daily Star*," Leg-acy.com. Accessed September 20, 2022, https://www.legacy.com/us /obituaries/tucson/name/philip-monzon-obituary?id=34678802.

4 "The Harried Housewife: Lemon Cheesecake Tarts," WKTV.com, April 27, 2001. Accessed September 20, 2022, https://www.wktv .com/community/harried-housewife/the-harried-housewife-lemon -cheesecake-tarts/video_2c786b25-623a-515c-bebf-8a064339cda3 .html.

5 Libby Torres, "Hulu's 'Candy': Where the Real-Life Candy Montgom-ery Is Now, and What Happened to Betty Gore's Children," Insider, May 13, 2022. https://www.insider.com/where-is-candy-montgomery -now-hulu-series-jessica-biel-2022-5.

6 Dele Ogunyemi, "Gunmen Abduct Housewife, Children in Delta Community," *Punch Newspapers*, May 14, 2022, https://punchng .com/gunmen-abduct-housewife-children-in-delta-community/.

7 Daily Trust, "How Bandits Who Plotted to Rape Housewife Were Nabbed in Kaduna Forest," Daily Trust, May 15, 2022, https://daily trust.com/how-bandits-who-plotted-to-rape-housewife-were-nabbed -in-kaduna-forest/.

8 "Housewife Stabbed Dead in Ctg," United News of Bangladesh, May 8,

2022. Accessed September 20, 2022, https://unb.com.bd/category /bangladesh/housewife-stabbed-dead-in-ctg/92437.

9 "One Arrested over Rape of Housewife in Pirojpur," New Age Bangladesh, May 16, 2002. Accessed September 20, 2022, https://www .newagebd.net/article/170646/one-arrested-over-rape-of-housewife -in-pirojpur.

10 "Croatian Domacica Biscuits Spark Sexism, Feminism Debates." Accessed May 18, 2023, https://www.total-croatia-news.com/made -in-croatia/62578-croatian-domacica-biscuits.

11 "Housewife," Online Etymology Dictionary. Accessed September 20, 2022, https://www.etymonline.com/word/housewife.

12 "Woman," Online Etymology Dictionary. Accessed September 20, 2022, https://www.etymonline.com/word/woman.

13 Anatoly Liberman, "Were Ancient 'Wives' Women?," *OUPblog*, October 12, 2011, https://blog.oup.com/2011/10/wife/.

14 "From 'Housewife' to 'Hussy,'" *Grammarphobia* (blog), June 1, 2016. Accessed September 20, 2022, https://www.grammarphobia.com /blog/2016/06/housewife-hussy.html.

15 Ad in *The Morning Call* (San Francisco), April 28, 1890, Page 6, Image 6, Chronicling America, Library of Congress. Accessed September 20, 2022, https://chroniclingamerica.loc.gov/lccn/sn94052989/1890-04 -28/ed-1/seq-6/.

16 Ad in the *Sunday School Times*, May 3, 1890. Google Books. Accessed September 20, 2022, https://www.google.com/books /edition/Sunday_School_Times/Z_4iAQAAMAAJ?hl=en&gbpv =1&dq=%22The+housewife+publishing+co%22+ny+city&pg =PA288&printsec=frontcover.

17 Ad in the *Huntsville Gazette* (Huntsville, AL), February 18, 1888, Image 2, Chronicling America, Library of Congress, https://chronicling america.loc.gov/lccn/sn84020151/1888-02-18/ed-1/seq-2/.

18 Ad in the *Huntsville Gazette* (Huntsville, AL), December 12, 1891, Image 4, Chronicling America, Library of Congress, https://chronicling america.loc.gov/lccn/sn84020151/1891-12-12/ed-1/seq-4/.

19 "Housewives' League near Serious Split," *New York Times*, November 17, 2015. Accessed September 20, 2022, https://timesmachine .nytimes.com/timesmachine/1915/11/17/105047432.pdf.

20 Eleanor Gurnett, "THE HOUSEWIVES' LEAGUE," *Public Health Journal* 5, no. 3 (1914): 168–71. http://www.jstor.org/stable/45246142.

21 Wm. H. Bell, "Open Letter," *Afro-American Courier* (Yazoo City, Miss.), November 1, 1941, Library of Congress, Christmas Holiday Issue, Image 4, https://chroniclingamerica.loc.gov/lccn/sn88067171/1941 -11-01/ed-1/seq-4/.

22 Conor Friedersdorf, "A Trove of History as 1970s Housewives Lived It," *The Atlantic*, January 25, 2014. Accessed September 20, 2022, https://www.theatlantic.com/politics/archive/2014/01/a-trove-of -history-as-1970s-housewives-lived-it/283307/.

23 Jessica Grose, "Why Do We Call Them 'Stay-at-Home Moms'? There Must Be a Better Term," Slate, March 26, 2013. Accessed September 20, 2022, https://slate.com/human-interest/2013/03/housewife -homemaker-or-stay-at-home-mom-what-should-we-call-women -who-don-t-do-paid-work.html.

24 Mary Johnson, "The Magazine Exec Who Gave a Voice to Working Moms," *Bizwomen*, September 23, 2016. Accessed September 20, 2022, https://www.bizjournals.com/bizwomen/news/profiles -strategies/2016/09/media-the-magazine-exec-who-gave-a-voice -to.html.

25 Grose, "Why Do We Call Them 'Stay-at-Home Moms'?"

26 Stephanie Coontz, *The Way We Never Were: American Families and the Nostalgia Trap* (New York: Basic Books, 2000), xxix.

27 Jennifer Jolly, "LinkedIn Adds Stay-at-Home-Mom to Job Titles List; Will It Help Women Re-enter the Workforce?," *USA Today*, April 17, 2022. Accessed September 28, 2022, https://www.usatoday.com /story/tech/2022/04/17/linkedin-stay-home-mom-dad-official-job -titles/7332804001/.

28 S. E. Cupp (@secupp), Twitter, May 9, 2022. Accessed September 20, 2022, https://twitter.com/secupp/status/1523870211048366080.

29 Coontz, *The Way We Never Were*, xxix.

30 Effervesser, "Is a 'Stepford' Wife Fetish a Thing?," Reddit Post, *R/ AskRedditAfterDark*, December 31, 2018, www.reddit.com/r/AskRed ditAfterDark/comments/abac4b/is_a_stepford_wife_fetish_a_thing/.

31 Noona Hora (@HoraNoona), Twitter. Accessed September 20, 2022, https://twitter.com/HoraNoona.

## CHAPTER 2

1 Rebecca Solnit, "The Housewife Theory of History," *Orion*, n.d. Accessed September 21, 2022, https://orionmagazine.org/article/the -housewife-theory-of-history/.

2 Randall Haas et al., "Female Hunters of the Early Americas," *Science-Advances* 6, no. 45, November 4, 2020. Accessed December 3, 2021, https://www.science.org/doi/10.1126/sciadv.abd0310.

3 Charlotte Hedenstierna-Jonson et al., "A Female Viking Warrior Confirmed by Genomics," *American Journal of Physical Anthropology* 164, no. 4, September 8, 2017. Wiley Online Library. Accessed September 19, 2022, https://onlinelibrary.wiley.com/doi/10.1002 /ajpa.23308.

4 "Viking Warrior Queen," *Secrets of the Dead*, season 18, episode 4, PBS. Accessed September 29, 2022, https://www.pbs.org/wnet /secrets/viking-warrior-queen/5180/.

5 Akson Russian Science Communication Association, "Archaeologists Found the Burial of Scythian Amazon with a Head Dress on Don," EurekAlert!, AAAS, December 25, 2019. Accessed September 19, 2022, https://www.eurekalert.org/news-releases/517672.

6 Wallace Ludel, "Archaeologists Uncover Evidence That Legendary Amazons Were Based on Real Women Warriors," *The Art Newspaper*, January 22, 2020, https://www.theartnewspaper.com/2020/01/22 /archaeologists-uncover-evidence-that-legendary-amazons-were -based-on-real-women-warriors.

7 Scott Armstrong Elias, "The Conversation: First Americans Lived on Bering Land Bridge for Thousands of Years," *Scientific American*, March 4, 2014. Accessed November 15, 2021, https://www.scientificamerican .com/article/first-americans-lived-on-bering-land-bridge-for-thou sands-of-years/.

8 Haas, "Female Hunters of the Early Americas."

9 Ludel, "Archaeologists Uncover Evidence That Legendary Amazons Were Based on Real Women Warriors."

10 Heather E. Heying, *A Hunter-Gatherer's Guide to the 21st Century:*

*Evolution and the Challenges of Modern Life* (Portfolio, 2021), 113–14, https://libcat.arlingtonva.us/Record/240858.

11  Jeanine M. Pfeiffer and Ramona J. Butz, "Assessing Cultural and Ecological Variation in Ethnobiological Research: The Importance of Gender," *Journal of Ethnobiology* 25, no. 2 (September 2005): 240–78, https://doi.org/10.2993/0278-0771_2005_25_240_acaevi_2.0.co_2.

12  *Baka, People of the Forest* (Washington, D.C.: The Society, 1990).

13  Hetty Jo Brumbach and Robert Jarvenpa, "Ethnoarchaeology of Subsistence Space and Gender: A Subarctic Dene Case," *American Antiquity* 62, no. 3 (1997): 414–36, https://doi.org/10.2307/282163.

14  Pfeiffer and Butz, "Assessing Cultural and Ecological Variation in Ethnobiological Research."

15  Irena Lazar et al., "The Archaeologist of the Future Is Likely to Be a Woman: Age and Gender Patterns in European Archaeology," *Archaeologies* 10 (December 1, 2014): 257–80, https://doi.org/10.1007/s11759-014-9263-6.

16  Haas, "Female Hunters of the Early Americas."

17  Michael Balter, "Ancient DNA Yields Unprecedented Insights into Mysterious Chaco Civilization," *Scientific American*, November 22, 2017. Accessed November 14, 2021, https://www.scientificamerican.com/article/ancient-dna-yields-unprecedented-insights-into-mysterious-chaco-civilization/.

18  "Chaco Culture National Historical Park," U.S. National Park Service. Accessed September 19, 2022, https://www.nps.gov/chcu/index.htm.

19  Douglas J. Kennett et al., "Archaeogenomic Evidence Reveals Prehistoric Matrilineal Dynasty," *Nature Communications* 8, no. 1 (February 21, 2017): 14115, https://doi.org/10.1038/ncomms14115.

20  Hannah Booth, "The Kingdom of Women: The Society Where a Man Is Never the Boss," *Guardian*, April 1, 2017. Accessed September 19, 2022, https://www.theguardian.com/lifeandstyle/2017/apr/01/the-kingdom-of-women-the-tibetan-tribe-where-a-man-is-never-the-boss.

21  Sabrina P. Ramet, *Gender Reversals and Gender Cultures: Anthropological and Historical Perspectives* (Psychology Press, 1996), 58.

## CHAPTER 3

1 Michele W. Berger, "How the Appliance Boom Moved More Women into the Workforce," Penn Today, January 30, 2019. Accessed September 20, 2022, https://penntoday.upenn.edu/news/how-appliance -boom-moved-more-women-workforce.

2 Glenna Matthews, *"Just a Housewife": The Rise and Fall of Domesticity in America* (New York: Oxford University Press, 1987), 4.

3 Matthews, *"Just a Housewife,"* 6.

4 Matthews, *"Just a Housewife,"* 4.

5 Matthews, *"Just a Housewife,"* 4.

6 Coontz, *The Way We Never Were*, 86.

7 Coontz, *The Way We Never Were*, 13.

8 Coontz, *The Way We Never Were*, 85.

9 Coontz, *The Way We Never Were*, 86.

10 Coontz, *The Way We Never Were*, 3.

11 Kate Egner Gruber, "Republican Motherhood," American Battlefield Trust, February 3, 2022, https://www.battlefields.org/learn/articles /republican-motherhood.

12 "Mary Wollstonecraft on Women's Education," Online Library of Liberty. Accessed May 21, 2023, https://oll.libertyfund.org/quote/mary -wollstone-craft-womens-education.

13 Rush, "Thoughts upon Female Education," Boston, 1787. Accessed September 20, 2022, https://www.swarthmore.edu/SocSci/rbannis1 /AIH19th/female.html.

14 Pamela Smith Hill, "Laura Ingalls Wilder Historical Timeline," *Little House on the Prairie* (blog), December 28, 2018, https://littlehouse ontheprairie.com/history-timeline-of-laura-ingalls-wilder/.

15 Coontz, *The Way We Never Were*, 90.

16 John Radzilowski, "Poles," Encyclopedia of the Great Plains. Accessed September 27, 2022, http://plainshumanities.unl.edu/encyclopedia /doc/egp.ea.030.

17 Coontz, *The Way We Never Were*, 90.

18 Coontz, *The Way We Never Were*, 88.

19 Coontz, *The Way We Never Were*, 87–89.

20 Dolores Hayden, *Redesigning the American Dream: The Future of Housing, Work, and Family Life* (W. W. Norton & Company, 2002), 87.

21 Janet L. Yellen, "The History of Women's Work and Wages and How It Has Created Success for Us All," *Brookings* (blog), May 7, 2020, https://www.brookings.edu/essay/the-history-of-womens-work-and-wages-and-how-it-has-created-success-for-us-all/.

22 Rosalind Rosenberg and Eric Foner, *Divided Lives* (New York: Farrar, Straus and Giroux, 1992), 14.

23 Lucinda MacKethan, "The Cult of Domesticity," n.d., 31.

24 "Women in Law, History and Literature: A Study of the Historical and Contemporary Legal Status of Women in American Society as Infused with the Liberal Arts – Faculty Resource Network." Accessed May 18, 2023, https://frn.hosting.nyu.edu/symposium/november-2013/women-in-law-history-and-literature-a-study-of-the-historical-and-contemporary-legal-status-of-women-in-american-society-as-infused-with-the-liberal-arts/.

25 Coontz, *The Way We Never Were*, 50.

26 Coontz, *The Way We Never Were*, 4.

27 Coontz, *The Way We Never Were*, 65.

28 Coontz, *The Way We Never Were*, 52.

## CHAPTER 4

1 Elaine Tyler May, *Homeward Bound: American Families in the Cold War Era* (Basic Books, 2017), 50.

2 National Housewives' League of America, "National Housewives' League of America Records, circa 1918–1996," University of Michigan Bentley Historical Library. Accessed September 21, 2022, https://findingaids.lib.umich.edu/catalog/umich-bhl-0080.

3 Annelise Orleck, "'We Are That Mythical Thing Called the Public': Militant Housewives during the Great Depression," *Feminist Studies* 19, no. 1 (1993): 148, https://doi.org/10.2307/3178357.

4 Eleanor Roosevelt, "It's Up to the Women" (Bold Type Books, 2017). Accessed September 20, 2022, https://www.google.com/books/edition/It_s_Up_to_the_Women/GLLUDAAAQBAJ.

5 "Great Depression Facts," FDR Presidential Library & Museum.

Accessed September 20, 2022, https://www.fdrlibrary.org/great-depres sion-facts.

6 "Marriage Rates in the United States, 1900-2018." Accessed September 20, 2022, https://www.cdc.gov/nchs/data/hestat/marriage_rate_2018 /marriage_rate_2018.htm.

7 Gaby Galvin, "U.S. Marriage Rate Drops to Record Low," *US News and World Report*, April 29, 2020. Accessed September 20, 2022, https:// www.usnews.com/news/healthiest-communities/articles/2020-04 -29/us-marriage-rate-drops-to-record-low.

8 U.S. Department of Labor, "#15–The Economic Situation of Negroes in the United States," HathiTrust Digital Library. Accessed September 20, 2022, https://babel.hathitrust.org/cgi/pt?id=umn.31951d0339743 6s&view=1up&seq=15.

9 May, *Homeward Bound*, 38–40.

10 May, *Homeward Bound*, 38.

11 Coontz, *The Way We Never Were*, 9.

12 Spencer Howard, "The Economy Act of 1932," *Hoover Heads* (blog), July 29, 2020, https://hoover.blogs.archives.gov/2020/07/29/the-econ omy-act-of-1932/.

13 May, *Homeward Bound*, 48.

14 William Henry Chafe, *The Unfinished Journey: America Since World War II* (Oxford University Press, 2003), 15.

15 Jonathan Rowe, "What History Books Left Out About Depression Era Co-Ops," *Yes!* magazine, September 14, 2018. Accessed September 21, 2022, https://www.yesmagazine.org/issue/issues-5000-years-of -empire/2018/09/14/what-history-books-left-out-about-depression -era-co-ops.

16 George D. Tselos, "Self-Help and Sauerkraut: The Organized Unem- ployed, Inc. of Minneapolis," *Minnesota History*, Winter 1977, 16.

17 "International Ladies Garment Workers Union," Shalvi/Hyman Ency- clopedia of Jewish Women, Jewish Women's Archive. Accessed Sep- tember 21, 2022, https://jwa.org/encyclopedia/article/international -ladies-garment-workers-union.

18 "Activist Clara Shavelson Leads Butcher Shop Boycott, May 27, 1935," This Week in History, Jewish Women's Archive. Accessed January 5, 2023, https://jwa.org/thisweek/may/27/1935/clara-shavelson.

19 Emily E. LB. Twarog, *Politics of the Pantry: Housewives, Food, and Consumer Protest in Twentieth-Century America* (Oxford University Press, 2017).

20 Sue Weston and Susie Rosenbluth, "Radical Housewives: Twentieth-Century Jewish Women's Activism on the Lower East Side and Beyond," The Jewish Voice & Opinion. Accessed January 5, 2023, https://thejewishvoiceandopinion.com/radical-housewives-twentieth-century-jewish-womens-activism-on-the-lower-east-side-and-beyond/.

21 Damon Mitchell, "These 1930s Housewives Were the Godmothers of Radical Consumer Activism," Narratively Hidden History. Accessed September 20, 2022, https://narratively.com/these-1930s-housewives-were-the-godmothers-of-radical-consumer-activism/.

22 Claire Goldberg Moses, Heidi I. Hartmann, and Heidi Hartmann, *U.S. Women in Struggle: A Feminist Studies Anthology* (University of Illinois Press, 1995), 202.

23 Mitchell, "These 1930s Housewives Were the Godmothers of Radical Consumer Activism."

24 Georg Schrode, "Mary Zuk and the Detroit Meat Strike of 1935," *Polish American Studies* 43, no. 2 (1986): 5–39, http://www.jstor.org/stable/20148202.

25 Mitchell, "These 1930s Housewives Were the Godmothers of Radical Consumer Activism."

26 Annelise Orleck, *Rethinking American Women's Activism* (Routledge, 2022), 47.

27 Associated Press, "Buyers Trampled by Meat Strikers; Women Picket Butcher Shops in Detroit Suburb, Slap, Scratch, Pull Hair," *New York Times*, July 28, 1935. Accessed September 21, 2022, https://www.nytimes.com/1935/07/28/archives/buyers-trampled-by-meat-strikers-women-picket-butcher-shops-in.html.

28 Schrode, "Mary Zuk and the Detroit Meat Strike of 1935," 9.

29 Moses, Hartmann, and Hartmann, *U.S. Women in Struggle*, 203.

30 Moses, Hartmann, and Hartmann, *U.S. Women in Struggle*, 202.

31 Annelise Orleck, *Common Sense and a Little Fire: Women and Working-Class Politics in the United States, 1900–1965* (University of North Carolina Press, 2000), 213.

32 *Training to Be Housewives, 1930's. Archive Film 96082*, 2016, https://www.youtube.com/watch?v=-1LeQLFVQ1I.

33 Solnit, "The Housewife Theory of History."

34 Orleck, *Rethinking American Women's Activism.*

35 "How Journalists Ella Baker and Marvel Jackson Cooke Exposed Domestic Work's 'Slave Market,'" New-York Historical Society, September 1, 2021. Accessed September 21, 2022, https://www.nyhistory.org/blogs/how-journalists-ella-baker-and-marvel-jackson-cooke-exposed-domestic-works-slave-market.

36 The Crisis Publishing Company Inc. *The Crisis* (The Crisis Publishing Company, Inc., 1935), 330.

37 *What a Housewife Must Know (1934)*, 2016, https://www.youtube.com/watch?v=xcqjgQj6tJk.

38 Orleck, "We Are That Mythical Thing Called the Public."

39 Mitchell, "These 1930s Housewives Were the Godmothers of Radical Consumer Activism."

40 Herb Boyd, "Mrs. Fannie B. Peck, Founder of the National Housewives' League," New York Amsterdam News, June 29, 2017. Accessed September 21, 2022, https://amsterdamnews.com/news/2017/06/29/mrs-fannie-b-peck-founder-national-housewives-leag/.

## CHAPTER 5

1 "'The Donna Reed Show' Just a Housewife (TV Episode 1960)–IMDb." Accessed September 21, 2022, https://www.imdb.com/title/tt0564243/.

2 Coontz, *The Way We Never Were*, xxii.

3 Hayden, *Redesigning the American Dream*, 21.

4 Garth Jowett and Victoria O'Donnell, *Propaganda and Persuasion* (Sage, 2006), 207–358.

5 Sarah Stroman, "Food, Comfort, and Care: Women Workers at Kaiser's WWII Child Service Centers," Oregon Historical Society, March 22, 2022. Accessed September 21, 2022, https://www.ohs.org/blog/women-wwii-childcare-workers.cfm.

6 Stephen J. Dubner, "The Coolest Child Care Program You've Never

Heard Of," *Freakonomics* (blog), January 6, 2014, https://freako nomics.com/2014/01/the-coolest-child-care-program-youve-never -heard-of/.

7 Chris M Herbst, "Universal Child Care, Maternal Employment, and Children's Long-Run Outcomes: Evidence from the U.S. Lanham Act of 1940," n.d., 63.

8 Office for Emergency Management. Office of War Information. Domestic Operations Branch. Bureau of Special Services, *WOMEN IN WAR INDUSTRY*, Series: World War II Posters, 1932–1947, 1942.

9 May, *Homeward Bound*, 68.

10 Office for Emergency Management. Office of War Information. Domestic Operations Branch. Bureau of Special Services, *House- wives! Save Waste Fats for Explosives!*, Series: World War II Posters, 1932–1947, 1942.

11 Rosenberg and Foner, *Divided Lives*, 131.

12 Christina A. Samuels, "Study: 1940s-Era Universal Child Care Pro- gram Had Positive Effects on Children," EducationWeek, January 15, 2014. Accessed September 21, 2022, https://www.edweek.org/teaching -learning/study-1940s-era-universal-child-care-program-had-posi tive-effects-on-children/2014/01.

13 Coontz, *The Way We Never Were*, 33.

14 Betty Friedan, "Excerpts from *The Feminine Mystique* (1963)," n.d., 4.

15 May, *Homeward Bound*, 165.

16 May, *Homeward Bound*, 159.

17 May, *Homeward Bound*, 66.

18 Coontz, *The Way We Never Were*, 30–32.

19 Rebecca Francis Isaacs, "The Feminine Mystake: Betty Friedan and the Dogma of Domesticity in 1950s America," ETheses Repository. Accessed September 29, 2022, https://nanopdf.com/download/the -feminine-mystake-etheses-repository_pdf.

20 May, *Homeward Bound*, 151.

21 Coontz, *The Way We Never Were*, 35.

22 Ferdinand Lundberg and Marynia Lundberg, *Modern Woman: The Lost Sex* (New York: Harper & Brothers Publishers, 1947), v.

23 May, *Homeward Bound*, 100.

24  May, *Homeward Bound*, 139.

25  May, *Homeward Bound*, 96.

26  May, *Homeward Bound*, 141.

27  May, *Homeward Bound*, 204.

28  May, *Homeward Bound*, 109.

29  "FBI Law Enforcement Bulletin," January, 1957.

30  May, *Homeward Bound*, 138.

31  "Biography: J. Edgar Hoover," American Experience, PBS.org. Accessed February 22, 2023, https://www.pbs.org/wgbh/americanexperience /features/eleanor-hoover/.

32  Coontz, *The Way We Never Were*, xxviii.

33  May, *Homeward Bound*, 147–49.

34  Coontz, *The Way We Never Were*, 96.

35  Hayden, *Redesigning the American Dream*, 23.

36  May, *Homeward Bound*, 171.

37  Hayden, *Redesigning the American Dream*, 29.

38  Hayden, *Redesigning the American Dream*, 23.

39  Myron Orfield and Thomas F. Luce, "America's Racially Diverse Suburbs: Opportunities and Challenges," *Housing Policy Debate* 23, no. 2 (April 2013): 395–430, https://doi.org/10.1080/10511482.2012.756 822.

40  William H. Whyte, *The Organization Man* (University of Pennsylvania Press, 2013), 300.

41  May, *Homeward Bound*, 95.

42  May, *Homeward Bound*, 164–67.

43  History.com Editors, "The Interstate Highway System," History, June 7, 2019. Accessed September 21, 2022, https://www.history.com /topics/us-states/interstate-highway-system.

44  May, *Homeward Bound*, 109.

45  May, *Homeward Bound*, 107.

46  May, *Homeward Bound*, 105.

47  Federal Civil Defense Administration. Region I. 1951–1958 (Predecessor) and Office of Civil and Defense Mobilization. Region 1. 1958–1961, *Governor Muskie's Family Prepare Their Grandmas Pantry*, Series: Civil Defense Photographs, 1947–1962, 1951.

48 May, *Homeward Bound*, 105.
49 Peter Kerr, "Donna Reed, Oscar Winner and TV Star, Is Dead at 64," *New York Times*, January 15, 1986. Accessed September 21, 2022, https://www.nytimes.com/1986/01/15/obituaries/donna-reed-oscar -winner-and-tv-star-is-dead-at-64.html.
50 "Enjoli Commercial 1978," YouTube.

## CHAPTER 6

1 James P. Caruso and Jason P. Sheehan, "Psychosurgery, Ethics, and Media: A History of Walter Freeman and the Lobotomy," *Neuro-surgical Focus* 43, no. 3 (September 1, 2017): E6, https://doi.org /10.3171/2017.6.FOCUS17257.
2 Jack El-hai, "The Lobotomist," *Washington Post*, February 4, 2001. Accessed September 22, 2022, https://www.washingtonpost.com /archive/lifestyle/magazine/2001/02/04/the-lobotomist/630196c4 -0f70-4427-832a-ce04959a6dc8/.
3 Hugh Levinson, "The Strange and Curious History of Lobotomy," BBC News, November 8, 2011. Accessed September 22, 2022, https:// www.bbc.com/news/magazine-15629160.
4 Emma Dibdin, "The Controversial History of the Lobotomy," Psych-Central, May 6, 2022. Accessed September 22, 2022, https://psych central.com/blog/the-surprising-history-of-the-lobotomy.
5 Caruso and Sheehan, "Psychosurgery, Ethics, and Media."
6 Walter Freeman and James W. Watts, "Prefrontal Lobotomy in the Treatment of Mental Disorders," *Southern Medical Journal* 30, no. 1 (1937): 23–31.
7 W. Freeman and J. W. Watts, *Psychosurgery* (Oxford, England: Charles C. Thomas, 1942).
8 "Egas Moniz—Facts," NobelPrize.org. Accessed September 22, 2022, https://www.nobelprize.org/prizes/medicine/1949/moniz/facts/.
9 Andrea Tone and Mary Koziol, "(F)Ailing Women in Psychiatry: Lessons from a Painful Past," *CMAJ: Canadian Medical Association Journal* 190, no. 20 (May 22, 2018): E624–25, https://doi.org/10.1503 /cmaj.171277.

10 Tom Buckley, "Transsexuality Expert, 90, Recalls 'Maverick' Career," *New York Times*, January 11, 1975, sec. Archives, https://www.nytimes.com/1975/01/11/archives/transsexuality-expert-90-recalls-maverick-career.html.

11 Tone and Koziol, "(F)Ailing Women in Psychiatry."

12 Jenell Johnson, *American Lobotomy* (University of Michigan Press, 2014), 50.

13 Coontz, *The Way We Never Were*, 35.

14 Caruso and Sheehan, "Psychosurgery, Ethics, and Media."

15 Tone and Koziol, "(F)Ailing Women in Psychiatry."

16 Johnson, *American Lobotomy*, 58.

17 Bob Ostertag, *Sex Science Self: A Social History of Estrogen, Testosterone, and Identity* (University of Massachusetts Press, 2016), 27.

18 Carol S. North, "The Classification of Hysteria and Related Disorders: Historical and Phenomenological Considerations," *Behavioral Sciences* 5, no. 4 (November 6, 2015): 496–517, https://doi.org/10.3390/bs5040496.

19 Robert W. Baloh, "Early Ideas on Hysteria," in *Medically Unexplained Symptoms* (Copernicus, Cham, 2020).

20 Ada McVean, "The History of Hysteria," McGill University Office for Science and Society, July 31, 2017. Accessed September 22, 2022, https://www.mcgill.ca/oss/article/history-quackery/history-hysteria.

21 Baloh, "Early Ideas on Hysteria."

22 Ostertag, *Sex Science Self*, 27.

23 Emmanuel Broussolle et al., "History of Physical and 'Moral' Treatment of Hysteria," *Hysteria: The Rise of an Enigma* 35 (2014): 181–97, https://doi.org/10.1159/000360242.

24 Ostertag, *Sex Science Self*, 28.

25 *Huntsville Gazette* (Huntsville, AL), April 11, 1885, Chronicling America, Library of Congress, https://chroniclingamerica.loc.gov/lccn/sn84020151/1885-04-11/ed-1/seq-4/.

26 El-hai, "The Lobotomist."

27 "The Lobotomist," *American Experience*, PBS. Accessed September 22, 2022, http://www.shoppbs.pbs.org/wgbh/amex/lobotomist/stories/ionesco_qt_lo.html.

28  "My Lobotomy," StoryCorps. Accessed September 22, 2022, https://storycorps.org/stories/my-lobotomy/.

29  "A Lobotomy Timeline," NPR, November 16, 2005, https://www.npr.org/templates/story/story.php?storyId=5014576.

30  "My Lobotomy," StoryCorps."

31  "The Lobotomist," *American Experience.*

32  "'My Lobotomy': Howard Dully's Journey," *NPR*, November 16, 2005, https://www.npr.org/2005/11/16/5014080/my-lobotomy-howard-dullys-journey.

33  Paula Schleis, "The Drug That Became Prescription for Trouble," *Washington Post,* May 8, 2005, https://www.washingtonpost.com/archive/lifestyle/2005/05/08/the-drug-that-became-prescription-for-trouble/2ebf91cc-a16c-4b38-881c-0c4112e8aa0c/.

34  tiadmin, "Mother's Little Helper at 50," *Proto* Magazine, September 22, 2013, https://protomag.com/medical-history/anniversary-valium-turns-50/.

35  David Herzberg, "'The Pill You Love Can Turn on You': Feminism, Tranquilizers, and the Valium Panic of the 1970s," *American Quarterly* 58, no. 1 (2006): 79–103, http://www.jstor.org/stable/40068349.

36  Jonathan M. Metzl, "'Mother's Little Helper': The Crisis of Psychoanalysis and the Miltown Resolution," *Gender & History* 15, no. 2 (August 2003): 228–55, https://doi.org/10.1111/1468-0424.00300.

37  tiadmin, "Mother's Little Helper at 50."

38  Stephen Taylor, "The Suburban Neurosis," n.d., 1.

39  May, *Homeward Bound*, 174.

40  H. J. H. Claassens, "'Housewives Disease' a Modern Psychosomatic Syndrome," *South African Medical Journal* 38, no. 7 (1964): 533, https://www.ajol.info/index.php/samj/article/view/181037.

41  Ruth Cooperstock et al., "Some Social Meanings of Tranquilizer Use," *Sociology of Health & Illness* 1, no. 3 (1979): 331–47, https://doi.org/10.1111/1467-9566.ep11007101.

42  Paul R. Albert, "Why Is Depression More Prevalent in Women?" *Journal of Psychiatry & Neuroscience : JPN* 40, no. 4 (July 2015): 219–21, https://doi.org/10.1503/jpn.150205.

43  Metzl, "'Mother's Little Helper.'"

44 Jonathan Metzl, *Prozac on the Couch: Prescribing Gender in the Era of Wonder Drugs* (Duke University Press, 2003), 71.

45 Herzberg, "The Pill You Love Can Turn on You."

46 Herzberg, "The Pill You Love Can Turn on You."

47 Judith Warner, "Valium Invalidation: What If Mother (and Father) Really *Did* Need a Little Help?" *Time*, October 5, 2012. Accessed September 22, 2022, https://ideas.time.com/2012/10/05/valium-invalidation-what-if-mother-and-father-really-did-need-a-little-help/.

48 "The Lobotomist," *American Experience.*

## CHAPTER 7

1 News Office, "Fifty Years Later, Friedan Survey Finds Women's Roles Changed, Frustrations Remain," Smith College, June 18, 2007. Accessed January 12, 2023, https://www.smith.edu/newsoffice/releases/BettyFriedan.html.

2 Betty Friedan, *The Feminine Mystique* (New York: Norton, 2013), 35.

3 Friedan, *The Feminine Mystique*, 1.

4 Rachel Shteir, "Why We Can't Stop Talking About Betty Friedan," *New York Times*, February 3, 2021. Accessed September 22, 2022, https://www.nytimes.com/2021/02/03/us/betty-friedan-feminism-legacy.html.

5 "PHT (Putting Husband Through) Degrees Being Awarded at the University of Florida," University of Florida Archives, 1960. Accessed January 17, 2023, https://original-ufdc.uflib.ufl.edu/UF00032286/00001/citation.

6 "Awakening," YouTube. Accessed September 22, 2022, https://www.youtube.com/watch?v=0A1UdwGCZUM.

7 Friedan, *The Feminine Mystique*, 19.

8 Rae Alexandra, "The Extraordinarily Sexist History of Laundry Detergent Commercials," KQED, February 6, 2018. Accessed September 22, 2022, https://www.kqed.org/pop/101669/the-extraordinarily-sexist-history-of-laundry-detergent-commercials.

9 Hayden, *Redesigning the American Dream*, 95.

10 Caitlin Flanagan, "Housewife Confidential," *Atlantic*, September 1,

2003, https://www.theatlantic.com/magazine/archive/2003/09/house
wife-confidential/302778/.

11 Friedan, *The Feminine Mystique*, 24.

12 Friedan, *The Feminine Mystique*, 405.

13 America: A Narrative History, 6th Edition, Chapter 34; Inventing America, Chapter 30; Give Me Liberty, Chapter 25 "Women's Liberation: The Feminine Mystique (1963)." Accessed September 22, 2022, https://wwnorton.com/college/history/archive/reader/trial/direc tory/1959_1970/18_ndh.htm.

14 Louis Menand, "Books as Bombs," *New Yorker*, January 16, 2011. Accessed September 22, 2022, https://www.newyorker.com/maga zine/2011/01/24/books-as-bombs.

15 Coontz, *The Way We Never Were*, 40.

16 Friedan, *The Feminine Mystique*, 377.

17 Friedan, *The Feminine Mystique*, 406, 412.

18 Friedan, *The Feminine Mystique*, 430.

19 Coontz, *The Way We Never Were*, 90.

20 "Labor Force Participation–an Overview | ScienceDirect Topics," Marriage and the Dual-career Family: Cultural Concerns. L. J. Waite, in International Encyclopedia of the Social & Behavioral Sciences, 2001. Accessed September 22, 2022, https://www.sciencedirect.com /topics/social-sciences/labor-force-participation.

21 Bernard Ineichen, "Neurotic Wives in a Modern Residential Suburb: A Sociological Profile," *Social Science & Medicine (1967)* 9, no. 8 (August 1, 1975): 481–87, https://doi.org/10.1016/0037-7856 (75)90077-3.

22 Ali Haggett, "'Desperate Housewives' and the Domestic Environment in Post-War Britain: Individual Perspectives." *Oral History* 37, no. 1 (2009): 53–60.

23 Friedan, *The Feminine Mystique*, 439.

24 Katie McLaughlin, "5 Things Women Couldn't Do in the 1960s," CNN.com, August 25, 2014. Accessed September 22, 2022, https:// edition.cnn.com/2014/08/07/living/sixties-women-5-things/.

25 "Equal Credit Opportunity Act," Ballotpedia. Accessed September 22, 2022, https://ballotpedia.org/Equal_Credit_Opportunity_Act.

26 Kyla Bishop, "A Reflection on the History of Sexual Assault Laws in the

United States," *Arkansas Journal of Social Change and Public Service*, April 16, 2018, https://ualr.edu/socialchange/2018/04/15/reflection-history-sexual-assault-laws-united-states/.

27 Friedan, *The Feminine Mystique*, 430.

28 Moses, Hartmann, and Hartmann, *U.S. Women in Struggle*, 215.

29 "Commission on the Status of Women," Encyclopedia.com. Accessed September 22, 2022, https://www.encyclopedia.com/history/encyclopedias-almanacs-transcripts-and-maps/commission-status-women.

30 U.S. Department of Labor, "The Negro Family: The Case for National Action," March 1965. Accessed January 11, 2023, https://www.dol.gov/general/aboutdol/history/webid-moynihan.

31 Robert Staples, "The Myth of the Black Matriarchy," *The Black Scholar* 12, no. 6 (1981): 26–34, https://www.jstor.org/stable/41066853.

32 Daniel Patrick Moynihan, *Daniel Patrick Moynihan: A Portrait in Letters of an American Visionary* (PublicAffairs, 2010), 96.

33 "Blacks in the U.S. Army, Then and Now." Accessed January 11, 2023, https://api.army.mil/e2/c/downloads/572478.pdf.

34 May, *Homeward Bound*, 13.

35 May, *Homeward Bound*, 222.

36 May, *Homeward Bound*, 224.

37 Coontz, *The Way We Never Were*, xxii.

38 "About Ms.," *Ms.* Accessed September 22, 2022, https://msmagazine.com/about/.

39 May, *Homeward Bound*, 223.

40 Laura Berberian, "Research Guides: American Women: Topical Essays: The Long Road to Equality: What Women Won from the ERA Ratification Effort," research guide. Accessed September 22, 2022, https://guides.loc.gov/american-women-essays/era-ratification-effort.

41 "Special Message to the Congress on the Nation's Antipoverty Programs. | The American Presidency Project." Accessed September 22, 2022, https://www.presidency.ucsb.edu/documents/special-message-the-congress-the-nations-antipoverty-programs.

42 H.R.1083—93rd Congress (1973–1974): Comprehensive Child

Development Act, Congress.gov, Library of Congress. Accessed September 22, 2022, https://www.congress.gov/bill/93rd-congress/house-bill/1083.

43 H.R. 968, 104th Congress, February 15, 1995. Accessed September 22, 2022, https://www.govinfo.gov/content/pkg/BILLS-104hr968ih/html/BILLS-104hr968ih.htm.

44 Elizabeth Rose, *The Promise of Preschool: From Head Start to Universal Pre-Kindergarten* (Oxford University Press, 2010), 60.

45 Olivia B. Waxman, "The U.S. Almost Had Universal Childcare 50 Years Ago. The Same Attacks Might Kill It Today," *Time*, December 9, 2021. Accessed September 22, 2022, https://time.com/6125667/universal-childcare-history-nixon-veto/.

46 "Excerpts from Nixon's Veto Message," *New York Times*," December 10, 1971. Accessed September 22, 2022, https://www.nytimes.com/1971/12/10/archives/excerpts-from-nixons-veto-message.html.

47 Proposed Amendment to the United States Constitution (Equal Rights Amendment). Accessed September 22, 2022, https://www.govinfo.gov/content/pkg/STATUTE-86/pdf/STATUTE-86-Pg1523.pdf.

48 "Griffiths, Martha Wright," US House of Representatives: History, Art & Archives. Accessed September 22, 2022, https://history.house.gov/People/Listing/G/GRIFFITHS,-Martha-Wright-(G000471)/.

49 Rosenberg and Foner, *Divided Lives*, 220.

50 Eric C. Miller, "Phyllis Schlafly's 'Positive' Freedom: Liberty, Liberation, and the Equal Rights Amendment," *Rhetoric and Public Affairs* 18, no. 2 (2015): 277–300, https://doi.org/10.14321/rhetpublaffa.18.2.0277.

51 "S-Leg_162_005_part1_d.Pdf." Accessed September 22, 2022, https://dolearchives.ku.edu/sites/dolearchives.ku.edu/files/docs/ERA_additions/s-leg_162_005_part1_d.pdf.

52 Annelise Orleck, *Rethinking American Women's Activism* (Taylor & Francis, 2022), 203.

53 Dareh Gregorian, "The Equal Rights Amendment Could Soon Hit a Major Milestone. It May Be 40 Years Too Late," NBC News, January 11, 2020. Accessed September 22, 2022, https://www.nbcnews.com

/politics/congress/equal-rights-amendment-could-soon-hit-major
-milestone-it-may-n1112581.

54  Lauren Lewis, "Women Who Want to Be Women [Association of the
W's]," Texas State Historical Association, June 29, 2021. Accessed
September 22, 2022, https://www.tshaonline.org/handbook/entries
/women-who-want-to-be-women-association-of-the-ws.

55  "Ratification By State," Equal Rights Amendment. Accessed September 22, 2022, https://www.equalrightsamendment.org/era-ratification
-map.

## CHAPTER 8

1  Francesca Donner, "The Household Work Men and Women Do,
and Why," New York Times, February 12, 2020. Accessed September
22, 2022, https://www.nytimes.com/2020/02/12/us/the-household
-work-men-and-women-do-and-why.html.

2  May, Homeward Bound, 223.

3  Coontz, The Way We Never Were, xix.

4  Larry Prochner, Ailie Cleghorn, and Jennifer Drefs, "Our Proud
Heritage: The 200-Year Legacy of Infant Schools," Young Children 70,
no. 2, May 2015. Accessed September 30, 2022, https://www.naeyc
.org/resources/pubs/yc/may2015/infant-schools.

5  Marjorie Hansen Shaevitz and Morton H Shaevitz, The Superwoman
Syndrome (New York: Warner Books, 1984).

6  Cheryl L. Woods-Giscombé, "Superwoman Schema: African
American Women's Views on Stress, Strength, and Health," Qual-
itative Health Research 20, no. 5 (May 2010): 668–83, https://doi
.org/10.1177/1049732310361892.

7  Coontz, The Way We Never Were, xix.

8  Amanda M. Pollitt, Brandon A. Robinson, and Debra Umberson, "Gender Conformity, Perceptions of Shared Power, and
Marital Quality in Same- and Different-Sex Marriages," Gender
& Society 32, no. 1, November 20, 2017. https://doi.org/10.1177
/0891243217742110.

9  "An Unequal Division of Labor," Center for American Progress (blog).

Accessed September 22, 2022, https://www.americanprogress.org/article/unequal-division-labor/.

10 Rick Rojas, "What Happened to Etan Patz?" *New York Times*, January 30, 2017. Accessed January 14, 2023, https://www.nytimes.com/2017/01/30/nyregion/what-happened-to-etan-patz.html.

11 Paul M. Renfro et al., "The New 'Crime Wave' Panic and the Long Shadow of John Walsh," *The New Republic*, August 13, 2021, https://newrepublic.com/article/163235/crime-wave-john-walsh-americas-most-wanted.

12 Anna K. Danziger_Halperin, "Biden Has Chance to Reverse 50 Years of Failure on Child-Care Policy," *Washington Post*, July 16, 2021. Accessed September 22, 2022, https://www.washingtonpost.com/outlook/2021/07/16/biden-has-real-chance-reverse-50-years-failure-child-care-policy/.

13 "The Coronavirus Will Make Child Care Deserts Worse and Exacerbate Inequality," Center for American Progress. Accessed September 22, 2022, https://www.americanprogress.org/article/coronavirus-will-make-child-care-deserts-worse-exacerbate-inequality/.

14 Tara Law, "Women Are Majority of Workforce, but Still Face Challenges," *Time*, January 16, 2020. Accessed September 22, 2022, https://time.com/5766787/women-workforce/.

15 "The Wage Gap," 81cents.com. Accessed September 22, 2022, https://www.81cents.com/thewagegap.

16 Anne-Marie Slaughter, "Why Women Still Can't Have It All," *Atlantic*, July/August 2012. Accessed January 14, 2023, https://www.theatlantic.com/magazine/archive/2012/07/why-women-still-cant-have-it-all/309020/.

17 "A Record Number of Women Are Serving in the 117th Congress," Pew Research Center. Accessed September 23, 2022, https://www.pewresearch.org/fact-tank/2021/01/15/a-record-number-of-women-are-serving-in-the-117th-congress/.

18 "Most Americans Say Children Are Better Off with a Parent at Home," Pew Research Center. Accessed September 23, 2022, https://www.pewresearch.org/fact-tank/2016/10/10/most-americans-say-children-are-better-off-with-a-parent-at-home/.

19 Claire Cain Miller, "Nearly Half of Men Say They Do Most of the Home Schooling. 3 Percent of Women Agree," *New York Times*, May 6, 2020. Accessed October 28, 2020, https://www.nytimes.com/2020/05/06/upshot/pandemic-chores-homeschooling-gender.html.

20 "Women in the Workplace," McKinsey, October 18, 2022. Accessed October 22, 2022, https://www.mckinsey.com/featured-insights/diversity-and-inclusion/women-in-the-workplace.

21 Claire Ewing-Nelson, "Nearly 2.2 Million Women Have Left the Labor Force Since February," *National Women's Law Center*, November 2020, https://nwlc.org/wp-content/uploads/2020/11/October-Jobs-Day.pdf.

22 Deepa Mahajan et al., "Don't Let the Pandemic Set Back Gender Equality," *Harvard Business Review*, September 16, 2020. Accessed September 23, 2022, https://hbr.org/2020/09/dont-let-the-pandemic-set-back-gender-equality.

23 Amanda Taub, "Pandemic Will 'Take Our Women 10 Years Back' in the Workplace," *New York Times*, September 26, 2020. Accessed September 23, 2022, https://www.nytimes.com/2020/09/26/world/covid-women-childcare-equality.html.

## CHAPTER 9

1 "Services for Displaced Homemakers," New York State Department of Labor. Accessed September 22, 2022, https://dol.ny.gov/services-displaced-homemakers.

2 Charles A. Jeszeck et al., "The Nation's Retirement System: A Comprehensive Re-Evaluation Is Needed to Better Promote Future Retirement Security," *SSRN Electronic Journal*, 2017, https://doi.org/10.2139/ssrn.3062574.

3 Kim Parker and Renee Stepler, "Americans See Men as the Financial Providers, Even as Women's Contributions Grow," *Pew Research Center* (blog). Accessed September 22, 2022, https://www.pewresearch.org/fact-tank/2017/09/20/americans-see-men-as-the-financial-providers-even-as-womens-contributions-grow/.

4 "Quick Facts on Paid Family and Medical Leave," Center for American

Progress. Accessed September 22, 2022, https://www.americanprog
ress.org/article/quick-facts-paid-family-medical-leave/.

5 Alyson Byrne and Julian Barling, "Does a Woman's High-Status
Career Hurt Her Marriage? Not If Her Husband Does the Laundry,"
*Harvard Business Review*, May 2, 2017. Accessed September 22, 2022,
https://hbr.org/2017/05/does-a-womans-high-status-career-hurt
-her-marriage-not-if-her-husband-does-the-laundry.

6 Suqin Ge, Elliott Isaac, and Amalia Miller, "Elite Schools and Opting
In: Effects of College Selectivity on Career and Family Outcomes,"
National Bureau of Economic Research, August 2019. Accessed Sep-
tember 22, 2022, https://www.nber.org/papers/w25315.

7 Schneider, Daniel, "Lessons Learned from Non-Marriage Experi-
ments," *The Future of Children* 25, no. 2 (2015): 155–178. doi:10.1353
/foc.2015.0017.

8 "The Motherhood Penalty," American Association of University
Women. Accessed September 22, 2022, https://www.aauw.org/issues
/equity/motherhood/.

9 "Table 6. Employment Status of Mothers with Own Children under
3 Years Old by Single Year of Age of Youngest Child and Marital Status, 2020–2021 Annual Averages—2021 A01 Results," U.S. Bureau of
Labor Statistics. Accessed September 22, 2022, https://www.bls.gov
/news.release/famee.t06.htm.

10 "Work-Family Benefits: Which Ones Maximize Profits? On JSTOR."
Accessed September 22, 2022, https://www-jstor-org.proxy2.hamp
shire.edu/stable/40604332.

11 YoonKyung Chung et al., "The Parental Gender Earnings Gap in the
United States," U.S. Census Bureau, November 2017. Accessed September 22, 2022, https://www2.census.gov/ces/wp/2017/CES-WP-17
-68.pdf.

12 Michelle J. Budig, "The Fatherhood Bonus and the Motherhood Penalty: Parenthood and the Gender Gap in Pay," Third Way, September
2, 2014. Accessed January 19, 2023, https://www.thirdway.org/report
/the-fatherhood-bonus-and-the-motherhood-penalty-parenthood
-and-the-gender-gap-in-pay.

13 "Learn More about Financial Abuse," National Network to End

Domestic Violence. Accessed February 19, 2023, https://nnedv.org
/content/about-financial-abuse/.

## CHAPTER 10

1  Fay Mitchell, "Happy Birthday President Polk," North Carolina Department of Natural and Cultural Resources, November 8, 2018. Accessed
   September 22, 2022, https://www.ncdcr.gov/blog/2018/11/08/happy
   -birthday-president-polk.
2  "First Lady Sarah Childress Polk," *Our White House | Looking In,
   Looking Out* (blog), National Children's Book and Literacy Alli-
   ance. Accessed September 23, 2022, https://ourwhitehouse.org/sarah
   -childress-polk/.
3  "Sarah Polk Biography," National First Ladies' Library. Accessed September 22, 2022, http://archive.firstladies.org/bibliography/results
   .aspx?firstlady=12.
4  Bryan Alexander, "Melania Trump's Christmas Decorating Curse
   Leaks; Twitter Reacts," *USA Today*, October 2, 2020. Accessed September 22, 2022, https://www.usatoday.com/story/entertainment
   /celebrities/2020/10/01/melania-trump-christmas-decorating
   -curse-leaks-twitter-reacts/5890795002/.
5  "Roles of the First Lady: Classroom Resource Packet," White House
   Historical Association. Accessed September 22, 2022, https://www
   .whitehousehistory.org/teacher-resources/roles-of-the-first-lady.
6  Gabrielle Olya, "What Does It Cost to Live in the White House?,"
   Yahoo! Finance, April 21, 2023, https://finance.yahoo.com/news
   /does-cost-live-white-house-130039548.html.
7  Kate Bennett, "Melania Trump's Popularity Jumps in New CNN
   Poll," CNN, May 7, 2018, https://www.cnn.com/2018/05/07/politics
   /melania-new-cnn-poll/index.html.
8  Gallup Inc., "Last Trump Job Approval 34%; Average Is Record-
   Low 41%," Gallup.com, January 18, 2021, https://news.gallup.com
   /poll/328637/last-trump-job-approval-average-record-low.aspx.
9  Eric Garcia, "Trump Serves McDonald's at His CPAC VIP Party, Continuing His Fast Food Obsession," *Independent*, February 27, 2022.
   Accessed September 22, 2022, https://www.independent.co.uk/news

/world/americas/us-politics/trump-cpac-mcdonald-s-fast-food
-b2024192.html.

10 "Dolley Madison Biography," National First Ladies' Library. Accessed
September 22, 2022, http://www.firstladies.org/biographies/firstladies
.aspx?biography=4.

11 "Hillary Clinton Manages Family Cash," *South Florida Sun Senti-
nel*, August 3, 1992. Accessed September 22, 2022, https://www.sun
-sentinel.com/news/fl-xpm-1992-08-03-9202230179-story.html.

12 Susan Saulny, "Michelle Obama Thrives in Campaign Trenches,"
*New York Times*, February 14, 2008, sec. U.S., https://www.nytimes
.com/2008/02/14/us/politics/14michelle.html.

13 Pollitt, Robinson, and Umberson, "Gender Conformity, Perceptions
of Shared Power, and Marital Quality in Same- and Different-Sex
Marriages."

14 Constance L. Shehan, *Gender Roles in American Life: A Documentary
History of Political, Social, and Economic Changes* [2 Volumes] (ABC-
CLIO, 2018).

15 Gregory Krieg, "The President Gets Paid $400,000 a Year. The First
Lady Should Too," Mic, April 16, 2015. Accessed September 22, 2022,
https://www.mic.com/articles/115658/the-president-gets-paid-400
-000-a-year-the-first-lady-should-too.

16 Natalie Gonnella-Platts and Katherine Fritz, "A Role Without a Rulebook: The Influence and Leadership of Global First Ladies," Bush Center,
March 28, 2017. Accessed March 22, 2022, http://www.bushcenter.org
/publications/resources-reports/reports/role-without-a-rulebook.html.

17 Gonnella-Platts and Fritz, "A Role Without a Rulebook."

18 "Letter, Martha Washington to Fanny Bassett Washington, October
23, 1789," George Washington's Mount Vernon. Accessed September 22, 2022, https://www.mountvernon.org/education/primary
-sources-2/article/letter-martha-washington-to-fanny-bassett
-washington-october-23-1789/.

19 Kimberly J. Largent, "The Life of Mary Todd Lincoln," eHistory, Ohio
State University. Accessed February 19, 2023, https://ehistory.osu
.edu/articles/life-mary-todd-lincoln.

20 *ABC Primetime with Howard & Judy Dean—January 22, 2004*, 2018,
https://www.youtube.com/watch?v=KyJFMfcsRAE.

21 *Hillary Clinton on "Baking Cookies,"* 2008, https://www.youtube.com /watch?v=8EGranwN_uk.

22 Kathleen Hall Jamieson, *Beyond the Double Bind: Women and Leadership* (Oxford University Press, 1995), 24.

23 Daniel White, "Hillary Clinton's Chocolate-Chip Cookies: A Brief History," *Time*, August 19, 2016. Accessed September 22, 2022, https://time.com/4459173/hillary-bill-clinton-cookies-history/.

24 *Ass'n of Am. Physicians Surgeons v. Clinton*, 997 F.2d 898 | Casetext Search + Citator. Accessed September 22, 2022, https://casetext.com /case/assn-of-am-physicians-surgeons-v-clinton.

25 Connie Schultz, "First Ladies Should Keep Their Jobs and Their Opinions," *New York Times*, March 9, 2016. Accessed September 22, 2022, https://www.nytimes.com/roomfordebate/2016/03/09/how-should -the-role-of-first-spouse-change/first-ladies-should-keep-their-jobs -and-their-opinions.

26 Danielle Smyth, "Salary of Staff for the First Lady," Chron, October 2, 2022. Accessed October 22, 2022, https://work.chron.com/salary -staff-first-lady-29562.html.

27 Serena Marshall, "White House Salaries Revealed," ABC News, July 1, 2014. Accessed September 22, 2022, https://abcnews.go.com/Politics /white-house-salaries-revealed/story?id=24382955.

28 Gregory Korte, "22 White House Staffers Make $172,200 a Year," *USA Today*, July 1, 2014. Accessed September 22, 2022, https://www .usatoday.com/story/theoval/2014/07/01/white-house-staffer-salaries -2014/11916165/.

29 Adam Andrzejewski, "Trump's Leaner White House Payroll 2017 Projected to Save Taxpayers $22 Million," *Forbes*, July 2, 2017. Accessed September 22, 2022, https://www.forbes.com/sites/adam andrzejewski/2017/07/02/trumps-leaner-white-house-payroll-pro jected-to-save-taxpayers-22-million/.

30 Juliana Kaplan, "White House Interns Will Be Paid for the First Time This Fall, Opening the Doors of the Prestigious Program to Lower-Income Applicants," Business Insider, June 2, 2022. Accessed September 22, 2022, https://www.businessinsider.com/white-house -internships-paid-for-first-time-unpaid-internships-unequal-2022-3.

31 Sarina Finkelstein, "Want to Fix Wage Inequality? Start with the

First Lady," *Money*, April 12, 2016. Accessed March 21, 2022, https://money.com/wage-gap-first-lady/.

32 Bob Collins, "A Letter from Jackie," NewsCut, Minnesota Public Radio News, November 22, 2013. Accessed September 22, 2022, https://blogs.mprnews.org/newscut/2013/11/a-letter-from-jackie/.

## CHAPTER 11

1 Carrie Blazina, "Fast Facts on Views of Workplace Harassment amid Allegations against New York Gov. Cuomo," *Pew Research Center* (blog), August 6, 2021. Accessed January 25, 2022, https://www.pewresearch.org/fact-tank/2021/08/06/fast-facts-on-views-of-workplace-harassment-amid-allegations-against-new-york-gov-cuomo/.

2 "Women in the Workplace," McKinsey.

3 Pollitt, Robinson, and Umberson, "Gender Conformity, Perceptions of Shared Power, and Marital Quality in Same- and Different-Sex Marriages."

4 Maureen Perry-Jenkins and Karen Folk, "Class, Couples, and Conflict: Effects of the Division of Labor on Assessments of Marriage in Dual-Earner Families," *Journal of Marriage and the Family* 56, no. 1 (1994): 165–80, https://doi.org/10.2307/352711.

5 Kayla Van Gorp, "The Second Shift: Why It Is Diminishing but Still an Issue," 2013, 9.

6 Nicole Civettini, "Housework as Non-Normative Gender Display Among Lesbians and Gay Men," *Sex Roles* 74, no. 5 (March 1, 2016): 206–19, https://doi.org/10.1007/s11199-015-0559-9.

7 Theodore N. Greenstein, "Economic Dependence, Gender, and the Division of Labor in the Home: A Replication and Extension," *Journal of Marriage and Family* 62, no. 2, May 2000. Accessed September 22, 2022, https://onlinelibrary.wiley.com/doi/abs/10.1111/j.1741-3737.2000.00322.x.

8 "III. Millennials' Attitudes about Marriage," *Pew Research Center's Social & Demographic Trends Project* (blog), March 9, 2011, https://www.pewresearch.org/social-trends/2011/03/09/iii-millennials-attitudes-about-marriage/.

9 Jennifer Wright, "Millennial Men Want 1950s Housewives after They

Have Kids," *New York Post*, May 7, 2022, https://nypost.com/2022/05/07 /millennial-men-want-1950s-housewives-after-they-have-kids/.

10 Debra Michals, "Lucy Stone," National Women's History Museum, 2017. Accessed September 20, 2022, https://www.womenshistory.org /education-resources/biographies/lucy-stone.

11 Betty Friedan, *The Feminine Mystique*, 92.

12 Neely Tucker, "Stone/Blackwell Marriage: To Love and Honor, but Not 'Obey,'" *Library of Congress Blogs* (blog), May 5, 2020, http://blogs.loc .gov/loc/2020/05/stone-blackwell-marriage-to-love-and-honor-but -not-obey/.

13 Olivia B. Waxman, "'Lucy Stone, If You Please,'" *Time*, March 7, 2019. Accessed September 20, 2022, https://time.com/5537834/lucy-stone -maiden-names-womens-history/.

14 US Census Bureau, "U.S. Census Bureau Releases CPS Estimates of Same-Sex Households," Census.gov. Accessed January 10, 2022, https://www.census.gov/newsroom/press-releases/2019/same-sex -households.html.

15 Pollitt, Robinson, and Umberson, "Gender Conformity, Perceptions of Shared Power, and Marital Quality in Same- and Different-Sex Marriages."

16 Harry Howard and James Tapsfield, "Lesbian Couples Are TWICE as Likely to Divorce as Married Gay Men, ONS Data Reveals," *Daily Mail Online,* November 17, 2020. Accessed March 11, 2022, https://www .dailymail.co.uk/news/article-8960185/Lesbian-couples-TWICE -likely-divorce-married-gay-men-ONS-data-reveals.html.

17 Christopher Carrington, *No Place Like Home: Relationships and Family Life among Lesbians and Gay Men* (University of Chicago Press, 1999), 176.

18 Dawn Ennis, "Three Years Later," *Life After Dawn* (blog), August 6, 2016, https://lifeafterdawn.com/2016/08/06/three-years-later/.

19 *Before Dawn, After Don*, 2016, https://vimeo.com/193265569.

## CHAPTER 12

1 *#TRADWIVES: Rethinking Feminism?*, 2020, https://www.youtube .com/watch?v=CjTjMrBnXJY.

2 "About the Darling Academy, Founder and Traditional Housewife Alena Kate Pettitt," The Darling Academy etiquette books. Accessed February 21, 2022, https://www.thedarlingacademy.com/about/.

3 "Alena Kate Pettitt | Housewife Life on Instagram: 'The New Stepford ♡,'" Instagram. Accessed September 22, 2022, https://www.instagram.com/p/B4nS7iqnpko/.

4 *The Russian Schools Training Women to Be Housewives*, 2016, https://www.youtube.com/watch?v=G-rhH1Xg67I.

5 *How I Went from Raging Feminist to Feminine Traditional Wife *HIGHLY REQUESTED**, 2021, https://www.youtube.com/watch?v=3byEo63NnA8.

6 "Tradwife on Instagram: 'Are You Also Preparing for a Wonderful Weekend, Ladies? Enjoy Every Minute of It! ♡♡,'" Instagram. Accessed September 22, 2022, https://www.instagram.com/p/CZRbCDGNcTm/.

7 "Tradwife on Instagram: 'How Can I Be a Good Tradwife? First of All: A Traditional Woman's Place Is Not under a Man's Feet, but under His Wing, by His Side. A Traditional Housewife Chooses Her Husband Based on His Ability to Care for People, Provide for Their Children, and Most Importantly upon His Integrity and Values. Having Such a Partner Enables You to Take Pleasure in Traditional Domestic Duties While Promoting Feminine Submissiveness, Domesticity, and Wifehood. As a Wife, You Are Expected to Serve Your Husband, Preparing Food, Clothing and Other Personal Needs. As a Mother, You Take Care of the Children and Their Needs, Including Education. As a Housekeeper You Run the Show. Develop Traits Such as Nurturance, Sensitivity, Sweetness, Supportiveness, Gentleness, Warmth, Passivity, Cooperativeness, Expressiveness, Modesty, Humility, Empathy, Affection, Tenderness, and Being Emotional, Kind, Helpful, Devoted, and Understanding. You Will Be Even More Feminine and Desirable. As a Real Tradwife,'" Instagram. Accessed September 22, 2022, https://www.instagram.com/p/CXTJtU3N2wk/.

8 "Tradwife on Instagram: 'How Can I Be a Good Tradwife?'"

9 Martha Cliff, "I Trained to Be a Doctor but Traded It All in to Be a Tradwife—I Spend All Day Cleaning, I Love Serving My Husband,"

*Sun*, June 7, 2021. Accessed September 22, 2022, https://www.thesun
.co.uk/fabulous/15163758/trained-doctor-gave-up-become-trad
wife/.

10  Jennifer Reese, "*Why We Can't Sleep*, by Ada Calhoun, Book Review,"
*Washington Post*, February 7, 2020. Accessed September 22, 2022,
https://www.washingtonpost.com/entertainment/books/why-are
-gen-x-women-such-a-mess-a-new-book-explores-the-many-pos
sible-reasons/2020/02/06/96f6f75c-4768-11ea-bc78-8a18f7afcee7
_story.html.

11  "What Does the Bible Say About Submissiveness?" Accessed March 2,
2022, https://www.openbible.info/topics/submissiveness.

12  *Stacey Dooley Sleeps Over*, Series 2 Episode 1: "Tradwife," 2021, https://
www.youtube.com/watch?v=r4wkRhfR-ZY.

13  "Wife with a Psalm (@wifewithapurpose) • Instagram Photos and
Videos." Accessed September 22, 2022, https://www.instagram.com
/wifewithapurpose/.

14  "Gen Z Female (@typical.Tradwife) • Instagram Photos and Videos."
Accessed September 22, 2022, https://www.instagram.com/typical
.tradwife/.

15  Frankie Hope Sitler-Elbel, "From Swiffers to Swastikas: How the
#tradwife Movement of Conventional Gender Roles Became Synony-
mous with White Supremacy," n.d., 83.

16  Lisa Miller, "The Feminist Housewife: Can Women Have It All by
Choosing to Stay Home?" *New York*, March 15, 2013. Accessed September 22, 2022, https://nymag.com/news/features/retro-wife-2013-3/.

17  Ashley Morgan, "The Real Problem with Toxic Masculinity Is That It
Assumes There Is Only One Way of Being a Man," The Conversation,
February 7, 2019, http://theconversation.com/the-real-problem-with
-toxic-masculinity-is-that-it-assumes-there-is-only-one-way-of
-being-a-man-110305.

18  "Mum's Who Organise, Clean, Cook and Chat." Accessed March 1,
2022, https://www.facebook.com/groups/1028139730670506/.

19  Hannah Paine, "Mum's Housework Routine Sparks Debate on Facebook," News.com.au, February 5, 2020. Accessed September 22,
2022, https://www.news.com.au/lifestyle/relationships/marriage/do

-it-even-when-you-feel-like-not-doing-it-mums-housework-routine -sparks-debate-on-facebook/news-story/dcc5fffad027a20a89c489d 256f661ed.

20 *Tradwives Make Feminists JEALOUS*, 2020, https://www.youtube .com/watch?v=rBa9ZKLw-qw.

21 "Tradwife on Instagram: 'Traditional Women Who Live in a Patriarchal Family Are Happier and Healthier than Other Women.'" Instagram. Accessed September 22, 2022, https://www.instagram.com/p /CX8p-tfIDe0/.

22 D'vera Cohn and Andrea Caumont, "7 Key Findings about Stay-at-Home Moms," Pew Research Center. Accessed January 31, 2022, https://www.pewresearch.org/fact-tank/2014/04/08/7-key-findings -about-stay-at-home-moms/.

23 "Total Power Exchange, 'Cliche 1950s Housewife', Master/Slave Dynamics, and Much, Much More. AM(Almost)A? : ThekinkPlace." Accessed September 22, 2022, https://www.reddit.com/r/ThekinkPlace/comments /pln6l8/total_power_exchange_cliche_1950s_housewife/.

24 "How Much Do YouTubers Make? Facts and Figures for 2022," *MintLife* Blog (blog), May 24, 2022, https://mint.intuit.com/blog/relationships /how-much-do-youtubers-make/.

25 "Alena Kate Pettitt, Housewife Life on Instagram."

26 Aja Romano, "Doris Day's Complicated Legacy, Explained," Vox, May 13, 2019. Accessed September 22, 2022, https://www.vox.com/culture /2019/5/13/18617650/doris-day-life-films-legacy-rock-hudson-terry -melcher-manson.

27 *The Russian Schools Training Women to Be Housewives*, 2016, https:// www.youtube.com/watch?v=G-rhH1Xg67I.

28 Richard V. Reeves, "Of Boys and Men," *Brookings* (blog), June 8, 2022, https://www.brookings.edu/book/of-boys-and-men/.

## CHAPTER 13

1 Nancy Folbre and Marjorie Abel, "Women's Work and Women's Households: Gender Bias in the U.S. Census," *Social Research* 56, no. 3 (1989): 545–69. http://www.jstor.org/stable/40970556.

2 "Marshall Plan for Moms." Accessed September 23, 2022, https://marshallplanformoms.com/.

3 Reshma Saujani, "COVID Has Decimated Women's Careers—We Need a Marshall Plan for Moms, Now," *The Hill* (blog), December 7, 2020, https://thehill.com/blogs/congress-blog/politics/529090-covid-has-decimated-womens-careers-we-need-a-marshall-plan-for/.

4 Gallup Inc., "Children a Key Factor in Women's Desire to Work Outside the Home," Gallup.com, October 7, 2015, https://news.gallup.com/poll/186050/children-key-factor-women-desire-work-outside-home.aspx.

5 Livingston, "About 1 in 5 U.S. Moms and Dads Are Stay-at-Home Parents."

6 Christopher [D-CT Sen. Murphy, "Text–S.1211–118th Congress (2023–2024): Social Security Caregiver Credit Act of 2023," legislation, April 19, 2023, 04/19/2023, http://www.congress.gov/.

7 "Aid to Families with Dependent Children (AFDC) and Temporary Assistance for Needy Families (TANF)–Overview," Office of the Assistant Secretary for Planning and Evaluation, U.S. Department of Health and Human Services. Accessed January 15, 2023, https://aspe.hhs.gov/aid-families-dependent-children-afdc-temporary-assistance-needy-families-tanf-overview.

8 Mohamed Basyir, "Government to Introduce Housewife Social Security Scheme Next Year," New Straits Times Online, August 9, 2021, https://www.nst.com.my/news/nation/2021/08/716578/government-introduce-housewife-social-security-scheme-next-year.

9 Ross D. Parke and Armin A. Brott, *Throwaway Dads: The Myths and Barriers That Keep Men from Being the Fathers They Want to Be* (Houghton Mifflin Harcourt, 1999).

## CHAPTER 14

1 Molly Gamble, "34 States Where Child Care Costs More than College Tuition," Becker's Hospital Review, February 17, 2022. Accessed January 17, 2023, https://www.beckershospitalreview.com/rankings-and

-ratings/34-states-where-child-care-costs-more-than-college-tuition
.html.

2  "Child Care Costs in the United States," Economic Policy Institute.
   Accessed September 30, 2022, https://www.epi.org/child-care-costs
   -in-the-united-states/.

3  "Universal Child Care and Early Learning Act," Office of Senator
   Elizabeth Warren, February 2019. Accessed September 23, 2022,
   https://www.warren.senate.gov/imo/media/doc/Universal_Child
   _Care_Policy_Brief_2019.pdf.

4  Cory Turner, "The Expanded Child Tax Credit Briefly Slashed Child
   Poverty," NPR, January 27, 2022. Accessed September 23, 2022,
   https://www.npr.org/2022/01/27/1075299510/the-expanded-child
   -tax-credit-briefly-slashed-child-poverty-heres-what-else-it-d.

5  Robert E. Rubin and Jacob J. Lew, "A Plan to Help Kids Without
   Increasing Inflation," *New York Times*, May 2, 2022. Accessed September
   23, 2022, https://www.nytimes.com/2022/05/02/opinion/child
   -tax-credit.html?smid=tw-share%0A.

6  "December Child Tax Credit Kept 3.7 Million Children from Poverty,"
   Columbia University Center on Poverty and Social Policy. Accessed
   September 23, 2022, https://www.povertycenter.columbia.edu/news
   -internal/monthly-poverty-december-2021.

7  Evangel Penumaka, Isa Alomran, and Abby Steckel, "Memo: Majority of Voters Support a Guaranteed Income," Data for Progress, July
   8, 2021. Accessed September 23, 2022, https://www.dataforprogress
   .org/memos/voters-support-a-guaranteed-income.

8  Heartland Signal (@HeartlandSignal), Twitter, January 26, 2022.
   Accessed September 23, 2022, https://twitter.com/HeartlandSignal
   /status/1486376470859628558?mc_cid=9ceca6e2a4&mc_eid=e6a
   72ba2ca.

9  Pete Sweeney, "Japanese Inequality Lives in a Retirement Home,"
   Reuters, January 26, 2022, sec. Asian Markets, https://www.reuters
   .com/markets/asia/japanese-inequality-lives-retirement-home-2022
   -01-26/.

10 Kristin Donnelly et al., "Attitudes Toward Women's Work and Family Roles in the United States, 1976–2013," *Psychology of Women*

*Quarterly* 40, no. 1, June 26, 2015. Accessed February 22, 2023, https://journals.sagepub.com/doi/full/10.1177/0361684315590774.

11 Coontz, *The Way We Never Were*, xxxvi.

12 Yusuf George, "The 14 Companies Taking the Lead on Parental Leave," JUST Capital, June 20, 2019. Accessed September 23, 2022, https://justcapital.com/news/companies-taking-the-lead-on-parental-leave/.

13 S. Dixon, "Meta: Gender Distribution of Global Employees 2022," Statista, August 16, 2022. Accessed September 23, 2022, https://www.statista.com/statistics/311827/facebook-employee-gender-global/.

14 "Of 41 Countries, Only U.S. Lacks Paid Parental Leave," Pew Research Center. Accessed September 23, 2022, https://www.pewresearch.org/fact-tank/2019/12/16/u-s-lacks-mandated-paid-parental-leave/.

15 Jacob Alex Klerman, "Family and Medical Leave in 2012: Technical Report," *Final Report*, n.d., 174.

16 "Zero Weeks." Accessed January 17, 2023, https://www.zeroweeks.com/.

17 "Employee and Worksite Perspectives of the Family and Medical Leave Act: Results from the 2018 Surveys," n.d., 80.

18 "State-Paid-Family-Leave-Laws.Pdf." Accessed September 23, 2022, https://www.nationalpartnership.org/our-work/resources/economic-justice/paid-leave/state-paid-family-leave-laws.pdf.

19 "Work–Life Balance," sweden.se, June 1, 2021, https://sweden.se/life/society/work-life-balance.

20 Libby Kane, "Sweden's Maternity Leave, Paternity Leave Policies Create 'Latte Dads,'" Business Insider, April 4, 2018. Accessed September 22, 2022, https://www.businessinsider.com/sweden-maternity-leave-paternity-leave-policies-latte-dads-2018-4.

21 US Census Bureau, "College-Educated Women and Non-Hispanic White Women More Likely to Work During First Pregnancy," Census.gov. Accessed September 22, 2022, https://www.census.gov/library/stories/2021/09/two-thirds-recent-first-time-fathers-took-time-off-after-birth.html.

22 Richard J. Petts and Chris Knoester, "Paternity Leave-Taking and Father Engagement," *Journal of Marriage and Family* 80, no. 5,

October 2018. Accessed September 22, 2022, https://onlinelibrary
.wiley.com/doi/abs/10.1111/jomf.12494.

23 Alana Romain, "These Studies Show Going Back to Work Too Soon Is
Bad for Moms' Health," Romper, August 21, 2017. Accessed September 23, 2022, https://www.romper.com/p/these-studies-show-going
-back-to-work-too-soon-is-bad-for-moms-health-77458.

24 "Paid Leave Is Essential for Healthy Moms and Babies." Accessed September 23, 2022, https://nationalpartnership.org/report/paid-leave
-is-essential-for/.

25 Reshma Saujani, "Childcare Is Infrastructure, and Our Country Is
Crumbling," Medium, September 28, 2021. Accessed September
23, 2022, https://medium.com/@reshmasaujani/childcare-is-infra
structure-and-our-country-is-crumbling-b6e5b8246896.

26 "Meng Introduces Marshall Plan for Moms," Office of Congresswoman
Grace Meng, February 16, 2021. Accessed September 23, 2022, https://
meng.house.gov/media-center/press-releases/meng-introduces-mar
shall-plan-for-moms.

27 "Breadwinning Mothers Continue to Be the U.S. Norm," Center for
American Progress.

28 Coontz, *The Way We Never Were*, xxvii.

29 Liz Alderman, "Paid to Stay Home: Europe's Safety Net Could Ease
Toll of Coronavirus," *New York Times*, March 6, 2020. Accessed September 23, 2022, https://www.nytimes.com/2020/03/06/business
/europe-coronavirus-labor-help.html.

30 Jackie Mader, "How 7 Countries Are Supporting Child Care and
Families during Coronavirus," the Hechinger Report, October 29,
2020. Accessed September 23, 2022, https://hechingerreport.org
/how-7-countries-are-supporting-child-care-and-families-during
-the-pandemic/.

## CONCLUSION

1 "History," MADD. Accessed September 23, 2022, https://madd.org/
our-history/.

2 Coontz, *The Way We Never Were*, 85.